# The Overlooked Pillar

# The Overlooked Pillar

## Making a Case for Cultural Sustainability

ALISA V. MOLDAVANOVA

**SUNY**
**PRESS**

Published by State University of New York Press, Albany

For information, contact State University of New York Press, Albany, NY
www.sunypress.edu

**Library of Congress Cataloging-in-Publication Data**

Name: Moldavanova, Alisa V., author.
Title: The overlooked pillar : making a case for cultural sustainability / Alisa V.
  Moldavanova.
Description: Albany : State University of New York Press [2024] | Includes
  bibliographical references and index.
Identifiers: ISBN 9781438498942 (hardcover : alk. paper) | ISBN 9781438498959
  (ebook) | ISBN 9781438498935 (pbk. : alk. paper)
Further information is available at the Library of Congress.

*For my mother, Zoia Osypova, who instilled in me, from an early age, my passion for arts and culture, and for my daughter, Mariya Moldavanova-Artman, who gave me the perspective of future generations*

# Contents

# Foreword

With *The Overlooked Pillar: Making a Case for Cultural Sustainability*, Alisa Moldavanova offers an original perspective in the sustainable development discourse by emphasizing the importance of culture and cultural institutions in facilitating societal sustainability in its ecological, social, and environmental dimensions. By focusing on different organizational types and contexts in the arts and humanities, the book systematically explores the benefits of applying organizational thinking to sustainability concerns and thus positions sustainability as an organizational logic and routine. This, in turn, furthers the critical notion that genuine long-term sustainability that secures the rights and interests of future generations requires sustainable organizational stewardship today. Management strategies to achieve sustainability stewardship, Moldavanova argues, must be grounded in the communities in which the organization is embedded and must fully recognize the active stakes that communities hold.

In foregrounding the importance of cultural organizations as an overlooked pillar of sustainability, Moldavanova drills down on the cultural development objectives of the Sustainable Development Goals (SDGs). Drawing on rich empirical material that encompasses diverse sets of cultural organizations in a variety of cultural subfields—museums, literature, and music and performing arts—the book's significant contribution lies in the systematic conceptualization of the intersection between culture, cultural organizations, and sustainable development. It provides numerous examples and settings in which cultural organizations advance community sustainability goals, thus arguing that principles and practices of internally sustainable management resonate with organizational external outcomes, enable cultural organizations to foster sustainability in their communities, and ultimately are the transmission belt for the implementation of the SDGs' cultural development objectives.

Organizational thinking has long been underplayed in sustainability and development discourse with its general focus on policy-level development interventions. However, as Moldavanova convincingly demonstrates, sustainability should be understood as an institutional logic that has to be routinely enacted in organizational decision-making by taking the consequences of future generations' actions into account. On this basis, the book differentiates principles of sustainable thinking from those aligned with a more conventional strategic management. Framing the conceptual argument around a logic that emphasizes both institutional resilience and distinctiveness allows Moldavanova to suggest managerial strategies that offer a sensible blueprint for cultural organizations: one that helps them achieve organizational sustainability and pursue adaptations with positive future benefits.

Moldavanova's framework is grounded in the exploration of the differences and similarities among the arts and humanities subfields included in the study, as much as the particular local ecosystem of Metropolitan Detroit in which they are explored. This approach, along with the diversity of the organizations themselves, allows for compelling storytelling about organizational perseverance and immediate adaptation in the face of significant external shocks, principally among them the Great Recession of 2007–2009, which in many ways caused a perfect storm for Detroit's cultural infrastructure.

The novel contribution of this book lies in clearly linking ethical sustainability considerations to intentional managerial strategies: helping cultural organizations to sustain themselves over time by adapting to increasingly more complex environmental and other challenges. In sum, while sustainability is recognized as an important societal goal to which arts and humanities organizations aspire, sustainability must also be viewed as an institutional logic that unfolds within specific organizational settings. This crucial insight has clear significance beyond the arts and culture context that Moldavanova explores here and ought to be taken up by scholars researching the role of other public and nonprofit organizations in achieving sustainable development.

Stefan Toepler
Professor of Nonprofit Studies
Schar School of Policy and Government, George Mason University

# Preface

The idea of this book dates back to the first years of my job as assistant professor at Wayne State University in Detroit, Michigan. I distinctly remember marching together with the Detroiters in front of the Detroit Institute of Arts in Fall 2013 in the midst of the Grand Bargain controversy and the debate about a possible sale of its assets following the City of Detroit's filing for Chapter 9 bankruptcy on July 18, 2013. The purpose of the march was to express public support for the institution and protest against the sale of its assets.

However, the experiences that inform the book are rooted in the work that I had done in my home country of Ukraine while working with nonprofit cultural organizations, artists, the Ministry of Culture and Tourism of Ukraine. While my own educational background was not in the arts, I had been fortunate to engage with local arts organizations in a variety of arts management and support roles for a number of years in late 1990s and early 2000s. This work included serving as a strategic management consultant for The Center for Applied Cultural Management located in my hometown Odesa, Ukraine, and funded by the Swiss Cultural Program, as well as volunteering for the Two Days and Two Nights of New Music—a contemporary music festival held annually in Odesa since 1995.

The resilience of local cultural institutions in the face of the many economic crises, institutional transformations and, more recently, the Russian Federation's war against Ukraine, is truly remarkable and has taught us a lot about the value of such institutions for the current and future generations, as well as the remarkable commitment of their leaders and the community at large to preserving such institutions for posterity. And while this book's empirical material is grounded in the U.S. context, its insights about the importance of cultural institutions and cultural heritage are now relevant for Ukraine as well, in light of the current war and all the damage and destruction that has been caused to cultural sights and landmarks.

This book had largely materialized during my time as a faculty member at Wayne State University, an urban research university located in midtown Detroit. Wayne State University had served as an excellent home for my research and writing, as its location in Metropolitan Detroit provided me with access to the many cultural organizations with unique experiences with regard to their engagement in urban revival agendas as well as recovering from the Great Recession. Additionally, the university itself had created a unique interdisciplinary environment for this kind of research and exploration, and my research had greatly benefited from the various forums and interdisciplinary groups. Frequent engagements with the many colleagues in the Department of Political Science, the Humanities Center, and the Center for Urban Studies have been instrumental to this book's research and writing.

# Acknowledgments

Research for this book has benefited from the following funding sources: Paul A. Volcker Endowment for Public Service Research (American Political Science Association); Humanities Center Faculty Fellowship (Wayne State University), Research Enhancement Program in the Arts and Humanities of the Office of the Vice President for Research (Wayne State University); and the Joseph R. Biden Jr. School of Public Policy and Administration at the University of Delaware.[1]

The author would like to thank the managers of the arts and humanities organizations who participated in this study and shared their experiences, arts management experts who generously shared their insights, as well as the network organization CultureSource, which supported the research process in Detroit, Michigan.

The book has also benefited from the valuable feedback of the many colleagues (John C. Pierce, Laurie Paarlberg, Marjorie Sarbaugh-Thompson, Kelly LeRoux, Naim Kapucu, Mark Greenberg, John J. Kennedy, Walter Edwards, Bernhardt Wulff, Rolf Keller, and others), the work of several graduate and undergraduate research assistants (some of whom are now colleagues in the field), and from the editorial work of Anthony Ambrogio.

I am also very grateful to Stefan Toepler for kindly writing an excellent foreword for the book, one that highlights its unique contributions to the literature on sustainable development as well as the field of public and nonprofit management. I am also deeply grateful to the reviewers

---

1. Portions of the text in this book appeared in the following publication: A. Moldavanova, Two narratives of intergenerational sustainability: A framework for sustainable thinking. *The American Review of Public Administration*, 46(5) (2016): 526–545. https://doi.org/10.1177/0275074014565.

whose time and expertise helped to highlight the book's key argument and strengthen its presentation.

Finally, the author would like to thank SUNY Press Senior Acquisitions Editor Michael Rinella for his guidance and for shepherding this book through the publication process.

Chapter 1

# Introduction

## The Overlooked Pillar

In the 21st century, humans have achieved notable technological progress and increased global collaboration, especially in the fields of science and technology. However, despite all the progress, we continue to struggle with various natural and man-made environmental, social, and economic problems; international conflicts; and global pandemics. Despite the invention of energy-efficient and environmentally friendly technologies, human-induced activities continue to produce high levels of pollution. Despite advances in disaster prediction, we seem to be insufficiently prepared to deal with hurricanes, earthquakes, and tornados. Despite notable signs of improvement, revitalized urban centers continue to suffer from social and economic inequities, casting doubt on the very progress that economic development has engendered. The persistence and increasing complexity of these various issues lead one to conclude that perhaps some aspects of the progress achieved to date might be short-sighted or not fully sustainable and need to be critically examined in more holistic ways.

Following this line of thinking, scholars and practitioners alike continue grappling with the problem of sustainability—the vaguely defined term that unites these diverse issues under the three interrelated dimensions—environment, economy, and sociopolitical systems (Adams, 2006; Dale, 2001; Edwards & Onyx, 2007; Fiorino, 2010; Nurse, 2006; Wang, Hawkins, Lebredo, & Berman, 2012; Stazyk, Moldavanova, & Frederickson, 2016). While the concept of sustainability and our understanding of it is constantly evolving, most agree with the definition of sustainability developed by the World Commission on Economic Development (WCED 1987), also known as the Brundtland Commission. In its 1987 proceedings, WCED defined sustainable development as "the development that meets the needs of the present without compromising the ability of future generations to meet their own needs" (p. 16). Thirty years later, while many may question the developmental aspect of sustainability, as some developments are clearly unsustainable, it is clear that sustainability, as an idea, is rooted in the care of future generations. Following this logic, this book is dedicated to the idea of sustainability understood in intergenerational terms, whose successful enactment depends on the quality of institutions and organizations created collectively by many generations of humans.

Furthermore, since the rapid expansion of the environmental or ecological movement in the 1960s and 1970s, we came to recognize that the environmental framing of sustainability is incomplete without recognizing its interconnectedness with social and economic pillars. However, we seem to overlook the no-less-important pillar of sustainability, which is culture. Yet a recognition of culture—broadly defined as human values and belief systems accumulated and transferred from one generation to another, as well as more narrowly construed as institutions and organizations of the cultural sector that are tasked with preserving and transferring cultural heritage and values from the past into the future (Williams, 1983)—is critical to a holistic understanding of sustainability. While acknowledging the significance of culture as shared norms and beliefs, this book specifically focuses on organizations in the cultural sector, and it makes a case for the importance of such organizations for understanding the very intention and logic of intergenerational sustainability.

The argument about the importance for sustainability of the arts, humanities, creativity, and cultural institutions through which creative impulses flourish, is not new (Matarasso, 2001; Moldavanova, 2013, 2014; Nurse, 2006; Throsby, 1995, 2005; Tubadji, 2010; Tubadji, Osoba, & Nijkamp, 2015). In fact, cultural sustainability scholarship has emerged in response to a policy effort to add cultural governance to Agenda 21 for sustainable development initially approved by the United Nations at the Rio Earth Summit in 1992. While, at the outset, the ecological dimension of Agenda 21 was dominant, many governments incorporated cultural development into their sustainable development goals, and, in 1998, the World Bank and UNESCO both endorsed the inclusion of culture in their sustainable development strategy (Duxbury, Cullen, & Pascual, 2012). The scholarship on the subject, however, fell short of properly conceptualizing the intersection between culture and cultural organizations and sustainable development, which is the task that this book undertakes.

The key premise of this book is that organizations are an important, albeit often overlooked, level of sustainability. Yet sustainability as an institutional logic unfolds in organizations, and it is enacted by managers who make decisions and engage in sustainable thinking on a daily basis, leading them to reconcile current organizational realities and the need to adapt to those realities while considering the needs of future generations. Organizations represent the meso level of sustainable development that functions alongside the macro (societal or policy) and the micro (individual) levels (Leuenberger & Bartle 2009). The macro level seeks to define and pursue sustainability at a societal or community level (Adams, 2006; Dale, 2001; Edwards & Onyx, 2007; Fiorino, 2010; Nurse, 2006; Portney & Cuttler, 2010; Wang et al., 2012). The micro-level positions individuals as change agents in fostering or inhibiting sustainability (Domask 2007; Smith Voß & Grin 2010; Thistlethwaite & Paterson 2016). The meso level affords a crucial role to organizations in advancing societal sustainability goals (Leuenberger & Bartle 2009; Guthrie et al., 2010; Osborne et al., 2014; Portney & Berry, 2015; Stazyk et al., 2016; Moldavanova & Goerdel, 2018), and it concerns itself with the "long-term success and preservation of organizations" (Leuenberger & Bartle 2009, p. 4).

The emphasis on organizations in the sustainable development literature is inspired by the growing corporate social responsibility discourse that emphasizes a commitment of a corporation to generate profits while remaining socially and environmentally responsible (Elkington, 1994; Moldavanova & Goerdel, 2018; Osborne et al., 2014; Paulraj, 2011; Schaltegger et al., 2014; Smith 2012; Stead & Stead, 2013; Thomas & Lamm, 2012). Public management scholars, likewise, have begun to use the term "socially responsible organization" to refer to an organization that engages in internally and externally sustainable practices, such as, for example, the advancement of social equity (Stazyk et al., 2016). Sustainability in the public-sector context, however, should be distinguished from its framing in the corporate world due to the different goals and missions that organizations in both sectors pursue (Bansal & DesJardine, 2014; Moldavanova & Goerdel, 2018).

The book takes an organizational approach to sustainability (March & Olsen, 1989), drawing attention to the importance of organizational thinking about sustainability, which has been lacking in the past. The book relies specifically on the context of organizations found within the domain of the arts and humanities, as a representative case of institutions created collectively by many generations while considering the needs of future generations, to unpack and describe sustainability as an organizational logic and routine. The book systematically conceptualizes the intersection between culture and sustainability by considering different types of organizations (university-affiliated and freestanding) as well as different subfields of the arts and humanities (museums, literature, music and performing arts). While the focus here is on the classical forms of culture, questions of sustainability also affect new and emerging cultural industries, such as streaming companies and virtual arts, and the key lessons of the book are also relevant for those kinds of industries.

The theoretical framework of organizational sustainability presented in the book, which could be applied to a variety of public-serving organizations, is the result of over five years of research and fieldwork that incorporated a variety of cultural organizations located in seven U.S. states as well as an arts ecosystem formed in one particular area: metropolitan Detroit. This approach, however, is not without limitations, as organizations included in the study are embedded in particular political and social environments, and the findings are impacted by such environments. For example, levels of support for arts and culture institutions in the United States vary by geographical location, and this support affects organizations' baseline for sustainability. Therefore, it is important to take into account local conditions when applying the framework to new contexts.

On the surface, the intent to explore the logic of organizational sustainability via the arts and humanities may appear unique, particularly because of its emphasis on cultural preservation, and that supports the preservation of cultural heritage, objects, and institutions for future generations (Alivizatou, 2016; Cerisola, 2019; Duxbury et al., 2012; Rubio, 2014). However, the logic of sustainability that unfolds within arts and humanities organizations, as well as broader managerial implications that we can draw from this context, is nearly universally applicable to all public-serving institutions, including both nonprofits and governments. Importantly, the significance for sustainable development of the arts, humanities, creativity, and institutions through which creative impulses flourish goes well beyond cultural preservation. Cultural institutions make important contributions to the economy, environment, and social systems in their communities (Kangas, Duxbury, & De Beukelaer, 2017; Matarasso, 2001; Moldavanova, 2013, 2014; Nurse, 2006; Throsby, 1995, 2005; Tubadji, 2010; Tubadji, Osoba, & Nijkamp, 2015).

The book's novelty lies in its recognition of the connection that exists between sustainability as an ethical intention and aspiration and sustainability as a deliberate organizational and management strategy: one that ensures cultural organizations can flourish across generations by effectively coping with environmental and common but increasingly complex structural problems. In other words, while sustainability is recognized here as an important societal goal to which institutions of arts and humanities contribute, sustainability is also viewed as an institutional logic that unfolds within specific organizational settings.

The ability of cultural institutions to advance sustainability in society depends on their own survival but also depends on organizational contributions to their communities and effective participation in various societal discourses. There are many examples of how modern-day cultural organizations make themselves relevant: from orchestras providing discounted or free tickets to museums exhibiting their collections in public places, there is a sense of larger social responsibility that penetrates the creative sector and its organizations that aspire to achieve or advance sustainability. Some have been arguing that it is about time to add "A" into the STEM acronym (STEAM), thereby adding to the already common scientific and technological modes of human discovery a more humanistic approach to the sustainability problem that includes contributions by arts and culture institutions.

A founder and executive director of a children's theater in Michigan, with whom I spoke while researching this book, provided a convincing analogy for the importance of the arts and humanities and creativity as helping to provide solutions to the various problems that humans face. He compared the role of the arts in a community to that of the highly valued O-Negative blood type to the Red Cross by saying that the arts, too, are "universal donors . . . We [the arts] can only take O-Negative, but every other blood type can take O-Negative. We solve everybody's problem; that's what the arts do" (Personal Communication, 2015). Indeed, the arts and humanities play many important roles in their communities, from instrumental, such as contributing to local economic development, revitalizing buildings, beautifying neighborhoods, and providing entertainment, to intrinsic, such as being a public good and value in themselves (Belfiore, 2002; Belfiore & Bennett, 2008; Kim, 2016; Markusen, 2014; Moldavanova, 2013, 2014). They also engage in semi-instrumental roles, such as serving as a source of social capital and societal values—including sustainable thinking and social justice (Moldavanova 2013, 2014;

Moldavanova & Wright, 2020). By influencing individual and collective values, the arts' contributions to local communities affect both current and future generations.

Many scholars of the arts and humanites, as well as cultural managers themselves, tend to prioritize the importance of instrumental over more intrinsic types of roles, particularly focusing on cutural organizations' contributions to economic development (Rushton & Landesman, 2013). This happens in part because instrumental roles result in measurable outcomes and provide a commonly acceptable justification for supporting the arts (often framing such support as a return on investment) and in part because these types of contributions are easier to grasp and directly observe. However, cultural organizations' missions have been shifting toward an emphasis on the semi-instrumental roles that affect individual and collective values and perceptions, thus contributing to sustainable communities in the long run.

As John Dewey argued, aesthetic experiences are often the longest-remembered experiences possessing a predictive capacity: "The first strings of dissatisfaction and the first intimations of a better future are always found in works of art" (Dewey, 1934). One of the properties of such experiences is their endurance: art in which meanings have received objective expression endure because they become part of the environment and ensure the transmission of cultural meaning over time, which in turn ensures their continuity in the life of civilization (Dewey, 1934). Following this line of thought, this book shows how, by contributing to the sustainability of communities and societies both now and in the future, cultural institutions build the basis for their own intergenerational sustainability. Furthermore, the book argues that cultural organizations, by pursuing strategies that allow them to continue in their role as sustainable stewards of cultural heritage, are in essence working today to protect the rights and interests of future generations.

This intergenerational view of sustainability adds to the existing sustainable development scholarship by considering the longer-term or intergenerational aspect of sustainability, as opposed to focusing primarily on short-term survival. Such immediate focus on sustainability as organizational survival is quite common in organizational sustainability literature (Bowman, 2011; Garvare & Johansson, 2010; Miragaia, Brito, & Ferreira, 2016; Stead & Stead, 2013; Van der Heijden, 2004), resulting primarily from the practical difficulty of thinking beyond current generations (Catron, 1996; Frederickson, 2010). The focus on short-term survival is also influenced by the strategic management paradigm and business-like management approaches adopted by many public-sector organizations in the aftermath of the New Public Management movement (Bryson, 2018; Koteen, 1997).

This book offers an alternative point of view. It conceives organizational sustainability as a two-level concept that includes both institutional survival as a necessary baseline for sustainability and intergenerational or longer-term sustainability, understood as the ability of institutions to persist and fulfill their social missions in the long run (Moldavanova, 2016). This understanding is consistent with a normative view of sustainability that treats sustainability as a form of intergenerational equity and implies that future generations should be treated as a priority (Parfit, 1984) or at least given as much consideration as current generations (Barry, 1997; Catron, 1996; Tremmel, 2009). Organizational sustainability conceived in this way is fundamentally about ethics and ethical organizational practices, whether those practices affect natural environment, economy, social systems, or organizations themselves. In many ways, human instinct aimed at creating cultural institutions to preserve and transmit cultural heritage and values from one generation to another is an example of pursuing intergenerational sustainability in action and displaying care for those yet to be born.

While intergenerational sustainability could be viewed as an extension of organizational survival (thus appearing as a self-serving goal), it is uniquely important for ensuring larger societal outcomes that cultural organizations aspire to produce both in their local communities and globally. When applied to the cultural sector, the definition of sustainability advanced here is particularly relevant, as it ensures that cultural organizations are able to pursue their foundational mission: the protection, accumulation, and intergenerational transfer of collective cultural heritage and values. Moreover, the view of organizational sustainability presented here shows that, in order to sustain themselves, organizations must engage in a variety of strategies that address both internal organizational and external environmental concerns. More specifically, the concept of intergenerational sustainability unfolds via specific institutional logics and the day-to-day managerial practices in arts and humanities organizations.

As such, the book seeks to answer two primary research questions. First, what are the main long-term sustainability strategies developed by organizations that allow transforming immediate institutional survival into longer-term sustainability? Second, what strategies ensure the commitment of organizations to future generations? In answering these questions, the book offers a theoretical framework for intergenerational organizational sustainability, and identifies and describes mechanisms and strategies, adopted by managers of cultural organizations, that maintain and enhance intergenerational sustainability. The broader message of the book is that intergenerational sustainability is not an outcome—it is a process and an ethic.

## Organizational Sustainability Argument

The book's argument is based on the interplay of the two interconnected narratives of intergenerational sustainability—institutional resilience and institutional distinctiveness—and the explanation of how these two narratives foster organizational survival and sustainability via sustainable managerial thinking. Cultural organizations engage in a wide range of strategies that ensure their social relevance and lead to improved institutional resiliency, while also helping them to remain unique. Together, institutional resilience and distinctiveness lead to the formation of institutional capital, which helps formalized organizations to sustain themselves. Organizational capital may exist in many forms: financial (operational funds, endowments), physical (buildings and collections), virtual (websites, digital collections), human (artists, board, management, staff and volunteer capacity, community of donors and friends), and intangible (intrinsic value for society). Sustainability capital functions like a bank savings account: when money is tight and times are hard, organizations can spend some of their capital to bounce back after environmental shocks, or they can choose to use such capital for future investment and exploration of new paths.

Institutional resilience is understood here as "the capacity to cope with unanticipated dangers after they have become manifest, learning to bounce back" (Wildavsky, 1988, p. 77), the capacity that incorporates "both the ability of a system to persist despite disruptions and the ability to regenerate and maintain existing organization" (Gunderson & Pritchard, 2002, p. 4). Due to lack of information about the future, long-term planning strategies (risk aversion) are less important for cultural organizations' resilience strategies (immediate system responses, risk taking). This observation is consistent with the work of Aaron Wildavsky (1988) and with James G. March's decision theory (1994). The latter maintains that successful managers take risks in ways that are different from what rational-choice theory would suggest: managers take risks based on their own previous experiences, and they tend to be confident in their ability to influence the external environment. In many ways, cultural managers approach risky situations with confidence; they act boldly and astutely in the face of uncertainty.

The resilience of cultural organizations cannot be reduced to merely seeking system efficiency. Rather, similar to other fields, resilience is both about the capacity of the system "to deal with shocks and disturbances" and to use "such events to catalyze renewal, novelty, and innovation" (Krasny, Lundholm, & Plummer, 2011, p. vii). Institutional resilience can be described as adaptability, flexibility and change, innovation, capitalizing on failure, and turning challenges into opportunities.

The second narrative of intergenerational sustainability is the institutional distinctiveness narrative. The purpose of this narrative is to enhance sustainability by promoting the institutional distinctiveness of the sector as a whole, as well as that of particular organizations. Institutional distinctiveness implies that organizations identify a unique institutional niche and direct their focus toward occupying that niche but also staying true to their missions and establishing the value of a particular art form or a particular organization without reducing it to a commodity. Managers' unwavering commitment to keeping institutional purpose in mind while making operational decisions is key to the distinctiveness narrative.

Compared to the institutional resilience narrative that is often voiced in museums' strategic plans, the institutional distinctiveness narrative is much less explicit. It is rooted in the interpretive institutional and managerial order rather than in specific programmatic documents, statutes, or other formalized routines. While the resilience narrative is important for ensuring the survival of different types of organizations and systems (including environmental, health and safety, disaster mitigation, and high-reliability systems), the distinctiveness narrative is particularly prominent in cultural organizations since their survival as well as intergenerational sustainability would be impossible without the distinct character that each of these organizations seeks to establish (and indeed the unique value that cultural organizations contribute to society). In the long run, these narratives together serve as the basis for the intergenerational sustainability of cultural organizations.

In a sustainable organization, the two narratives constitute a duality, both complementing and contradicting one another. Together, the resilience and distinctiveness narratives produce what has been described by Astley and Van de Ven as the "strategy/natural selection" dichotomy (Astley &

Van de Ven, 1983). For instance, distinctiveness allows an organization to occupy a unique institutional niche, which ensures its survival in the process of natural selection; at the same time, proactive strategic choices by institutional managers can also result in sustainable organizations. The natural selection paradigm has been developed by scholars of organizational ecology (Amburgey & Rao, 1996; Carroll, 1984; Hannan & Freeman, 1989) and implies that organizations have limited capacity to adapt their internal structure to changing environments, meaning that their chances of survival are determined by how well they "fit" into specific niches. The notion of strategic choice, meanwhile, is embedded in the strategic management literature (Brown, 2010; Bryson, 2018; Koteen, 1997; Varbanova, 2013); it recognizes the importance of adaptive organizational change. Thus, while natural selection implies that organizations are at the mercy of their environments, strategic choice recognizes the proactive role of organizational managers in fostering organizational change. Both approaches, however, are important for understanding the complex interplay among the narratives of sustainability.

## What We Know about Organizational Sustainability

This book does not offer a universal prescription for organizational sustainability. Rather, the book advocates for a special kind of anticipatory thinking, an institutional and managerial rationality that considers questions of legacy and considers the needs of future generations, thus leading to sustainability. Sustainable thinking, therefore, represents a mindset or a mental framework that managers of cultural institutions engage in on a daily basis. Although there is no singular correct path for every institution to achieve sustainability, there are common lessons about sustainable organizations that can nevertheless be drawn. Moreover, the book's lessons about sustainable thinking in the arts and humanities are relevant to a wide range of public and nonprofit organizations beyond the arts and humanities. For example, one of the book's findings, based on the analysis of both university-affiliated and freestanding cultural institutions, is that while institutional arrangements are important predictors of a choice of sustainability strategies, the form itself does not determine long-term sustainability: the ability of managers to make sustainable choices on a daily basis defines outcomes favorable to intergenerational sustainability. This lesson is important for any organization aspiring to achieve sustainability.

The starting point in thinking about organizational sustainability as presented here is to recognize it as both an internal and an external construct. Externally, business management literature defines sustainable organizations as those that pursue the idea of Triple Bottom Line by maximizing economic returns while also minimizing any negative social and environmental outcomes of their profit-making strategies (Elkington, 1994; Osborne, Radnor, Vidal, & Kinder, 2014; Paulraj, 2011; Smith & Smith, 2012; Stead & Stead, 2013; Schaltegger, Beske, & Seuring, 2014; Thomas & Lamm, 2012). In the public sector, mission-driven organizations are tasked with even more ambitious goals beyond the harm-minimization narrative—they seek to create positive effects in a form of social, environmental, and economic outcomes for their local communities. Cultural organizations, for example, contribute to sustainable communities via instrumental, intrinsic, and semi-instrumental roles (Moldavanova 2013, 2014; Moldavanova & Wright, 2020), as discussed above.

Internally, sustainability is about the ability of organizations to withstand various internal and external pressures to continue their social missions. Thus, organizational survival serves as a baseline for sustainability. An important argument developed in this book is that the internal and external layers of sustainability are interconnected because by engaging in practices that contribute to sustainability in their communities, organizations simultaneously improve their own chances for immediate survival and long-term sustainability. At a certain point, internal sustainability challenges may affect all organizational types, no matter their age, size, or genre. Even old organizations may face the prospects of closure, thus making organizational sustainability a compelling problem for all.

This was, for example, the case of the Belle Isle Aquarium in Detroit, Michigan: a living aquatic museum and the oldest continually operating public aquarium in the United States at over a hundred years old. It closed its doors to the public in 2005, prior to the start of the Great Recession, due to financial problems and a lack of commitment on the part of the city's leadership to save it. But the museum was since brought back to life in 2012 by dedicated volunteers and supporters. Likewise, large and famous organizations, too, may struggle with the sustainability challenge. A good example from the same metropolitan area is the Detroit Institute of Arts, whose collections were viewed in 2013 as valuable monetary assets, and some of which the City of Detroit, upon declaring its own bankruptcy, considered selling in order to cope with its financial debts. The collections were preserved as a result of a "Grand Bargain" that involved a judicial system, state government, Detroit citizens and public officials, and private foundations working together to find a viable compromise.

In the aftermath of the Great Recession, the sustainability challenge affected many performing arts institutions as well, some of which ceased to exist, such as the Florida Philharmonic Orchestra, the San Jose Repertory Theatre and San Jose Symphony, the Tulsa Philharmonic, the Colorado Springs Symphony, and the San Antonio Symphony, to name a few. The most stable of cultural institutions, public libraries, also may face closures, especially during economic recessions, as financially struggling local governments may prioritize supporting other types of services for their citizens. Other literary organizations, especially publishing houses, have seemed on the verge of extinction for the last 20 years or so, partially due to fluctuating reading rates, and partially due to the spread of online publishing and open access–type models. Yet, sustainability of all these institutional types is critical when it comes to preserving and intergenerationally transmitting collective cultural heritage, as well as educating the young about the humanistic values embedded in literature, music, historic artifacts, and other forms of embedded and living culture.

While each institutional story is in many ways unique, there are common lessons about sustainability that could be derived by looking at the experiences of those organizations that avoided collapse and have done quite well in becoming sustainable as both organizations and societal actors. What distinguishes those organizations is the balancing act in which they engage via institutional routines and managerial practices to reconcile the various tensions, and the ability of managers to balance such tensions while finding their sustainability models. Before introducing more details on how this balancing unfolds, it is important to mention several broader lessons about organizational sustainability that this book offers.

## What Organizational Sustainability Is and Is Not

The first broader lesson about organizational sustainability, and the one that may displease some in the cultural community, is that sustainability is not about buildings, artifacts, or artistic excellence alone. Without a doubt, the quality of cultural artifacts, creative works, and performances—as well as the aesthetic appeal of museum buildings and performance halls in which such artifacts are exhibited and plays are performed—contribute tremendously to establishing the societal value of cultural institutions.

However, it is not the quality of buildings or the artistic value of collections that explains how organizations achieve sustainability. Likewise, although artistic excellence contributes to organizational sustainability, at the end of the day, it is not the ultimate factor that makes it or breaks it, as many high-quality institutions whose examples were given above did not survive the pressures of time. Rather, organizations that are able to transcend the boundaries of their buildings and physical locations, and that are capable of reaching out to their external environment, making local and global connections, and achieving overall social relevance, are the ones that achieve sustainability in a meaningful intergenerational sense.

Furthermore, sustainability itself is much more about intangible social connectedness than it is about buildings and other assets that cement institutional presence in their communities. Social connectedness and community embeddedness, to which connectedness leads, are among the most important building blocks of organizational social capital, which in turn ensures a different kind of cementing in local communities—via cultural experiences, individual insights, and social reflections about the nature of the human condition that cultural institutions offer. The very nature of experiences delivered via cultural institutions, their deliberate intent and instinctual focus on preserving human legacy for future generations, constitutes the important intangibles that communities value intrinsically. However, social connectedness, as an intangible construct and a form of organizational social capital, can also be transformed into very tangible organizational benefits and resources essential for both organizational survival and long-term sustainability. Thus, organizations that are well-connected are also more sustainable. Therefore, it is no surprise that many organizations pursue social connectedness as part of their strategy. Some even adopt connectedness as part of their mission. The Charles Wright Museum of African American History in Detroit, for example, is a case in point. As part of its postrecession revival strategy, the museum has been developing ways to connect with and become more relevant to a wider community of its stakeholders rather than positioning itself as a niche institution primarily focusing on African American stakeholders. Museum managers and the board of directors realized that organizational lack of social connectedness and its reliance on primarily bonding-type ties, which are formed among similar actors, are unsustainable in the long term.

At the local level, social connectedness results in a sense of community ownership and civic pride that protects organizations even during the hardest of times. Globally, connectedness is often achieved with the help of technological innovations. As an example, many publishing houses and literary magazines have been exploring the value of web platforms as a way to better connect with their global readers. Others, such as Words Without Borders—a nonprofit organization located in Brooklyn, New York, which positions itself as a global literature initiative—support a range of web-based literary-translation projects that allow communicating literature to wider global audiences despite the language barriers.

When it comes to social connectedness as a path to greater organizational sustainability, it is hard to overemphasize its significance, especially for certain organizational types. For example, social connectedness plays an especially important role when it comes to the sustainability of urban organizations. Such organizations, on the one hand, benefit from plugging themselves into local social discourses that are relevant to the urban core, but they also benefit greatly from reaching out to communities beyond their immediate geography. In fact, for them, focusing too much on the local environment may deprive them of the ability to diversify their resource base, and thus position them too narrowly.

Reaching out to external communities and building bridging-type ties, which are formed among diverse actors, often involves relying on partnerships with other institutions. Such inter-organizational partnerships need to be formed organically, and with trusted actors; otherwise, they would not serve as effective bridges to geographically distant communities. Furthermore, in the cultural field, efforts of foundations and other donors to artificially induce such partnerships are often met with skepticism. Moreover, starting new partnerships requires time and other resources that some organizations, especially smaller ones, may lack. It is no surprise, then, that partnerships are often initiated by larger and more resourceful organizations, and, even then, smaller organizations may be concerned about preserving their institutional distinctiveness and about being "subsumed" by larger organizations.

There is also a problem with cross-jurisdictional partnerships, especially in environments that are characterized by a strong city-suburb divide. An example of such a divide is the Detroit metropolitan area, where community cultures and institutional mindsets are quite different, making it difficult for organizations to engage in meaningful collaborations across jurisdictional lines. Some suburban organizations, in particular, are wary of partnering with Detroit-based organizations, in part due to the unique historical legacy of this metropolitan area, the discussion of which goes beyond the scope of this book, but also because of the expectation that urban organizations may lack resources and exhibit greater dependency, whereas partnerships work best among equals. There is also a similar culture of suspicion in the urban core itself, where organizations are skeptical of connecting with and relying on others, which is not a sustainable attitude. To that extent, other actors—such as universities, schools, and social-service nonprofits—appear to be important members of the arts and culture eco-system, bridging divides among its various parts.

The second lesson about organizational sustainability is that organizational sustainability cannot be reduced to financial sustainability, albeit that the terms are frequently used as synonyms. In fact, many organizational managers and board members see organizational fiscal health (having a proper mix of revenue sources, including at least some reliance on earned income; balancing revenues with expenses; and establishing stronger endowments) as their primary focus. While such strategies are generally associated with greater prospects for organizational survival, they may not necessarily lead to intergenerational sustainability. Similarly, when it comes to internal operations, organizational capacity (particularly the quality of human resources, staff, board, and volunteers) is very important for organizational sustainability. Likewise, engaging in systematic strategic planning is important, too, but sustainability is not about following a perfect plan or having the most qualified staff. Moreover, strategic plans that outline goals for "achieving" sustainability may not be enough to ensure that the institutions and systems we hope to bequeath to future generations will actually survive long enough to meet those goals.

Organizational survival is, without a doubt, conditioned upon a healthy bottom line and strong organizational capacity, as well as the ability to use the strategic planning process to address environmental dependencies. However, organizational sustainability, in substantive terms, is more about the mission and the ability of organizations to continually pursue their core missions for generations to come. Not every institution with a large financial endowment, for example, would be considered fully sustainable. Good examples of the distinction are the two historical estates in the Detroit metropolitan area associated with the prominent Ford family. One is the Henry Ford House located in Dearborn, a culturally diverse suburb of Detroit; and another one is the Eleanor and Edsel Ford House located in Grosse Pointe Shores, which is a more homogenous and economically well-off suburb of Detroit. The first organization was temporarily closed due to much-needed renovations and the lack of funds to do such renovations without closing. In response to long-standing financial pressures, the organization was eventually moved under the larger umbrella of the Henry Ford Estates. Earlier in its history, the Henry Ford House likewise ran out of funds and was "gifted" to the University of Michigan Dearborn. Despite its financial insecurities, the Henry Ford House is a respected institution that enjoys substantial public recognition and is well-embedded within its community. At the same time, the Eleanor and Edsel Ford House possesses an unusually substantial endowment that guarantees its long-term financial safety. However, the organization is much less connected with the larger community, and it is seeking to establish its broader social relevance. In this example, it is the less financially well-off institution that has managed to establish its relevancy and to have a lasting intergenerational impact, and it is the more financially well-off institution that has struggled to become socially meaningful and intergenerationally significant.

The third lesson about organizational sustainability is that even though "maintenance" is embedded in its meaning, sustainability is not about stability and status quo. Organizational sustainability is more about change and adaptation than it is about stability. This is partially because the external environment in which cultural organizations exist is always changing, presenting both new opportunities and new challenges and thus prompting organizations to respond and adapt. Partially, because sustainable organizations are dynamic internally, they may go through multiple periods of crisis and change: staff and board rotations, evolution in mission statements, and changes in core programs. Organizations that sustain are, therefore, those that are capable of changing, learning, and adapting in the face of internal and external transformations.

In many cases, some of these changes are driven from the bottom up by organizational staff or artists. One example is an institutionalization of a hospital initiative by the musicians of the Detroit Symphony Orchestra, where musicians decided to volunteer their time by performing in local hospitals. This started as an informal grassroots initiative based on musicians' own connections, but the management quickly realized that, if the orchestra is to keep up with its community-oriented mission, it needs to support the musicians in this endeavor and take on a leadership role. As a result, the orchestra was able to achieve greater social relevancy and also distinguish itself, thus serving as an example to others.

The fourth lesson about sustainability is about *not* avoiding stress. Stress is actually a good thing for organizations, as it pushes their managers to be more creative in figuring out what works. It also prompts managers to think whether their organizations are working on developing distinctive competencies and exploring the path of becoming more socially relevant. This message was stressed in many interviews I conducted for this book. Managers of organizations that suffered from stress and forced to engage in various traditional forms of downsizing were also forced out of their comfort zones to develop new strategic partnerships, wider public outreach, more inclusive and innovative programming, and other methods aimed at making their organizations more resilient. In particular, institutions located in urban settings, and those that also experienced high degrees of external stress, were the ones pushed to reinvent themselves, capitalizing on the diversity of their environment and the richness of ideas that such diversity carries with it.

While many organizational managers had regrets about the high levels of stress their institutions had suffered, they also acknowledged the importance of stress for longer-term organizational sustainability. Several of them explicitly stated that stress prevented their institutions from becoming complacent and stagnant. For example, in the context of the Detroit metropolitan area, an innovative and entrepreneurial response to stress is something that particularly large, struggling organizations used to set their institutions on a more sustainable path. External stress was effectively used as a driver toward greater innovation and adaptation by such major institutions as the Detroit Symphony Orchestra, the Detroit Institute of Arts, and the Henry Ford Museum, to name a few.

The fifth lesson about sustainability is that it is not solely in the hands of organizational managers and board members. At a certain point, it is the quality of the operational environment and community culture itself that explains why some organizations thrive and develop more than others. This lesson reflects the core idea of the systems-thinking theory developed in the context of museums by Yuha Jung and Ann Rowson Love (2017) and that implies that the world is open and interconnected, the parts are situated in context, and they shape the whole. Following a similar logic, this book identifies the profound connection that exists between cultural organizations and their environments. While some might consider this type of connection a sort of curse, it is actually a blessing in disguise. On the one hand, arts and culture organizations contribute to their communities in so many different ways that go above and beyond the widely recognized economic development, revitalization, and beautification roles. Cultural organizations generate social capital and foster values, including those associated with sustainability, and they also have intrinsic significance (Moldavanova, 2013, 2014; Moldavanova & Wright, 2020). On the other hand, their own vitality can fall prey to the problems that their communities experience, such as economic decline or demographic shifts.

What distinguishes communities in which arts and culture organizations thrive is a general sense of appreciation and support for arts and culture coupled with the overall sense of civic pride. This sense of civic pride is then transformed in a sense of ownership that exists in such communities in relation to their cultural amenities, and that is especially important in environments where public support for the arts is scarce. Consistent with Richard Florida's argument (2002), arts and culture tend to thrive in areas with high concentrations of educational infrastructure, especially in the presence of major universities. On the one hand, these types of areas are likely to be home to arts and culture donors with naturally high levels of appreciation for the arts. On the other hand, areas with high per-capita levels of education and the presence of educational institutions are also places where creative activities are often initiated in association with the aforementioned educational institutions. For example, many large universities have their own art galleries, museums, theaters, and performing arts centers. They also have departments that educate art professionals and others employed in the various related industries.

However, sustainability of arts and culture institutions is also a product of a particular community-level mindset that encourages the presence of vibrant arts and science centers, thriving libraries and historical museums, and well-attended community theater productions. Communities that have this mindset are places where people like to gather outside of their homes and where they view caring for community institutions, whether arts-related institutions or homeless shelters, as part of their lives and as part of their personal legacies. Typically, these are very diverse communities in terms of race, ethnicity, income, and professions, and such diversity is associated with particularly rich cultural expression. These are collaborative and connected kinds of communities, where people have a stake in each other and in community life, but these are not necessarily high-income communities, although the presence of resources is important for sustaining various forms of social infrastructure. Arts and culture organizations thrive in these kinds of communities. It is important, however, that arts and culture organizations foster the sense of community ownership by deliberately increasing their social relevance while also protecting their institutional distinctiveness.

However, even in declining communities, the arts can thrive if they are capable of embedding themselves into larger social discourses that are important for their communities. Libraries, museums, and theaters in struggling communities often bring a ray of light to the life of their residents, giving them hope, a sense of solidarity, and creative ideas on how to improve community life. Detroit Repertory Theatre is an example of an institution that plays these roles in the struggling city of Highland Park—one of Detroit's inner-ring cities that was severely affected by the downsizing of the car industry and subsequent population decline. Today, Highland Park is a high-crime and low-employment area riddled with abandoned houses and empty store fronts. This is where the Detroit Repertory Theater, a community-based professional theater, is located. It opened its doors in 1957 and survived its share of dark times in Detroit's history, including the race riots of 1967. The theater hires professional actors to present modern-day and classic plays to the Highland Park community, but it also forms an unseen web of social connections and serves as a "third" place for community residents who, due to their generally low-income status, are not traditionally viewed as core patrons of the arts. Yet, the theater has endured largely due to the support of its local community and because of the unique place it holds and the value it provides for that community. What this example shows is that it is not necessarily economically well-off communities that are able to sustain their cultural institutions; it is rather the value that communities place on their cultural institutions that determines organizational destiny.

Following the idea that cultural sustainability is a collective enterprise, and both cultural managers and communities have a responsibility for sustaining the arts, the sixth lesson about organizational sustainability is that it requires advance investment. In particular, more investment is needed to conquer the history of elitism that still permeates institutional structure and operations in many classical cultural institutions (Acevedo, & Madara, 2015; Garibay, 2009; Olivares & Piatak, 2022; Ostrower, 2020), thus creating an unwelcoming environment for many underrepresented visitors. Despite some advances that have been made in recent years to diversify organizational boards and staff and make programming more inclusive, more work needs to be done to improve cultural representation (Olivares & Piatak, 2022; Sandell, & Nightingale, 2012). Another form of important advance investment is in the early exposure to the arts via the public education function. Early exposure to reading, theater-going, and other cultural experiences forms long-term habits that people pass on to their children and grandchildren. Arts and culture institutions may appear too intimidating to those who have not visited an art museum or heard a symphony perform inside a concert hall early on in their lives; they may feel put off by the rules that one is expected to follow while attending an exhibition or play hosted by a classical cultural institution. That is why engaging with community and facilitating inclusive access is so important for arts and culture organizations' sustainability.

This also brings up the argument about the importance of public support for the arts. Even if modest, public funding serves as both a financial baseline and a symbol of larger societal legitimacy of the arts as a valued form of both living and embedded human heritage. Note that libraries that typically receive at least some public funding, and whose developed network owes a lot to the legacy of Andrew Carnegie's philanthropic efforts in the early 20th century, rarely suffer from the claims of elitism. Libraries are present in their communities, they are welcoming and accessible, and they perform multiple social roles. However, the lack of early exposure to libraries—and book reading more generally—can be damaging.

## Organizational Sustainability: The Balancing Nature of the Concept

While it is clear now what organizational sustainability is and is not, it is worth discussing a fundamental feature of organizational sustainability that emerged in the process of my research. If we were to use one word to describe organizational sustainability, it would be "equilibrium," meaning "balance." The balancing nature of organizational sustainability manifests itself in a dynamic interplay of complementary and/or opposing concepts. As this book argues, achieving proper balance between the two narratives—institutional resilience and institutional distinctiveness—is key to achieving intergenerational sustainability. To that extent, it is more likely that the strategies designed to enhance institutional resilience will conflict with institutional distinctiveness, rather than vice versa, especially when environmental pressures are high and cause significant competition due to resource scarcity. It might be tempting at those times to prioritize resilience strategies; yet maintaining institutional distinctiveness is of equally critical importance for intergenerational sustainability.

For example, many cultural organizations that were profoundly affected by the Great Recession of 2007–2009 sought to professionalize and adopt businesslike management approaches, viewing such approaches as a path to greater resilience. However, in the process of institutional adaptation and change (especially if such adaptation involved becoming "businesslike"), keeping focus on one's mission and institutional uniqueness was critically important for preserving institutional identity. Organizational sustainability, therefore, is not about perfect harmony but rather about a balancing act pursued by organizational managers on a daily basis. It is about the ability of institutions (at times on the verge of extremes) to find balance so they will be able to fight off a storm when it comes.

Having a clear institutional identity is important for organizational sustainability both at times of stress, when considering such identity may keep organizations on course while engaging in various innovative strategies, and also in stable times, when running their business as usual. In fact, organizations that struggle with establishing a strong identity are also typically uncertain of their future. One such example from Metropolitan Detroit is the Grosse Pointe War Memorial, an organization established in a suburb of Detroit in memory of veterans and soldiers of World War II. While, as the name suggests, serving veterans of World War II and other wars remains part of its mission, the organization pursues a wide range of activities, from hosting public concerts and presentations to rendering commercial services, such as wedding and party rentals. Some of these activities are primarily about culture, while others are income generating. Therefore, there is a certain level of dissonance between an actual and aspired identity coupled with confusion regarding what this organization's legacy should be. Yet, establishing a more streamlined identity is of critical importance for the future of this organization.

From a strategic management point of view, balancing between a more generalist orientation and a more specialist focus (Hannan & Freeman, 1989) in organizational programs and operations appears important as well. Hence, niche organizations may engage in diversification strategies, while generalist organizations may seek the development of distinct competencies. The idea behind this logic is to be prepared for both stable and changing times, particularly because shifts between such times can be sudden and unpredictable (Hannan & Freeman, 1989). It is also important to balance organizational professionalization, such as investing in its human resources and technologies, with attention to the external environment and the various stakeholders embedded in that environment. Organizations that disproportionally focus on professionalization may lose sight of their missions, and organizations that pay insufficient attention to professional skills may not be able to continuously pursue their missions. Organizational size itself appears to bring up some balancing considerations. On the one hand, keeping things small and frugal may allow for the prevention of sustainability crises caused by rapid growth. On the other hand, a small operational scale may also restrict organizational ability to scale its social impact. Organizational growth, therefore, increases the potential for higher impact, but it needs to be carefully balanced.

Another example of a balancing act in the name of sustainability is pursuing a more global focus while also emphasizing relevance to local communities in which cultural organizations are physically embedded. The importance of a more global orientation could be explained by the larger societal tendencies, including globalization pressures and the increasing importance of information technology that enables going-global efforts. However, a global focus needs to be balanced with achieving social relevancy locally, as cultural organizations are unequivocally tied to their local communities. Yet another example of sustainability pursuit is balancing the traditional focus of cultural organizations—especially the classical forms, on arts and culture scholarship and intellectual sophistication—with achieving greater content accessibility. This is perhaps one of the better strategies for countering the claims of elitism, achieving greater social relevance, and connecting with new audiences and potential supporters. Behind this balancing act is the idea that arts and culture are inherently public goods, and they should be presented to the public as such.

As these examples show, there is no true long-term sustainability without a balance. In fact, organizations are constantly facing all kinds of balancing dilemmas, and their managers have to make decisions about how to achieve a proper balance. The question then becomes, What sort of institutional and managerial thinking allows some organizations to achieve such balance more successfully than others? The answer this book offers lies in the idea of sustainable thinking—both an actual practice and an ethical obligation with which managers of sustainable organizations are tasked.

## Putting It All Together: Sustainable Thinking

The main argument of this book, as stated above, is based on the dynamic interplay of two sustainability narratives. In the long run, these narratives together serve as the basis for the intergenerational sustainability of organizations. Although the institutional resilience and institutional distinctiveness narratives are both necessary for institutional survival and sustainability, there is also a tension between them.

The state of equilibrium that allows organizations to properly balance complementary and at times competing narratives and strategies is achieved via sustainable thinking—a form of institutional logic that is fundamentally forward looking and that is distinct from strategic thinking. Unlike conventional strategic thinking, sustainable thinking factors in care for future generations and prioritizes institutional legacy over immediate outcomes. For example, when it comes to social connectedness as a factor of sustainability, engaging in strategic kinds of partnerships that provide access to resources and help broaden organizational missions would be an example of strategic thinking. At the same time, choosing partnerships that will be carefully aligned with the current mission and will also be beneficial for the long-term organizational legacy is an example of sustainable thinking.

In conventional terms, the focus of strategic thinking is on achieving results. Strategic thinking asks: What is my mission, and what are my goals? What steps do I need to take to accomplish these goals? How do I effectively use internal and external resources for maximizing outputs and outcomes? Sustainable thinking, on the other hand, transcends this logic. Instead of seeking results, sustainable thinking asks: What is important for my organization, and what kind of legacy would it want to leave for the future? What are its core values, and what would it take to preserve them? In other words, strategic and sustainable thinking are different, albeit connected, ideas. Indeed, sustainability often builds on strategic thinking. Strategic thinking improves the chances for organizational survival—a necessity for intergenerational sustainability, and it often becomes a baseline for sustainable thinking. By contrast, sustainable thinking allows for the reconciling of the two narratives of sustainability, and sustainable decisions over time translate into sustainability capital, which can be conceived of as an unseen endowment that sustains organizations in the long-term and safeguards the needs of future generations.

Organizational managers engage in sustainable thinking by devising strategies that safeguard the interests of future generations, but they sometimes do so unconsciously; it is instead a personal sense of what is right and what is ethical that guides their everyday work. By doing so, managers of cultural institutions almost inadvertently pursue an ethic of sustainability, thus upholding the interests of future generations while also preserving culture and helping to uncover and acknowledge the past in more direct ways. Following institutional theory (March & Olsen, 1989), sustainable decisions are made according to a logic of appropriateness and the idea of making sense of existing institutional and extra-institutional conditions, rather than in the rational pursuit of formalized strategic plans. This sense of appropriateness allows managers to reconcile the tensions embedded in the two narratives of intergenerational sustainability. Consistent with the decision-making theory by March and Olsen (1989), managers of sustainable organizations do not simply act as rational strategic planners when considering longer-term sustainability; instead, they try to make sense of the contemporary environmental and institutional contexts, while still making decisions with practical implications for future generations. Moreover, although a formal commitment to future generations is not always explicitly declared in institutional missions and strategic plans, such a commitment is nevertheless a guiding principle for managerial decisions.

Furthermore, in the face of future uncertainties, sustainability implies the presence of an ethical imperative—a concern for the rights and welfare of future generations—embedded in both organizational routines and managerial practices. Being intergenerationally sustainable means not only being effective but also being equitable toward future generations. The sustainability imperative is concerned with the legacy of institutions, and how modern-day policies and actions affect the ability of institutions to carry out their purpose across generations. Therefore, we can think of sustainable thinking as a process that extends strategic management by bringing it to a new level.

Likewise, when it comes to strategic management, greater reliance on earned income as a financial sustainability strategy, investment in professionalization and capacity building, and engagement in strategic planning are all manifestations of strategic thinking that is outcome oriented and seeks to produce primarily tangible impact. Sustainable thinking, on the other hand, is more about the balancing act and about reconciling tensions that may arise while pursuing conventional strategies. Sustainable thinking is also about constantly learning, which ensures the ability of organizations to stay relevant regardless of their actual age. Learning organizations are more sustainable, and those that stopped learning are on the path to eventual extinction.

Sustainable thinking requires having a bold vision, especially in organizations that face stress. Moreover, the strategic kind of boldness that comes with the appreciation of risks and innovations needs to be combined with the boldness of being able to look farther into the future, anticipating major societal shifts that are likely to affect humans' relation to culture. One example of sustainable thinking is anticipating technological changes and the role that they will play in reshaping the nature and forms of creative activity, or anticipating changing audience preferences and attitudes, and factoring in how these changes are likely to affect institutional missions and identities. In hiring future executives and recruiting board members, organizations need to make sure that they pay attention to both kinds of bold vision—the strategic and the intergenerationally sustainable.

## A Note on the Research Approach

The book is based on more than five years of research and fieldwork conducted on a variety of organizations within the domain of arts, culture, and humanities. This included in-depth interviews with managers of cultural organizations and cultural experts (66 interviews collected from 48 organizations, 21 located in seven U.S. states, and 27 in the Detroit metropolitan area); historical analysis of sustainability logic within the domains of museums, music and performing arts, and literature organizations; document analysis and analysis of best practices aimed at achieving sustainability that emerged in the field; and direct and participant observations. Rather than focusing on a smaller set of in-depth case studies, this book relied on analyzing institutional histories and managerial discourse collected from diverse cultural organizations. In order to understand the general context of institutional transformations, I also reviewed examples of innovative sustainability strategies within the cultural sector more generally and within the three subfields (museums, literary organizations, and music and performing arts) covered in the book, as well as discussions of such strategies in the media and on professional websites and blogs.

The conceptualization of intergenerational sustainability and the theoretical framework for intergenerational sustainability in the arts and humanities presented in this book were developed via the grounded theoretical approach (Clarke, Friese, & Washburn, 2018; Corbin & Strauss, 1990; Corbin & Strauss, 2008; Dunne, 2011; Glaser, 1978; McGhee, Marland, & Atkinson, 2007; Romzek, LeRoux, & Blackmar, 2012). This approach allowed for developing analytical categories that were then generalized into a framework that conceives intergenerational sustainability as an interplay between the two narratives—institutional resilience and institutional distinctiveness—and that relies on sustainable thinking as a way of enacting sustainability via day-to-day managerial practices and institutional routines.

Besides being used to generate cohesive theories, the grounded-theory approach has also been used by researchers as a means of generating new insights into their objects of study (Lansisalmi, Peiro, & Kivimaki, 2004). This book follows this tradition by presenting a framework of intergenerational sustainability obtained through the refinement and extension of existing theories (Dunne, 2011; McGhee et al., 2007; Snow, Morrill, & Anderson, 2003). This book, therefore, is a product of a dynamic interaction between an empirical inquiry and existing literature on sustainability, decision-making, and strategic management in public and nonprofit organizations. Furthermore, the book incorporates elements of the situational-analysis approach (Clarke et al., 2018), which reflects developments in the grounded theory beyond its initial positivist roots articulated in the 1950s and 1960s. The ultimate goals of the grounded-theory method that incorporates ideas of situational analysis are (1) to support theorizing as an ongoing process rather than the development of substantive and formal theories and (2) to give a researcher her own voice in interpreting the data as opposed to treating her as a mere objective observer. This latter interpretation of the grounded theory emphasizes not only similarities in the discovered patterns but also differences, and it enables a multimodal and more flexible research process that relies on the analysis of diverse sources ranging from discursive textual and historical and archival documents to ethnographic (interview and observational) transcripts and field notes (Clarke et al., 2018).

The main portion of the field-research component is composed of interviews with top and middle managers of the selected institutions, which provided for the acquisition of in-depth knowledge of the topic from a selected group of experts (Beamer, 2002; Dexter, 2006; Odendahl & Shaw, 2002). The purpose of such interviews was to better understand the topic from the perspective of the interviewees and to identify and analyze qualitative patterns and relationships among concepts (King, 2004). The interviews were based on a combination of closed (factual) and open (value) questions, which allowed subjects to explore the relationship between particular sustainability strategies and core institutional values. The reframing of research categories depended on data gathered from interviewees, as is common for grounded theory (Strauss, 1987).

Data for this book were collected via a two-stage process. The first set of data was collected over the course of three years, starting in 2011, from 21 U.S.-based museums, music and performing arts institutions, and literature organizations located in Kansas, Missouri, Colorado, Illinois, Iowa, New York, and Oregon. These organizational interviews were preceded by consultations with several experts, and they allowed for an investigation of institutional logics and intergenerational sustainability narratives via experiences of cultural organizations, most of which were at least 35 years old. The duration was chosen as an indication of institutional survivability and the ability of organizations to serve the needs of more than one generation. Initial selection was made via professional referrals and represented a convenience sample of diverse institutions within three cultural domains. All institutions from the sample are currently on the path to successfully pursuing their social missions.

The fieldwork allowed for the examination of the major differences among the three cultural domains (museums, music and performing arts institutions, and literary organizations); the tracing of intergenerational sustainability questions to the origins of recorded practices associated with creating and preserving significant artifacts; and the exploration of contemporary managerial thinking about institutional purposes and their evolution, future generations, current and future sustainability concerns, and how such concerns are being addressed. This part of my research has led to the development of the conceptual definition of both intergenerational sustainability and the two narratives—institutional distinctiveness and institutional resilience—that provide a substantive understanding of the institutional elements associated with intergenerational sustainability. Sustainable thinking also emerged as a way of reconciling tensions among the narratives and as a concept that explains how intergenerational sustainability is enacted.

The second set of data was collected over the course of two years, starting in 2014, in the Detroit metropolitan area. Data were collected from managers of 27 diverse cultural organizations that have suffered varying degrees of external stress due to the Great Recession of 2007–2009 and were able to recover. What prompted this second stage of data collection was the importance of local context as well as the varying levels of challenges that organizations may suffer on their path to sustainability. Firstly, placing the fieldwork in a geographically bounded area enabled me to investigate the role of the entire ecosystem in which arts and culture organizations exist, as well as the role of social connectedness as a critically important element of organizational sustainability.

Secondly, the outcomes of the Great Recession have made us question the very prospects of organizational survival, subsequently challenging the ability of cultural organizations to pursue intergenerational sustainability. Learning from different experiences of organizations from the same geographical area that were trying to balance their short-term survival with longer-term sustainability was particularly useful for understanding how sustainable thinking is enacted on a daily basis. Moreover, the second research phase was able to compare strategies used by organizations that have undergone varying degrees of stress in coping with the consequences of a major recession.

Organizations examined during the second phase of fieldwork were categorized into three groups based on the effects of stress: organizations that closed or considered closure as an option in response to stress were assigned to the highly stressed group; organizations whose operating budget was reduced by more than 25% or that engaged in downsizing, including staff and program cuts, were assigned to the medium-stress group; and organizations that did not experience any of these consequences were assigned to the low-stress group. There were more organizations that experienced high and medium levels of stress as compared to low-stress organizations in my sample, which comes as no surprise, as metropolitan Detroit was one of the U.S. regions hardest hit by the Great Recession. Although all organizations ended up surviving the recession, two of them were temporarily closed as a result of recession pressures. Insights provided by these organizations are particularly valuable in this investigation. They supplement the largely positive story about sustainability conveyed by organizations from the first round of research, with the profound struggles experienced and overcome with varying degrees of success by Detroit-based organizations.

The theoretical framework of intergenerational organizational sustainability presented in the book is, therefore, grounded in both a zoom-out approach that sketches the differences and similarities among the arts and humanities subfields included in the study, and a zoom-in approach that places organizations within a particular local eco-system (metropolitan Detroit). This type of approach, as well as the diversity of the organizations themselves, has allowed me to tell a story about organizational perseverance and adaptation in the face of significant external shocks, chiefly the Great Recession of 2007–2009. Furthermore, rather than focusing on organizational case studies, comparing broad-based insights with those derived from a particular local eco-system allowed for the painting of a more nuanced view of organizational sustainability as a concept that incorporates internal institutional logics as well as external routines through which organizations seek to interact with and contribute to sustainability in their local communities.

## Incorporating the Detroit Context: The Second Fieldwork

The Detroit metropolitan area proved to be a very fertile ground for researching organizational sustainability of the cultural sector and its institutions, both in terms of examples and for incorporating context. In some ways, the Detroit metropolitan area represents an extreme; in other ways, it perfectly mimics the many sustainability tensions that our society experiences, including the tensions among the three conventionally recognized sustainability pillars—environment, economy, and sociopolitical systems. The decline of the industrial city has brought with itself many environmental problems, many caused by deteriorating and closed plants or neighborhoods left behind by fleeing populations. While postrecession economic development has brought new infrastructure and improved transportation and mobility options, the benefits of those developments are unevenly distributed. The new economic growth and development that it created, as some would argue, has exacerbated social inequalities between the well-educated, dynamic, and entrepreneurial outsiders and the less-advantaged insiders. For example, while new business development increased the attractiveness of the downtown area, it has also pushed old-timers—both businesses and residents—further away from both the city center and the center of development.

These developments have affected long-standing major arts nonprofits, which have served as hubs or "warehouses" of cultural activity for the entire arts-and-culture ecosystem. Among these institutions are such major organizations as the Detroit Institute of Arts, Michigan Opera Theater, Detroit Public Library, Detroit Symphony Orchestra, as well as smaller but equally prominent actors, such the Belle Isle Aquarium or a more recently established Matrix Theater, located in southwest Detroit. Origins, history, and present concerns of these organizations are intertwined with the city of Detroit itself. For example, in their recent history, many downtown organizations have faced new competitive pressures as the new sports-and-entertainment district was erected on the ruins of several old buildings, some of which had to be demolished to make space for the new development, despite the many protests by historical preservation groups and area residents. The area—previously dominated by theaters and other performing arts institutions, as well as by small locally owned businesses—is now a new competitive space, pushing arts organizations, especially smaller ones, to think about their identity and their future in the downtown Detroit. Some, for example, the Detroit Puppet Theater—a long-standing downtown resident—had to find a new space in a nearby suburb. The new location is not as culturally vibrant as Detroit's downtown, but it does offer cheaper rent.

It is also critically important to acknowledge the racial tensions that are written into Detroit's history and are still affecting its present life, including the functioning of its cultural institutions (Binelli, 2013; Farley, Danziger & Holzer, 2000; LeDuff, 2013; Stone, 2017). In 1967, Detroit experienced one of the worst civil disturbances in U.S. history, due to entrenched, long-standing institutionalized racism (Farley et al., 2000; Stone, 2017). Depending on the source, events of 1967, when thousands of people took to the streets engaging in vandalism and overwhelming the law-enforcement system, have been labeled as "rebellion," "riot," "uprising," or "insurrection" (Stone, 2017). These events had exposed the many pains and ills of the postindustrial city, where economic decline caused by the auto industry reshaping was one of the many deep issues of social concern. Following 1967, Detroit experienced a major flight of white populations from racially mixed urban regions to more homogeneous suburban areas. As Farley et al. (2000) explain, while Whites were able to take advantage of subsidized home-loan programs to move to suburbs, African Americans' overall prospects for employment, education, and upward mobility were winding down, and many of the suburban locations were mostly closed to them (Farley et al., 2000). These dynamics have caused a major urban core-suburban divide that still affects the city's life today.

To be sure, the outer migration of White middle-class populations was not unique to Detroit, and it happened in many urban areas (e.g., Kansas City, Cleveland) during the civil rights movement in the 1960s. However, the impact on Detroit was particularly drastic, and it left the city with decades of fear, disinvestment, and racial segregation (Stone, 2017). Coupled with the auto-industry decline, Detroit was turning into an urban desert, as its population declined by more than 40 percent between 1970 and 2006. Once a place for unprecedented upward social mobility for blue-collar workers, many of whom were of minority backgrounds, by the early 1990s, Detroit had become a landmark example of rustbelt deindustrialization that disproportionally disadvantaged minority populations (Farley et al., 2000). Even today, when Detroit is experiencing an "upswing," and its politics and economy have changed, critical services for urban populations are still lacking, and many properties in the city remain unoccupied (Binelli, 2013; LeDuff, 2013; Stone, 2017). Despite the new opportunities coming its way, the city has one of the slowest population-growth trends in the U.S.

While many of Detroit's contemporary issues represent the universal urgency of the urban-revival problems, such as the questions of equity and access to various public amenities including the arts, metropolitan Detroit stands out in many instances, including the continuing presence in the city of deep segregation along racial lines even despite comparable socioeconomic status (Rushton, 2005). It is important to consider these dynamics in light of this book's subject—sustainability as an organizational logic and routine—as they provide valuable context for understanding consequences that many local cultural organizations experienced in the face of major shocks, such as the Great Recession of 2007–2009. For example, organizations located in the urban core suffered more from the Great Recession (Moldavanova & Akbulut, 2022), and many also experienced significant geographic accessibility issues as a result of the fragmented transportation infrastructure that supports access to various public amenities, especially by minority populations (Moldavanova, Meloche, & Thompson, 2022).

The Detroit metropolitan area is also still riddled with the problems of urban planning centered on the "car culture." As a result of the many social and economic transformations that happened over the course of the past 50 years, and despite their geographic proximity, Detroit's urban and suburban cultural institutions exist in very different spaces and very different realities. Approximately half of the organizations from the second research phase are located in the city proper and half in the suburbs. Therefore, comparing experiences of these organizations provided valuable lessons for the subject of this book. As the many Detroit-based examples in the book will show, these various path-dependent dynamics have had an impact on the logic of sustainable thinking that unfolds in cultural organizations.

The main lesson about organizational sustainability from the Detroit metropolitan area, however, aligns with insights obtained from the organizations located in other U.S. locations. When it comes to factors associated with future organizational success, interviewees emphasized the importance of pursuing strategies associated with both resilience and distinctiveness narratives. Being adaptable and engaging in innovative and strategic partnerships was seen as a sign of future success via the ability of organizations to maintain their social relevance. Preserving institutional identity and staying true to the mission, likewise, was deemed important for maintaining the distinctiveness narrative. Finally, the quality of local environment and the degree of organizational connectedness within such environment arose as an essential success factor. There was a general understanding that no matter how much internal sustainable thinking is going on in organizations, their long-term sustainability is conditioned upon a sense of civic pride and ownership that exists in their communities.

## The Structure of the Book

The concept of intergenerational sustainability developed here is based on the dynamic interplay of two narratives—institutional resilience and institutional distinctiveness. The two narratives are unpacked in the chapters focused on museums, music and performing arts, and literature organizations, investigating the evolving organizational missions, changing managerial roles, and values these organizations foster in their communities. Through engagement with theory and extensive fieldwork, the book shows that the narratives of sustainability (institutional resilience and institutional distinctiveness) and intergenerational equity are related in fundamental ways. The broader intellectual implication of the insights offered in this book encompasses the critical notion that genuine long-term sustainability (the kind that secures the rights of future generations) requires sustainable stewardship today. Such stewardship necessitates management strategies that pursue an ethic of sustainability within the context of organizations in which the community itself has a stake. While there are similarities among cultural subfields, each of them offers a unique contribution to our understanding of intergenerational sustainability from which other types of organizations can learn.

The book consists of five chapters. This introductory chapter 1 has offered an overview of the book's broader context, as well as the key argument and larger lessons about organizational sustainability that will be further detailed in the book. Chapters 2–4 present research findings that looked separately at museums, literature, and music and performing arts institutions. These chapters develop the concept of institutional capital for sustainability and show how each of these cultural subfields endeavors to develop it. The empirical chapters illustrate the interplay between the two narratives of intergenerational sustainability and the notion of sustainable thinking by providing historical and contemporary examples offered by museums, literature, and music and performing arts organizations. Each of the chapters explores organizational routines and the logic of sustainability by discussing (a) the institutional factors (university affiliation versus a freestanding nonprofit model) that influence the choices of sustainability strategies; (b) the evolution of institutional missions that has ensured greater organizational adaptability over time; (c) the changing managerial roles associated with sustainability; and (d) the various values different arts and humanities promote in their communities.

More specifically, chapter 2 shows that museums not only function as institutions of historical memory but also safeguard the interests of future generations by sharing culture and promoting the inclusion of culture into the societal sustainability discourse. Chapter 3 argues that the sustainability of literature institutions lies in their ability to transmit cultural capital across time and space. Thus, literature serves as a moral language between generations. Chapter 4 demonstrates that among all cultural organizations, music and performing arts are particularly capable of building symbiotic relationships with their communities. In the long run, this relationship with community results in greater institutional sustainability.

The concluding chapter 5 leads with the idea of sustainable thinking that has emerged from the examination of different cultural subfields, and the discussion of how sustainable thinking differs from more traditional strategic management. It highlights the importance of viewing organizational sustainability as a process, rather than an end result, to better understand how sustainability-related decisions are made and enacted, and how sustainability is embedded in institutional routines. Chapter 5 also discusses common themes and discoveries and outlines the key intellectual contributions of this book: in particular, how it advances our understanding of sustainability as an intergenerational concept.

The book's lessons about sustainable thinking in the arts and humanities, drawn from a diverse set of cultural organizations, are relevant to a wide range of public and nonprofit organizations beyond the arts and humanities. While the story of this book, building upon numerous examples from the cultural field, is largely context specific, the idea of intergenerational sustainability, the tensions embedded in this concept, and how those tensions are being reconciled by cultural managers on a daily basis, provide useful guidance to scholars and managers in and outside of the cultural field. These lessons offer a unique and innovative interpretation of the idea of organizational sustainability. By challenging the familiar expectations and conventions, the book calls upon students of organizational sustainability to expand their approaches to sustainable management by keeping in mind the needs and aspirations of future generations.

Chapter 2

# Museums

## Safeguarding the Interests of Future Generations

Within the domain of arts, culture, and humanities, a museum is perhaps the most obvious example of an institution specifically created for collecting and preserving historically significant objects and promoting humanistic values for future generations. From the very beginning, museums have served as institutions of intergenerational memory by ensuring the preservation of historically significant and socially meaningful objects. However, only after a museum has established itself as a truly public institution is it able to serve the interests of the public at large, whether currently living, or yet to be born. By ensuring the accumulation, transformation, preservation, and growth of cultural and social values, as well as their transmission to future generations, museums serve as an institutionalized form of sustainability.

The role of museums as institutions of intergenerational memory has been long acknowledged. Frederic A. Lucas, speaking as the director of Brooklyn Museum, during his 1907 address at the Staten Island Association of Arts and Sciences said,

> For nowadays the entire face of Nature is being altered by the energy of man, and natural conditions are changing so rapidly that in many places the present generation has little or no knowledge of what was there even fifty years ago . . . And it is one of the purposes of a museum . . . to carefully gather and preserve all objects that may aid in giving an idea of the

life that was here three centuries ago and to provide for the information of those who will be here three centuries hence. (Genoways & Andrei, 2008)

Considering the rapid change in technology and the effects of globalization, the problem described by Frederic A. Lucas one hundred years ago is even more urgent today. Indeed, by serving the interests of long-term future generations, museums function as social institutions that include future generations into the domain of their temporal public. Moreover, by offering a diverse range of cultural experiences and a plurality of ideas, as well as by attempting to reach various social groups, contemporary museums implement principles of justice toward current and future generations in practice, and thus inherently pursue an ethic of sustainability.

Museums as we know them today are the product of long years of growth and evolution, and they are still growing and changing. In 1970, the American Alliance of Museums (AAM), formerly the American Association of Museums, defined a museum as "an organized and permanent non-profit institution, essentially educational and aesthetic in purpose, with professional staff, which owns and utilizes tangible objects, cares for them, and exhibits them to the public on some regular schedule" (Alexander, 1983, p. 5). This definition was modified in 1988 to accommodate organizations that do not own collections on a permanent basis, such as art centers, planetariums, and science centers (Alexander & Alexander, 2008). The main functions of a museum recognized by AAM include collecting and conserving objects, research, exhibition, education, and interpretation. Historically, once the museum established itself as a public institution, the function of exhibition became dominant, and collecting, conservation, and research chiefly supported the development of exhibitions (Alexander et al., 2008).

The intergenerational continuity of museums as public-serving institutions is the result of their own organizational sustainability. Over the course of history, many political and economic systems collapsed; small and large countries changed their geographic borders; and numerous social institutions and ideologies—once prosperous and strong—collapsed, but many museums survived and even flourished. This tendency, of course, is not without exception, but the notable thing is that many museums located in both the developed and developing world managed to outlive their countries' political and economic systems, as well as various ideological regimes.

Despite their social significance and remarkable resilience, however, museums have always needed to justify their existence in order to cope with being underrated, underfunded, and underappreciated (Conn, 2010). In recent years, for example, many museums have been unable to survive a tough recessionary economy. Examples include Florida's Gulf Coast Museum of Art, the Bead Museum in Washington, D.C., and the Minnesota Museum of American Art. Other museums, including the Rose Art Museum at Brandeis University, the University of Connecticut's Benton Museum of Art, and the East Ely Railroad Depot Museum in Virginia City, have seriously considered either selling major works from their collections or loaning works of art to private galleries (Nazarov, 2011; Pollock, 2009).

In addition to economic pressures, contemporary museums also face environmental and man-made disasters, wars, and other cataclysms that may jeopardize their existence. When such loss occurs, however, it is not taken lightly by museum visitors, supporters, and larger society, as there is an understanding that, with every destroyed museum, a part of our collective cultural heritage is gone as well. One of the most recent and most devastating examples of such a situation is the fire in 2018 that destroyed the National Museum in Rio de Janeiro. About 10 percent of collections survived the fire, and some of the collections are replaceable, but it is clear that the museum as an institution is mostly gone. It surfaced that the museum had been losing funding and got behind on its infrastructure development projects, which may have contributed to the tragedy. The event was perceived as a true national tragedy, with some commentators referring to it as "a lobotomy in Brazilian memory" (Young, 2018). In other (but no less drastic) ways, the COVID-19 pandemic in 2020 caused many museums to close temporarily, cancel and downsize their programs, and lay off staff. After the pandemic subsided, many museums faced the problem of declining membership and attendance rates, leading to further budget shortfalls and operational downsizing (AAM, 2022). While governmental funding and access to the relief funds helped many museums to bounce back, some still experience challenges in filling open positions (AAM, 2022).

Despite the difficulties that museums face, many have nevertheless been successful in maintaining their status and significance for current and future generations, making museums a good subject for the study of intergenerational sustainability. What does it take for a museum to stand the test of time? What makes a museum sustainable? This chapter offers some answers to these questions by looking into museums' history, their present, and their future. The chapter draws upon a variety of museum types, from those that focus on arts, history, and natural history, to those that provide more interactive types of experiences, such as science centers. What they all have in common is the exhibition function that describes the nature of their work and the collections that they hold in public trust and for the generations to come.

The key lesson about sustainability that this chapter offers is that it is inherently about the balancing act, first and foremost, between the two institutional narratives (institutional resilience and institutional distinctiveness) that frame how sustainability is enacted in organizations with varying institutional structures. Further, a path toward intergenerational sustainability lies in the ability of museums to balance their naturally introspective focus on objects and collections with an outward-looking community-oriented perspective, and to promote socially important values while pursuing their own adaptive strategies. In following this path, museums enhance their own prospects for long-term sustainability while also contributing to the sustainability of their communities in a variety of tangible and intangible ways.

## Museum as an Institution of Intergenerational Memory: History and Evolution

Museums as formalized institutions date back to the third century BC, when the first famous museum containing the objects of art and nature was founded at Alexandria (Alexander et al., 2008). The modern museum as it is known to us is "a product of Renaissance humanism, of eighteenth-century enlightenment and nineteenth-century democracy" (J. Mordaunt Crook, quoted in Alexander et al., 2008). While museums started opening their doors to the public in the late 17th century—when the first university museum was opened in Basel in 1671, and not long after that the Ashmolean Museum was established at Oxford—the nineteenth century is often considered the museum's golden age, where nearly every country in Western Europe was able to build a comprehensive collection of art from ancient times to present (Alexander et al., 2008). This was also the time when the first Friends of the Museum organization in the world was established by Wilhelm Bode in Berlin, which enabled public museums to use private funds for purchasing desired collections.

The first formal museum opened in the United States was the Charleston Museum in Philadelphia, with branches in Baltimore and New York, founded in 1773 as a collection of natural history objects and portraits of Founding Fathers. Later, in 1846, the Smithsonian Institution was founded in Washington, D.C., as part of the will of the Englishman James Smithson, who was hoping that this institution would accumulate and infuse the scientific knowledge in America. In 1873, when George Brown Goode joined the Smithsonian, the museum started evolving into an interdisciplinary institution—a national museum of science, humanities, and the arts (Alexander et al., 2008). Finally, the United States gained a prominent place in the international museum community around 1870 with the establishment of three major museums—the American Museum of Natural History, the Metropolitan Museum of Art in New York, and the Museum of Fine Arts in Boston.

An early American museum was the combination of two competing models: one following the Louvre's idea of a museum as a palace, and the other following London's South Kensington complex, based on the idea of a museum as a place for enjoyment and education of working citizens (Conn, 1998). For instance, in the late nineteenth century, New York's Metropolitan Museum of Art chose the Louvre model, while Philadelphia's museum chose South Kensington's. As the role of objects continued to rise at the turn of the century, many prominent museums shifted away from the industrial model and moved toward the Louvre model (Conn, 2010). The separation between the two models is still alive—with larger museums preferring the Louvre orientation, and smaller community-based museums serving demand for education.

The establishment of the American museum as a separate entity is largely attributed to the initiatives of private collectors, as the tradition of object appreciation has old roots. Traveling to Europe was an important tradition for young wealthy people (primarily men) before they settled down; and once the Civil War was over and people were able to accumulate some capital, American travelers to Europe were also able to purchase expensive objects and bring them to their homeland (Spaeth, 1960). Museums emerged as elite institutions in the United States, but, over time, similar to their European counterparts, they opened their doors to the public. Only one major collector—Dr. Albert Barnes—refused to share his great collection of Impressionist and Post-Impressionist works with the public (Spaeth, 1960). They were locked in the doors of the

Barnes Foundation, which was open to the public only three days a week, and according to Barnes's will, his art collection could never be loaned or sold. After several court cases, in 2010 this private collection was finally moved to a new public museum in Philadelphia.

Compared to their European counterparts, American museums have historically been more egalitarian and democratic institutions. While European museums were created as instruments of the ruling classes to emphasize the glory of national culture, most American museums were created by individuals, families, and communities to celebrate local and regional traditions (Kotler, Kotler, & Kotler, 2008). Moreover, while European museums tended to rely on governmental support as a source of their financial sustainability, a distinctly American feature of museums was their reliance on various sources of financial support (Alexander et al., 2008). Funding for many American museums was based on the idea of combining local public and private support. The first major museums that embodied this type of arrangement were the Metropolitan Museum of Art and the American Museum of Natural History (Alexander, 1983).

The development of museums in America has paralleled the development of cities, which was an important factor in establishing a museum as a socially important and, in some instances, even instrumentally useful institution. When American cities were filled with many immigrants from around the world, many institutions, including museums, were functioning as places of "civilizing rituals" by instructing immigrants on the acceptable forms of behavior and turning them into good citizens (Conn, 1998). Thus, American museums have been pioneers in linking the ideal of community service to museums as public institutions. By 1900, many American museums evolved into centers of education and public enlightenment; a function that remains prominent today.

In the contemporary world, it is hard to underestimate the value of a museum as a mainstream cultural institution guided by the strong commitment to serving the public. Indeed, museums are perhaps among the most accessible cultural institutions. According to the American Association of Museums, at the start of the new millennium, there were approximately 15,000 museums in the United States, which translated into one museum for every 16,500 Americans (Genoways & Ireland, 2003). The majority of these museums (75%) are small, and nearly half (43 percent) are located in rural areas. The public significance of museums is also demonstrated by the sheer number of people who visit them: American museums averaged approximately 865 million visits per year, exceeding the yearly attendance at all professional sporting events (Genoways & Ireland, 2003). There is also convincing evidence of public involvement in the life of museums: one in 480 Americans over 18 years old is a museum volunteer.

Based on these sketches of the institutional history of museums, it is evident that from the beginning, museums have served as institutions of intergenerational memory by ensuring the preservation of historically significant and socially meaningful objects. However, only after the museum had established itself as a public institution was it able to serve the interests of the public at large—whether currently living, or yet to be born. This ability of museums to be more inclusive and open to the public is critical to understanding their organizational sustainability model—the subject to which this chapter turns next.

## From Preservation to Change: Developing a Museum Sustainability Model

While the emphasis on preservation and the concept of object-based thinking are important elements of a classical museum, in order to survive the various internal and external pressures and be able to continuously pursue their social missions for the generations to come, museums have had to develop a more balanced sustainability model that combines their collection-based introspective thinking with outward and very much externally focused work in response to the evolving social expectations. Along those lines, a science museum director whom I interviewed described a powerful speech he had heard during a national meeting of museum executives, and that changed his own view of what his museum should be as an institution:

> He started off his speech and said, "All of you, organizations with mission statements that say you're going to collect and preserve, you're going to die." And there was a really long awkward pause. He looked at me and said, "Those are fuzzy mission statements. Those of you who think you can rest on your laurels and that people can come and support you in the future, not going to grow; you're not going to sustain yourself. You're going to die." And then he read the new mission statement, which is basically using the collection, the place, to tell the story of how to optimize American institutions, to educate and inspire people to build a better future. (Personal Communication, 2015)

This reflection illustrates the importance of realizing the need for an adaptive change in museum purposes, and it also illustrates that change may be the "second" nature of organizational sustainability, contrary to conventional assumptions that view sustainability as stability and maintenance. Museums' sustainability is the result of their various institutional adaptations rather than their ability to remain essentially the same. Managers of museums that aspire to develop a more sustainable model are, for example, shifting from primarily focusing on the importance of collections to recognizing the significance of more externally oriented management strategies that foster both immediate survival and longer-term sustainability of museums. While pursuing this and other adaptive strategies, museum managers have been engaging in a balancing act of reconciling two different yet complementary organizational logics, referred to here as narratives, acknowledging that such narratives are derived from institutional and managerial discourses.

The first narrative, institutional resilience (the ability of museums to adapt in the face of internal and external pressures), is critical to understanding organizational sustainability as a dynamic rather than static concept. It implies that resilience is a cumulative experience achieved by particular organizations and the whole sector through withstanding various forms of stress via institutional adaptation and change. Furthermore, resilience cannot be reduced to merely seeking system efficiency; rather, institutional resilience can be described as adaptability, flexibility and change, innovation, capitalizing on past failure, and turning challenges into opportunities. It is essentially an adaptive learning process that engages both organizational structure and its cultural assumptions, thus producing a fundamentally new organizational logic.

The second narrative of sustainability, which complements resilience, is the institutional distinctives narrative. The purpose of this narrative is to enhance sustainability by promoting the institutional distinctiveness of the sector as a whole, as well as that of particular museum organizations. The distinctiveness narrative is particularly prominent in public and non-profit cultural organizations since their survival as well as intergenerational sustainability would be impossible without the unique character that each of these organizations seeks to establish and the unique value they contribute to society. The distinctiveness narrative is of critical importance for cultural-sector organizations because it supports their overall organizational purpose—the focus of individual organizations on unique ways to illuminate the human condition, whether we are talking about art, history, or scientific discovery.

Together, institutional resilience and distinctiveness lead to the formation of institutional capital for sustainability, which helps organizations to survive in the long term. Sustainability capital functions like a bank savings account: when resources are tight and times are hard, organizations can spend some of their capital to bounce back after environmental shocks, or they can choose to use such capital for investment in the future and exploration of new paths. In the arts and humanities, sustainability capital is best approximated by the idea of institutional endowments that essentially allow for putting resources aside as an organizational safety net. The concept of sustainability capital is critical to understanding museums' intergenerational sustainability, as it reflects the ability of immediately effective management strategies to build up or transform institutional capital, thus ensuring medium- and long-term organizational survival; it also reflects the cumulative nature of cultural capital itself, as something that many generations of cultural institutions contributed to collectively over the course of human history.

At an operational level, organizational capital may exist in many forms: financial (operational funds, endowments, etc.), physical (actual museum buildings and collections), virtual (websites, digital collections), human (artists, museum management and staff capacity, community of museum donors and friends), and intangible (a museum's value for society). There is also organizational social capital that comprises the various relationships and ties formed with various stakeholders. Many forms of sustainability capital could be transformed and converted into other forms; for example, one can leverage human capital to produce more income, or attract more talented staff by leveraging the unique value of a particular institution for society. Yet, organizational social capital, as an expression of overall organizational social connectedness, is particularly potent among other forms of capital when it comes to coping with external stress. For example, the Great Recession of 2007–2009 produced severe external pressures for museums and other cultural organizations due to its negative effects on multiple funding streams at once. The recession pressures added to the already challenging environment in which many cultural organizations existed—particularly the classic forms of culture. However, organizations that possessed various forms of sustainability capital were able to survive and thrive.

Take Detroit as an example: many Detroit museums and other cultural organizations have faced severe pressures, and some are still recovering from those pressures today. As vividly described by a history museum manager, the recession-induced stress in this metropolitan area was all encompassing, "What the public failed to realize is what we went through in 2006. The sky was falling. 'We're going to close the historical museum. We're going to close the zoo. We're going to shoot the animals.' All that kind of stuff" (Personal Communication, 2015). The typical pressures that Detroit-based institutions faced included financial problems associated with the declining public and private support, audience-related pressures, capacity building and infrastructure-maintenance pressures, as well as increased competition for both funding and audiences (Appendix A). Many of the immediate pressures were also among the future longer-term challenges, including financial, audience-related, capacity-building challenges, and competition. Notably, many organizations saw competition with the entertainment sector, such as the sports industry, as more of a future challenge while they saw competition with other cultural organizations as more of an immediate postrecession concern.

Ironically, Detroit's revitalization agenda and changing socioeconomic conditions in local communities were among the most pressing future challenges. Detroit's revitalization had created both opportunities and additional competitive pressures for local museums, as the revitalization attracted many new cultural organizations and individual artists to the city. The revitalization has brought with itself an inflow of resources and expertise, largely channeled via private foundations, some of which originated in Detroit. However, institutions of different sizes and prominence have been benefitting from these effects unevenly, and many, especially small and medium-sized organizations, expressed concerns about their ability to sustain competition with both newcomers and more established local institutions. To that extent, organizations with previously accumulated sustainability capital, whether financial endowments or productive relationships with key stakeholders, were able to handle the competition better.

Reflecting on the urgency of competitive pressures that many similar-sized organizations in the area faced, the director of a medium-sized museum had referred to the Detroit Institute of Arts, which is located in Detroit's midtown alongside many smaller museums, as "the thousand-pound gorilla across the street which gets all the buzz" (Personal Communication, 2015). While achieving more culturally vibrant communities with a greater number of institutions is, in fact, an intended goal of many revitalization efforts, the unintended outcome is the perceived and actual increased competition among organizations for the various forms of organizational capital. This competition poses challenges for developing interorganizational partnerships, which would otherwise have been quite beneficial as a collective stress-coping strategy for institutions located in the same area.

Another challenge in the context of Detroit is related to the city's bankruptcy context, and the fact that, despite relatively high volumes of activity within the philanthropic community, resource competition has also been driven by forces outside of the cultural sector. As described by the director of a historical museum, cultural institutions in Detroit compete with the city itself:

> I don't worry about the DIA for fundraising, or the Science Center, or the Henry Ford, or the Charles Wright Museum. In this community, the city of Detroit is propped up by the philanthropic community. I'm not competing with the other cultural institutions as much as I am competing with the city itself who's going to the philanthropic community for M1 police cars, fire, rape kits, blight removal—all good and important things that I support 1,000%. But that's a very different landscape than you see in many other areas. (Personal Communication, 2015)

Further, many managers indicated some skepticism regarding the role of the philanthropic community in supporting the arts and humanities in postrecession Detroit, particularly in two aspects—the inclination of foundations to stretch their resources further by frequently mandating that organizations create partnerships as a condition for grant application, and by expecting institutions to generate new programming rather than supporting the existing (in many cases much needed and already successful) programs. The first tendency is reflected upon by one of the Detroit-based museum managers:

> Sometimes funders force organizations like ours to do unnatural things to get their money by collaborating with other culture institutions or this artist group or this latest hipster and that kind of stuff. You know the foundations are going through a period now where they're trying to be progressive and hip and cool. They're making people do unnatural things that are counterproductive, and really all they result in is employment for the people at the foundation. My point is the people that

run and work in organizations like this know when they need to partner, know when they need to collaborate, are smart enough to make those decisions. You don't need an external force causing you to do it in an obscure, unnatural way in exchange to get their money. (Personal Communication, 2015)

These dynamics are hardly unique, as many organizations across the nation face similar pressures to which they attempt to respond in the hopes of both tackling their immediate survival pressures and developing more sustainable operational models for the long run. Along their path toward intergenerational sustainability, museum managers pursue various strategies that increase museums' institutional resilience while preserving their institutional distinctiveness.

## Institutional Resilience Narrative: The Story of Social Relevance and Connectedness

The idea of institutional resilience is based on the analogy with the natural environment and the laws of evolutionary survival, and, as expressed by a manager of a natural science museum, it rests on the premise that "you got to run as fast as you can just to stay in the same place" (Personal Communication, 2010). It assumes that external environment is generally competitive; however, there is more than one way to handle such competition, and, in fact, collaborative responses prove to be more beneficial for individual organizations and whole sectors. According to such an approach, successful and long-lasting museums have to be responsive and adaptable in the face of changes in their environment. In the long run, successful adaptations enhance institutional capital for sustainability, and successfully adapted organizations could subsequently use their capital to cope with future stress.

Resilience is an institutional property and cumulative experience that would not have happened in the absence of external pressures, which implies that stress is not necessarily an entirely negative concept. In fact, there is a dual perception of external stress by managers, who, on the one hand, are devastated by the actual or potential effects of stress on their institutions but on the other hand recognize the importance of stress for fostering productive organizational change. Depending on their age and size, institutions tend to be more or less open to change, and they may choose to be either reactive or proactive. More established institutions, which at least in theory have greater capacity to sustain change, are frequently among those less open to change in the face of environmental uncertainty, as compared to their younger and nimbler counterparts, as stability is embedded in their structure and organizational culture. Yet, change is a precursor of continuous successful adaptation, and it is, therefore, highly beneficial to all organizational types. As noted by a manager of a long-standing historical organization from one of the Detroit suburbs,

> A little bit of a stress point is beneficial because, when you're hungry or when you don't have all the resources, it's like the entrepreneurial spirit; it's like there's a fire, and you have something to prove. So, you're nimble and you're agile, you're flexible, you're adaptive. And you're spry and you're trying new things, and sometimes you're going to fail. But you have to . . . And, again, I hate to say this, museums—we're great about the past; we're not so good about the future. And I think we need to do a better job of that, too. I think it will solve a lot of issues down the road. (Personal Communication, 2016)

While not all adaptive strategies will be successful, undertaking change is nevertheless important for shaking organizational assumptions and moving an organization forward. In fact, environmental stress that organizations experience may serve as a powerful catalyst for both structural and cultural change. As an example, a manager of a Detroit-based art museum describes a paradigmatic change that was initiated by her institution during the Great Recession:

> The mission really started changing in 2007 with the reinstallation of [director's name], who came in and said, "You know, this museum needs to think about things differently." And I think that was pretty revolutionary. It was difficult for a 120-year-old organization to really start thinking about including community members, for example, in panels about exhibitions, to give us feedback on exhibitions. It's not just about the curator deciding what they want to do, but it really was about how you do it, what is important to community members, and why it is important. So that was the pivotal turning point in 2007. (Personal Communication, 2015)

The change described above represents both a structural change in the programming and a cultural shift in major institutional assumptions. This combination of structural modifications with the change in underlying assumptions is critical for understanding institutional resilience. Shifting to a more sustainable model requires instituting sustainable organizational culture, as undergoing structural change often involves resistance from both museum patrons and staff used to doing things "the same old way" and whose cultural assumptions long for stability. This is especially true in classical art museums whose own missions include academic-like sophistication and appreciation of highbrow art that requires special knowledge and can be out of reach for the average patron. However, this type of cultural assumption creates a barrier between a museum and its wider community, and therefore museums seeking to position themselves as public-serving institutions engage in various structural and cultural changes, to make museum experiences more accessible to ordinary visitors.

At an organizational level, institutional resilience results from two factors: structural adaptability and ability of museums to achieve social and community relevance (Table 2.1). Structural adaptability involves capitalizing on the differences in museum institutional forms, particu-

Table 2.1. Two Narratives of Intergenerational Sustainability: Museums

| Institutional Resilience Narrative | • Structural adaptability<br>• Social and community relevance | • Capitalizing on institutional structure<br>• Institutional change<br>• Institutional hybrids<br>• Public-private partnerships<br>• Interdisciplinary focus<br>• Utilizing technology and social media<br>• Diversifying and expanding community outreach |
|---|---|---|
| Institutional Distinctiveness Narrative | Capitalizing on institutional uniqueness and distinctiveness | • Staying true to the core mission<br>• Occupying unique institutional niche<br>• Promoting and cultivating socially important values<br>• Shifting towards semi-instrumental role<br>• Placing a distinct value on arts-based learning |

larly the freestanding model and a university-affiliated model, as well as moving toward a more balanced hybrid-type structural and operational model. The second set of strategies could be described as strategies aimed at achieving greater social and community relevance; those strategies reflect an external type of orientation that is required for a sustainable organization, as opposed to primarily focusing on the value of internal assets, such as collections or buildings. An illustration of this strategy is the increasing significance of museum-based public outreach and education. Other types of approaches aimed at increasing museums' social relevance include engaging in partnerships, pursuing a more interdisciplinary focus, and better utilization of technology. These strategies collectively enhance the overall social connectedness of a museum: the most valuable form of organizational capital for sustainability.

## Structural Adaptability: Moving toward a Hybrid

The first factor that matters for institutional resilience is structural adaptability. Structural adaptability implies institutional flexibility in dealing with external events and pressures through adaptation and change. In the case of museums, there are two common forms of organizational structure that matter in discussions of resilience: a freestanding nonprofit model and a model where a museum has a "parent" or a "patron" organization, such as a university or a municipality. There are also less-common intuitional configurations where a larger umbrella organization with a different social mission may establish a museum. One such example is the Arab American Museum in Detroit—one of the regional associates of the Smithsonian Institution in Washington, D.C.; it is not incorporated as a standalone nonprofit but instead is affiliated with the larger umbrella organization Arab Community Center for Economic and Social Services.

In terms of organizational sustainability, being a part of a larger umbrella organization is a double-edged sword. On the one hand, a "parent" or a "patron" organization tends to serve as a shield from external problems by providing baseline financial support and access to or complimentary infrastructure, to include both human resources, connections, and physical spaces, which is a positive factor. This type of baseline support is especially important in the face of recession pressures, and it is not as readily accessible to freestanding museums. In the aftermath of the Great Recession, for example, several major universities, such as Harvard,

Stanford, Yale, and the University of Chicago, decided to reinvest in their cultural facilities, seeing cultural campuses as the next big thing in attracting and retaining top-notch faculty and students (Russell, 2014). Some, like Princeton University, while transforming the New Jersey Transit Rail Station into the Lewis Center for the Arts, have gone so far as to acquire local historical and cultural access to make them part of the campus. Universities have also made significant strides to better connect the various university departments with on-campus cultural institutions, as a way of ensuring better utilization of those institutions. This type of symbiosis is quite beneficial to both museums and their patron organizations.

On the other hand, the quality of relationships may depend on the condition of a patron institution itself. As a matter of fact, there are several examples of museums across the nation whose future fell prey to the conditions of their patron institutions in attempts to cope with their own struggles. For example, Rose Art Museum at Brandeis University and the University of Connecticut's Benton Museum of Art struggled with these problems during the most recent recession. Without a doubt, patron institutions' attempts to question the future of their museums cause outcry within the museum professional community, from organizations such as the American Alliance of Museums or the American Association of Museum Directors. However, these national networks do not always succeed in saving local museums.

Likewise, municipally sponsored museums may face similar pressures. For example, many of Detroit's museums were established by elites from previous generations during the economic boom, with the expectation that they would always be supported by the taxpayers. However, factors such as the decline of the city and especially the Great Recession of 2007–2009 have questioned those assumptions, leading to the gradual disinvestment and deterioration of the cultural infrastructure. Moreover, for several prominent Detroit-based museums, such as the Charles Wright Museum of African American History, the Detroit Historical Society and Museum, the Detroit Institute of Arts, and Belle Isle Aquarium, to name a few, a close affiliation with the city of Detroit created a problem during the Great Recession.

As the city filed for bankruptcy protection in 2012, it failed to meet its financial obligations to its many creditors and public employees, which included its inability to support its cultural institutions, as was the case of the Detroit Institute of Arts, whose collections faced the prospect of deaccessioning in light of the substantial financial obligations incurred by the city. It quickly became clear that close ties with the struggling city can be harmful rather than beneficial for some cultural institutions, and several of those institutions responded by cutting or reducing those ties and forming independent nonprofit organizations to foster the needed sense of reinvention in both structural and cultural terms. In many instances, such structural changes were nonsystematic, but they ultimately proved useful for cultural shifts in institutional assumptions that became necessary for successful structural adaptation, as described by the manager of a historical museum:

> From 2006 to 2007, our budget was reduced by 75%; we went from 60 employees to 20. So, it was a drastic reduction, and it was an interesting dynamic because at that time the city of Detroit employees worked here up until 2006 and 20% of the floor was staffed by [name of organization] employees, including myself for a few years. There was an interesting cultural clash, where you had a kind of scrappy nonprofit group, and then you had an entitled group. If you ask the employees on the city side who they worked for, they didn't say [name of the organization]. They said the city of Detroit because they were entitled to the jobs and had very little idea of what they were supposed to do or how they were supposed to do it . . . So, actually, when we took over with fewer employees and a 75% budget reduction, we delivered much, much more than that group did. So, the perception was that independence from the city was a very good thing, and it was. (Personal Communication, 2015)

When comparing the two structural models, the freestanding nonprofit model has a number of advantages, including greater managerial autonomy and flexibility, greater institutional adaptability, and easier responsiveness to change (Appendix B). These factors become particularly important during times of turbulence, when the ability of an institution to adjust and reformat really matters. Nonprofit organizations can take advantage of their connections with local communities, greater proximity to their stakeholders, and access to broader funding opportunities. This enhances their prospects for survival and serves as a foundation for the future.

On the other hand, university-affiliated institutions also have a number of crucial advantages (Appendix B). Universities, for example, often serve as buffers from external shocks to museums by providing crucial baseline funding, which sustains arts organizations through hard times and provides access to quality human resources and built-in audiences. Other important advantages of university affiliation include access to technology and innovation, access to research and development, new ideas, a positive impact on organizational image, numerous opportunities for interdisciplinary and collaborative projects with other university divisions, and much less emphasis on commercial strategies than is prevalent in freestanding museums. However, while being a part of a university, in most cases, serves as an institutional protection for museums—as a shield against resilience pressures, museum managers report that their own choices are frequently constrained by too much regulation and a huge number of bureaucratic procedures, and they also note that universities often use museums as a source for generating research grants or solely for a public-relations function, which is a very narrow treatment of museums' value.

In light of its advantages and disadvantages, institutional structure does not by itself determine resilience. Instead, institutional resilience is achieved when organizational managers make decisions considering the peculiarities of particular structures, and when the structures themselves adapt, subsequently fostering the needed transformation in organizational cultural assumptions. Furthermore, managers interviewed for this book expressed that, in the long run, museums that would endure would be the ones with some sort of hybrid institutional structure that combines different institutional patterns.

One example of such hybridity at the operational level is the adoption of cross-structural strategies in order to strengthen museums' funding base and enhance their institutional resilience. For example, while there are notable differences between the two structural models, both university-based and freestanding museums increasingly realize the importance of diversifying museum revenue sources, which is considered a key to their financial success (Feldstein, 1991). This includes diversifying income sources, minimizing debt, creating a capable financial committee and a resourceful board of directors, sharing best practices with their museum colleagues, and engaging in long-term thinking by creating institutional endowments. Additionally, although universities still serve as their primary stakeholders, many university museums have already discovered that they need broader legitimacy and public support as much as freestanding museums, and they need to cultivate and serve their public in multiple ways. Therefore, they established public education departments and invested their resources in public outreach. Freestanding private and local community museums, likewise, in their attempts to resemble a university-affiliated structural model, try to become more academic and sophisticated in their programs.

Substantively, in their quest for intergenerational sustainability, museums are pursuing greater hybridity by balancing the scholarship part of their mission that takes more of a top-down perspective with more of a bottom-up approach to exhibition and interpretation that focuses on community outreach and engagement, as described by an art museum manager below:

> Not to say that that's not important to understand and to continue scholarship but to have a better balance between scholarship and the other side of relevance—making the museum a place for people. I think that's going to be a challenge structurally; I think there is going to be some tension. We tend to be interpreters of what people think about art and why it's relevant, and why it's important. That's going to start changing. We are going to have more of an individualized approach. You know, "Why is it important to me; why is it relevant to me?" And I think interpretation is going to be changing. As a result of that, we will probably receive more community input and more community involvement in the interpretation of the collection. (Personal Communication, 2015)

As museums move toward more hybridized and balanced models in both structural and substantive terms, the very definition of a museum as an institution begins to change. Institutions are increasingly being reconceptualized as a set of relationships, a "constellation of people and ideas" (Personal Communication, September 2011), rather than particular structures, rules, and routines. Further, looking into the future, it will matter less which building hosts museum collections; it will matter more which groups of populations a museum is able to reach, what kinds of relationships it is able to build, and what messages it is able to communicate to its publics. As the importance of museum buildings as architectural structures that merely hold artistically significant and culturally meaningful objects on display will continue to decline, it will continue giving way to the museum as a space for social and cultural inclusion, as reflected upon by history and science museum managers:

Different perspective altogether—that's also as a direct result of the philosophy of "We're not buttressing; we're not closing the gates and making them fit." We're going out and building bridges. We're going out and building. That's different altogether. (Personal Communication, 2015)

My guess for the long-term future would be that the museum like you see it today will disappear. I really think you're going to see something totally different. I think you're going to see something that is much more embedded in the community and in the region and not see a standalone architectural monument. I think that's going to go away. If you look forward, we're starting to talk about the idea that we are part of a whole downtown environment that celebrates science and technology and engineering. The real science center is out there, you know; we're just kind of emulating it internally. (Personal Communication, 2016)

**The role of organizational environment.** While structural adaptations are important for museums' resilience, the quality of their operational environment is critically important for successful institutional adaptations as well. That environment comprises what Jung and Love have called in their work on systems thinking "a complex, interdependent, and open web of things, people, and relationships that reside within the larger social, cultural, and natural environment that is continually in a state of flux" (Jung & Love, 2017, p. 3). For example, museums located in vibrant communities with high levels of cultural appreciation are more likely to maintain a constant flow of visitors and sustain their funding base via local supporters despite recession. It is not uncommon, for example, to ask local communities to support a tax millage for funding particular institutions, as for example happened with the Detroit Institute of Arts that was saved from closure in 2012 when voters of three metropolitan counties approved a 0.2 percent property tax to fund it. After receiving financial support from the millage, the DIA established free unlimited general admission for residents of these counties, expanded its programming for schools and seniors, and "gave back" to its community in other ways.

Similar initiatives to provide public funding to cultural institutions have been implemented on a more macro level. Many cities realized that, especially at the time of economic recession, public funding for the arts and the willingness of a local community to render its support matters for the long-term sustainability of the arts and humanities sector. One such example is the establishment of the Scientific and Cultural Facilities District in metropolitan Denver in 1988, where, in response to the loss of state funds, the citizens of the city voted to increase taxes in support of local arts (Hansberry, 2000). After Denver's success, cultural districts were created in Pittsburgh, Kansas City, and Salt Lake City under the realization that public support is increasingly seen as an investment in both present and future quality of life.

High levels of public appreciation for the arts and humanities as well as the desire to invest in vibrant cultural institutions can also be found in less economically privileged communities; however, members of such communities are not necessarily among the frequent museum visitors for a variety of reasons, ranging from economic and social barriers to the lack of transportation. In these communities, arts-and-culture institutions play a most critical role in providing access to collectively accumulated cultural capital now and for the generations to come. These types of communities represent a setting where the two sustainabilities—organizational and community—are synergistically related. An art museum manager compared population response to his institution's newly expanded outreach efforts between more and less well-off communities in the following way:

> We've been in over eighty different communities, so it's hard for me to say, but in general I would say that the communities that have the greatest response [to the extended programming] tend to be the communities that don't come to the museum. We've done a little bit of analysis to say, "Okay, in [name of an affluent city], they didn't do a lot of programming; they loved it in their community, but they didn't really do a lot to additionally engage their community members." But, if you go to a place like [names of low socio-economic status and geographically remote cities], actually, they hosted a series of walking tours, and informational sessions, and discussions about the art. They really worked to engage their residents in the art. It's the greatest impact, I would say, in those communities that don't normally engage with the arts, rather than those communities that regularly engage with the arts or have a strong arts foundation. (Personal Communication, 2015)

As is clear from the reflection above, communities that have less exposure to the arts are quite appreciative of the museum's outreach programs and physical presence in these communities. Local environment, especially community-level values and culture, as well as awareness of the cultural infrastructure, can be both an enabling and a constraining force for cultural institutions, regardless of their organizational form. Once again, these differences are not necessarily driven by the state of the local economy; rather, they are attributed to community-level cultural assumptions that may either enable or constrain a museum's adaptive strategy. The manager of a historical organization located in one of Detroit's affluent suburbs described cultural assumptions that constrain institutional reinvention like this:

> This is a stagnant community. No—well, it's dynamic, but it's stagnant in terms of population. It's also stagnant in terms of building. We maybe have a dozen new homes in the community in a three- or four-year period. We may have two or three improvements to existing public buildings. So, you know, we're not like [names of younger suburbs] that have a broader reach. Geographically we're pretty limited, and what we have is what we have. What we are becoming is a community of folks who have not lived here all their lives, and so, in that respect, we maybe tweak this mission statement to be a little more assertive in terms of helping people understand what this community is and what it has been and who we are. We have no place to grow except into the lake. We don't want to change. (Personal Communication, 2015)

Another important factor about local environment that contributes to museum sustainability is the proximity to educational infrastructure. Being in close proximity to a major research university is quite beneficial to nearby museums, even if they are not formally affiliated with that university. For example, Belle Isle Aquarium in Detroit has greatly benefitted from its partnership with Wayne State University. The partnership was initiated by a physiology professor from the university's School of Medicine who set up an invasive-species exhibition at the Aquarium after its reopening in 2012 and assumed informal leadership of the Aquarium's public outreach efforts. That exhibition led to regular educational programming at the Aquarium, the involvement of many other professors and students from local universities, as well as successful grant-seeking efforts which enabled regular programming with K–10 students. These efforts have transformed the Aquarium structurally and culturally, and have certainly set the institution on a more sustainable path.

Another example of a Metro Detroit institution that has capitalized on its close proximity to a major university is the Hands-On Museum in Ann Arbor, located in the vicinity of the University of Michigan as well as Eastern Michigan University and Washtenaw Community College. The museum's original positioning was to serve children and youths, but it managed to capitalize on its proximity to a major research university by transforming itself into a hub of cross-sectional community activity, where activities as diverse as scientific demonstrations, design shows, and engineering-discovery testing are regularly held. In undergoing the various structural transformations toward a more broadly positioned model, Hands-On Museum managed to capitalize on the vibrant educational resources as well as cultural values of its immediate community, as described by a museum representative:

> When I came here, the whole idea was that I was coming into a community that valued education, that valued learning, that valued diversity, that valued knowledge, and the idea of being able to really institute my philosophy of what I call community ownership and engagement really drew me to this organization and environment . . . What we realized right away is that all the talent that we could ever hope for in staff that we could not afford to hire was already here . . . And, to me, the number-one measure of our success is that people in our community . . . have a personal ownership stake in what we do here. (Personal Communication, 2016)

Overall, successful structural adaptation is a major element of institutional resilience of museums, and its success is conditioned upon both organizational and environmental factors, as well as the ability of museum managers to balance the strength and weaknesses of the various institutional set-ups while considering an increasing hybridization of museum structure.

## Social and Community Relevance: Aiming toward Greater Social Connectedness

The second element of the institutional resilience narrative is the ability of organizations to establish their social and community relevance. The attempts by museums to enhance their social and community relevance reflect the important role of cultural organizations as social, economic, and cultural actors, whose day-to-day activity translates into a variety of instrumental and intrinsic contributions to sustainable development in their local communities. The push for greater social and community relevance reflects the changing public expectations regarding the role of a museum in society and one of the fundamental changes in a museum's mission, as described by a history museum manager below:

> The other challenge that you face is the changing role of museums, that people don't need museums to get information. They need museums for places of community, for experiences, for interactions . . . The old mission was, "The [name] educates and inspires our community and visitors by preserving and portraying our region's shared history through dynamic exhibits and experiences." That's our old mission. Our new mission is telling Detroit stories and why they matter. And there is—in addition to being much simpler—a focus on relevance: why we matter as opposed to history for the sake of history. (Personal Communication, 2015)

> The idea of social and community relevance of the arts and humanities has been promulgated and supported by such major policymaking organizations as the National Endowment for the Arts, which funds museum projects aimed at fostering a symbiotic relationship between museums and local communities. As one of the art museum managers said, reflecting on the significance of such initiatives, their value is in demonstrating that "art, science, and society are in a synergetic relationship, where art is the force capable of creating and sustaining socially relevant narratives into the future" (Personal Communication, 2011)

The changing role of museums as inherently social institutions and their move toward adopting strategies that enhance their social and community relevance pushes them outside of the confines of their physical building and into the community, where they can become meaningful social, economic, and cultural actors. Managers of a historical and art museum from the Detroit metropolitan area reflect upon their institutions' shift toward greater social relevance in the following ways:

There's a lot of work, and it requires you to be very responsive to your community. To have a grassroots approach, to be connected at all times. You cannot work in isolation. With Southeast Michigan, when there's so much happening and evolving, even here in our corner, everything is changing, and we see our museum as an opportunity for the community. To use place as an opportunity for helping to drive the economy. For building community. For connecting with other communities. We're taking some of our museum programs out of the physical confines of the museum and embedding them in the community . . . we really want to see the city have a sustainable future, and be connected with the inner suburbs . . . We play a role as community-based institutions in helping to shape that future. (Personal Communication, 2015)

It's hard to tell what's going to happen in 100 years. But I would say that we're looking into the future to try to understand where we can be, and where we fit into the long-term place of Detroit not just as a museum. Like where do we fit as an organization in the new Detroit? I personally think we've got a tremendous opportunity to position ourselves as a beacon of inclusion and diversity. And have those spaces where people can talk about those difficult subjects, because we have so much in common around art. We can all come together around something that we all share. I think that that's probably the direction that museums in general will be heading. It is not so much just looking at the art on the wall but how you apply it to daily life and why is it important to daily life. (Personal Communication, 2015)

As is clear from the reflections above, social and community relevance is a multifaceted concept that reflects the diverse contributions that museums make to sustainable development in their local communities, ranging from fostering local economic development to contributing to a climate of diversity and inclusion. But social and community relevance strategies are also part of the larger intergenerational sustainability pursuit for museums themselves. Furthermore, by pursuing these types of strategies, museums are going through transformative changes by positioning themselves as a form of social glue that brings people and ideas together in one place, as reflected by a science museum manager's remarks:

> And then you start communicating the idea to the community that there's something new here. There's something additional happening here, and it really was the idea that it wasn't necessarily a [name of the institution]. It was a convener of people and ideas. It was a social learning experience, and, if you go out on our floor on any single day, you will find people that are exploring together and learning together, and I really think there would ever be people that they would know as friends or colleagues because there's such a diversity of people . . . So, really, the strategy was to operate in a very conservative manner initially to start fostering the idea of community engagement before we can foster community ownership and then to bring people to the table such that, instead of us investing in those ideas, other people did. So fast-forward to where we are now. We've been able to turn that into significant support from the community. We've raised millions of dollars in support of our programs and exhibits. (Personal Communication, 2016)

Specific operational strategies that result in museums' greater social and community relevance include their engagement in various public-private partnerships, expanding and diversifying community outreach, utilizing technology and social media, and implementing interdisciplinary projects (Table 2.1). Effective combination of these social relevance strategies fosters museums' institutional resilience. In a more practical sense, greater social relevance results in more stable funding, stronger public and private support, more powerful boards of directors, and loyal groups of visitors and friends. In the long run, greater social and community relevance also benefits museums by enhancing their overall capital for sustainability, including the attraction of steady financial resources as well as enhanced organizational reputation and legitimacy. Importantly, however, this strategy results in greater embeddedness of museums within their local communities and enables them to serve as a public forum for discussing and framing community visions of the future.

**Engaging in partnerships**. In their pursuit of greater social and community relevance, museums increasingly engage in various public-private partnerships. The resilience strategy of engaging in partnerships reflects the dynamic advantages of collective action, which implies that the productive interaction of multiple actors is likely to increase the resilience of individual organizations engaged in partnerships (Astley & Van de Ven, 1983). Despite the seemingly competitive environment surrounding museums lately, a collaborative approach allows institutions to stay relevant in their community and up to date: combining the strength of several institutions for a common goal, all institutions included in the collaboration benefit from the results. The benefits of partnerships include both resource- and mission-driven outcomes, and there is a realization that partnering with others will become more common in the future, as reflected upon by a history museum director:

> You will probably see a trend to more of that, and I think it is part of where museums are going in a couple of ways. Because these kinds of partnerships and collaborations allow you to connect with the community in a different way. So, we work with the public library a lot: we are close; we share some of the same constituency, and we found common paths, so it is driven by your ability to outreach and connect with the community. But it is also driven by the ability to share resources. So, I think it is driven by both; it is kind of an economic advantage but also a community-relationship building. (Personal Communication, 2012)

Public-private partnerships, in particular, allow museums to obtain the resources they need to pursue their programmatic goals; meanwhile, their partners derive numerous other benefits from such collaborations. For instance, when a private energy corporation funded summer art classes at the Lawrence Art Center (Lawrence, KS), its motivation went beyond direct financial gain or mere publicity. The company stood to benefit in other, more indirect ways as well. According to the director of the Arts Center, "They make wind turbines for wind energy in Kansas City, and they are believing that the type of employees they want are thinking in the way we teach people to think here" (Personal Communication, 2011). In other words, the private partner in this project derived primarily long-term intrinsic benefits from the art classes by fostering the kind of creative thinking that it valued in its employees. This type of partnership is also beneficial for the entire community, as it represents a long-term investment in its human capital via the arts.

Public-private partnerships are also seen as a way to enable larger social goals that museums pursue and that are consistent with the idea of more inclusive and more sustainable communities. For example, in order to provide more equitable access to museum experiences, especially in light of recession pressures, museums often form partnerships with non-arts-related businesses. For example, the Ford Learning Center at the Nelson-Atkins Museum of Art in Kansas City offers art classes for children as young as three years old that cost $92 to $280 per person. While relying on relatively high fees makes this educational program self-sustainable, it also makes it less accessible to the general population. Therefore, the museum has entered into a partnership with the Ford Motor Company Fund, which allows offsetting the high program cost by offering need-based scholarships based on the financial circumstances of a family. In this case, the goal of the partnership is to engage diverse visitors inside the museum by providing access to its programs.

Another common goal of pursuing partnerships with other organizations is stakeholder diversification. Museums increasingly engage in community-based programming outside of their buildings and in partnership with local community actors, which allows them to reach broader groups of stakeholders. These types of initiatives are guided by both pragmatic considerations aimed at diversifying the current supporter base as well as normative goals such as gaining institutional legitimacy by ensuring greater accessibility of cultural experiences to the traditionally underserved populations. In this case, community partners may provide financial and nonfinancial forms of support to cultural organizations.

One example of an outward-focused community-building program is the InsideOut initiative implemented by the Detroit Institute of Arts. As the name implies, the goal of the initiative is to get art out of the museum building and into the community, both figuratively and literally, by placing reproductions of museum paintings into public spaces in various urban and suburban communities. The museum has relied on a diverse set of partners to implement this program, including local government, other arts organizations, social-service nonprofits, and educational institutions, all of which have also benefitted from working with a nationally recognized art museum. The project has thus far had a significant impact on how art is perceived in the local communities, and it also had a transformational impact on the DIA itself by challenging the previously dominant cultural assumptions about its social role, as described by this DIA representative:

> InsideOut has been transformative for this museum. We've been doing this for six years now, and I think the reason it's

been transformative is because, when we first tried to do this, our curators were so against it. Everybody is like, "Putting fake art outside? Why, that doesn't make any sense." And, when the millage came around, people were able to see what type of collection we have. I think that made it very relevant to them and very personal to them . . . And InsideOut has not only made the collection really personal to people, but it also turned us around, and it has enabled us to develop relationships long term with organizations that we wouldn't normally be able to. InsideOut has been really instrumental in changing the way we as a museum engage with our community. (Personal Communication, 2015)

Reporting the positive effect in local communities, a representative of the DIA shared an anecdote about a community member calling to the DIA because this person thought that the work of art placed in their public park was stolen from the DIA, and they had an obligation to guard it. In addition to immediate publicity and recognition-type benefits, the project increased the overall social connectedness and embeddedness of the DIA within more diverse communities, thus adding significantly to the museum's sustainability capital. Moreover, by engaging a diverse set of local community partners, the project has been important for local communities by fostering the long-term relationships that support overall community development.

While engaging in partnerships as an expression of a collaborative ecosystem type of approach to enhancing institutional resilience is beneficial for the sustainability of organizations and their communities, we know that differences in organizational and community-level cultures shape the collaborative process and its outcomes. Some organizations and their local environments appear to be more open to collaboration than others, and there are also constraints to developing collaborations across geographical boundaries, as the case of Metropolitan Detroit illustrates. Managers of two historical museums, both located in Detroit suburbs, reflect upon the challenges of pursuing collaborative strategies:

What's important to understand is [city name] is like all of southeastern Michigan; it is very segmented and fragmented. People don't cross lines very well in this community. And we are the one place in the [name of the community] where people can come together without saying, "Okay I'm in this place, you know, in this one, or this one, or this one." And it's very much like Detroit. I mean, if you live in Hamtramck, you also know this, and if you live in Troy. It's very segmented and fragmented. (Personal Communication, 2015)

I mean, over here people are like, "Oh, you can't come." I mean, now we would never do that, but it's just (city name) and it's (another city name). You've got two different worlds. Quite frankly, I kind of relate more with (city 2), and I love the diversity that's there. And I think it's going to be a different audience. And so, even in our planning, we had to take that in mind because it's what they relate to. People are really different in life experiences, et cetera, et cetera; it's like different cultures and everything. And here's the funny thing. There is a great ownership to that place (city 2) out there because it defines who they are. And in (city 1), there is little ownership about it; everyone loves being here, but it's behind closed walls. It's kind of [as if] we are a world within our own. There we have to be part of the community, and it has to be at the core of that. It's just a very different philosophy. (Personal Communication, 2016)

Despite the challenges embedded in the collaboration process, engaging in partnerships with other organizations is beneficial for museums' institutional resilience, and it also enhances their ability to play important roles in their local communities beyond the main artistic and cultural functions.

**Adopting technology.** In line with the changing societal role of museums, their managers have realized that merely having quality objects on display is like trying to speak the language of a previous century. In their drive to be socially relevant, museums are, therefore, increasingly adopting technology and using social media. The onset of the COVID-19 pandemic in 2020 further pushed many museums to adopt remote and technology-based programming, which was then seen not just as a form of enhanced programming and a technological innovation but also as a lifeline for organizations that used to rely on object-based in-person programming (AAM, 2022). Examples of greater reliance on technology by museums today include digitizing collections, creating user-friendly museum websites, and hosting online forums. These initiatives help museums to achieve greater social relevance, particularly in their work with younger people and to ensure a more global outreach, both of which are critical to museums' intergenerational sustainability.

Museum managers continue to see technology as a valuable investment in the future as well as driving museum innovation, particularly when it comes to public education programming. For example, the public education department at the University of Kansas Natural History Museum designed a collaborative educational project involving physicists, museum educators, and computer designers. The project introduced young people to the concepts of scale and a particulate nature of matter through hands-on museum programs and a website with animated videos and games (MacDonald & Bean, 2011). The project has been very popular among young people, mainly because it utilizes tools that are already a part of young lives. As the use of technology becomes more and more prevalent in museum practice, museums are discovering ways of better connecting with both current and future generations.

As the digital orientation becomes a more prevalent interaction style and learning mode, museums grow stronger in their desire to exceed the boundaries of their communities. Technology—whether we are talking about digitizing the collections or using technology to conduct some of the programming remotely—is helpful for enabling broader public outreach. In fact, a more global orientation becomes part of museums' evolving missions, and it has several important outcomes for museums' sustainability. First, this global orientation contributes to the capital for museums' sustainability by sparking the interest of potential audiences and supporters from remote locations; second, it gives museums a global standing; third, it properly reflects intergenerational shifts in consumption modes since people in future generations are more likely to have greater mobility, access to, and appreciation of technology. Several museum managers reflect upon the intrinsic benefits of their technology-driven programs, including gaining a more global focus:

> For this organization to survive, it's not just about [city] anymore; we have to have a much more regional focus, and, in some instances, we need to have a global focus . . . . Technology helps our work to be local, national, and global simultaneously, being both much more focused on this specific community and more globally. (Personal Communication, 2015).

We also do this distance-learning piece. That's video conferencing, which is our pride and joy in that it doesn't just keep us locally or within a couple hours. It allows us to go anywhere. We'll actually put together the same programs we take into the classrooms, and we'll put together and send a kit to a school where they have all the materials. And then we will have a live interactive broadcast where we can see what every single student is doing. Walk them through the presentations and give them that same learning experience. Wildly successful—it's just wonderful being able to go into our lab and see us talking to students in Des Moines, or Australia, or Guam or any place else that we reach. (Personal Communication, 2016)

While relying on technology to go global is important, it is equally important to balance global virtual presence with physical experiences that collection-based institutions offer in their immediate communities, as those experiences help establish museum embeddedness with such communities. In other words, sustainable museums aspire to be "on the ground" as much as "in the air" and therefore to pursue their social and community relevance both globally and locally, as described by a science museum manager:

We're able to provide scholarships for school students within nine counties to come here. And that's all resulted in two hundred and eighty thousand people a year coming through our doors, the largest offsite outreach program in the state. But we also have an internationally known distance-learning program where our video-conferencing program is all over the world. It's relatively new. We broadcast it to Australia. We broadcast into the UK. All across the US, and that's all because of this idea of community ownership and engagement as our overarching philosophy. (Personal Communication, 2016)

Modern technology can also foster other types of wider accessibility for museums that go beyond geographical reach: a form of socially responsible behavior that is crucial for museums' long-term sustainability. For example, American Alliance of Museums reports that museums are increasingly relying on technology to make their collections and programming accessible to people with disabilities (McConnaughey, 2019).

This includes such initiatives as keeping the light and noise levels low for people on the autism spectrum, as well as producing touchable versions of museum objects and displays that rely on small metal sensors and recordings to explain what a visitor is touching. Two- and even three-dimensional displays can do wonders in making the cultural objects accessible to the blind and visually handicapped visitors.

Technology, therefore, appears to be a positive force for enhancing institutional resilience of museums in more than one way, particularly if they manage to balance their more global orientation with relevance and greater inclusiveness toward their local communities.

**Embracing interdisciplinarity.** In an effort to increase social and community relevance, museum practices have also become more interdisciplinary. The shift from focusing solely on the humanities to a more cross-disciplinary approach reflects the evolution of museum mission. While it is important for museum managers not to stray too far from their core focus on the arts and humanities, it is also imperative for museums to be able to challenge their comfort zone by taking part in unconventional projects. For example, the Watkins Community Museum in Lawrence, KS, which is primarily focused on local history and works primarily with older audiences, decided to expand its programming by initiating several innovative projects with local environmental activists. The program, which also involves collaboration with public schools, has allowed the museum to achieve greater social and community relevance by engaging with a wider set of social issues than it had traditionally done and expanding its outreach to younger audiences.

Being interdisciplinary is seen by museum managers as one of the most prominent resilience strategies, in part because it allows applying expertise that they already have in a particular domain to unconventional social settings, and thus demonstrating their broader social relevance, and in part because interdisciplinarity in action helps to bridge the divide between arts and humanities on the one end, and sciences and technology on the other, of the creativity spectrum. This false separation leads to defunding the arts and humanities in favor of keeping the funds for the STEM fields, which is especially devastating during recessions. This approach is especially prevalent in university-affiliated institutions, as the university administration places increasing pressure on faculty and university-affiliated units to raise external funds. Universities often see such funds as a sustainable revenue source, and donor agencies working in the STEM fields tend to award larger grants as compared to those working in the arts and humanities fields. Therefore, universities tend to prioritize the STEM agenda.

The engagement of arts and humanities in interdisciplinary projects, therefore, provides a justification of the important role that they play in advancing a holistic model of sustainable development. An art center manager reflects on this theme in the following way:

> That's where all current thinking is about art and science; that those two disciplines were falsely separated. And, if you'll notice, those classes are for young children, so they have themes and settings, like fifth-century B.C. Greece, Florence in the four-teenth century; a lot of them have settings where they're sort of golden age or Renaissance settings, and, in every golden age, the connection between science and art is clear. We sort of did that here as a reaction against what Kansas was doing, which was funding scientific research and defunding arts. We want to say it's not the same, but the type of thinking is the same . . . (Personal Communication, 2011)

The interdisciplinary strategy is especially prevalent in the world of university-based museums, which have a unique opportunity to capitalize on the strength of their parent institutions. Engaging in interdisciplinary projects helps to enhance museum capacity and may also result in substantial financial benefits because, through their engagement in such projects, museums get access to funding that is more readily available to the STEM fields, as explained by a natural science museum director:

> It increases our expertise, and there is certainly more money in the interdisciplinary grants, so, if you are asked to submit a proposal, for example, in dimensions of biodiversity, which is a five-million-dollar program, and you are going to require more expertise and resources, you are going to have to put together your own team. That's one of the secrets of certainly increasing research revenues, and the future is being more multidisciplinary and being able to put together the right competitive teams. (Personal Communication, 2010)

While engaging in deeper collaboration with disciplines outside the humanities improves museums' institutional capacity and provides access to untapped funding sources, it also contributes to museums' sustainability capital in more intrinsic ways, by creating and fostering symbiotic relationships with other disciplines and facilitating the process of mutual value enrichment that results from such symbiotic relationships. All parties involved in the symbiosis not only become more resilient as institutions but also grow qualitatively by offering deeper experiences to their stakeholders. This contributes to the long-term sustainability of museums and fosters a more holistic view of sustainability in their communities.

**Community outreach programs.** Modern museums invest significant resources in community outreach programs, which often engage the public in very nontraditional ways. One example is the Lunder Conservation Center, established by the Smithsonian American Art Museum. The Lunder Center is the first art conservation facility that allows the public to have a behind-the-scenes look at the work of art preservation. Processes as important to a museum's mission as conservation and preservation, which have historically been kept behind closed doors, are now being opened to the public. This shift from collection-driven institutions to visitor-centered organizations is an indication of a major paradigm shift within the museum world (Anderson, 2004). Under the old paradigm, museums were static, protective, and focused on the past; the new paradigm is much more forward-looking and welcoming, and it acknowledges that enticing the public to engage with the institution is one of the keys to their long-term sustainability.

The emphasis on community outreach and subsequent institutionalization of the public outreach function reflects the most important shift in the institutional purpose of museums—their transformation from elite to egalitarian institutions. While early museums primarily served narrow audiences of nobility, highly educated people, researchers, and scholars, serving an increasingly diverse audience that represents the range of social, cultural, and age groups becomes a primary goal of contemporary museums (Kotler et al., 2008). By ensuring a more comprehensive outreach under the new paradigm, museums act as socially responsible organizations that pursue overall public interest and advance societal sustainability goals. Additionally, there has also been an overall shift in the tonality of public outreach away from delivering the art to the public to greater engagement and even cocreation, where members of the lay public themselves contribute to the creation and interpretation of artworks (Hadley, 2021; Olivares & Piatak, 2022; Sandell, & Nightingale, 2012).

Museums that aspire to become intergenerationally sustainable have begun embracing the value of social equity, which most typically manifests in their public outreach practices aimed at ensuring greater public access, but it is also reflected in museums' attempts to diversify their boards, staff, and volunteers. Examples of specific outreach-related practices that are guided by the considerations of social equity include instituting flexible admission policies for the general public and need-based scholarships to attend museum educational programs for young people. These scholarships are based on egalitarian ethical principles and the idea of ensuring equal access to all, while providing additional opportunities to those in need. They are offered on the basis of the economic condition of a family that applies for assistance, rather than on the basis of a particular child's skills.

Equitable access to museum experiences is important for understanding museums' intergenerational sustainability, as the principles of egalitarian justice upheld within the current community are, over time, likely to extend to justice in relation to future generations. Moreover, young people will have the chance to benefit—many for the first time—from museum programming with the help of a scholarship, and they will eventually become parents who are likely to bring their children to the museum. By committing to the value of social equity, museum managers are applying the principle of intergenerational justice that implies treating somebody's children as their own (Parfit, 1984). Moreover, museum managers engage in intuitive thinking about how the adoption of certain initiatives today, despite the lack of perfect clarity regarding future conditions, could lead to sustainable outcomes in the long run, as reflected by an art center manager below:

> I don't know what will happen in 30 years. I hope that . . . it is less expensive for families to be here; that we never have to say no to someone who would like their children to be in a class here because of money. I think we can, perhaps, be in that situation because I know what we all believe in at the arts center as museum people do, that we sometimes feel that we are safeguarding something that is extremely important, and, at the end of the financial downturn, we want to still be here and still be standing and to have provided the experiences and performance and visual arts that make us human. (Personal Communication, 2011)

Museums also attempt to reach underprivileged audiences of various ages, including people with disabilities and the elderly, as part of their efforts to respond to community needs. These initiatives are fairly recent, but they prove useful for fostering greater social and community relevance of museums. While some of these programs are motivated instrumentally by increasing the number of visitors and patrons, as well as gaining access to foundation and governmental funding, there is also a normative driver behind these initiatives—namely, aspirations of broader organizational legitimacy and concerns about institutional legacy, as expressed by managers of art, history, and natural science museums:

> It started when I came here about two years ago, and we engage people with cognitive and physical disabilities, so the broad spectrum. We even engage elderly people with dementia and Alzheimer's disease. The reason we do it is because it's another audience we're trying to give access to the contemporary arts. I'd say they come to the museum probably about six or seven times a year; it's not a lot. The reason we started the program was because we had just put in an elevator, and, two years ago, before then, we had no elevator and no way to access the second floor. So, when I saw the elevator go in, I thought to myself, "Well, we just need to start these programs." So, we're able to hold workshops upstairs for people in wheelchairs; it's great. (Personal Communication, 2012)

> And with the summer festival, we've made it free for the community. We've taken the barrier of cost away. We have worked with a number of presenters that aren't organizations, but they represent people behind them. We're working with [name of a performing-art organization] where we were paying them, but they re-granting us something from [name of a governmental organization] . . . So, we are doing it in a different way than what we had done in the past. Now it's free, so everybody can come as opposed to just [city] residents. (Personal Communication, 2015)

> That's all part of the community engagement strategy. It's really understanding who our customer is and then getting to them. You know, the senior population, many of the neighborhood block clubs, they don't have technology; they don't have phones where they're going to get the apps and the emails and the

Facebook posts. They have probably never been on Facebook a day in their life. So, we bring fliers to all the block-club meetings and have them available, or work with the state representatives and district representatives to say, "You send out newsletters every month; can you put an entry in for [name of organization] and what we have coming up?" So, it's getting a little smarter about how we communicate with our constituencies. That's the public service, we want [the name of the organization] to be accessible for all (Personal Communication, 2014)

In their quest to reach the wider public, however, museums often face various kinds of barriers, including the institutional history of elitism that still permeates operations in classical museums as well as many other traditional cultural institutions (Acevedo, & Madara, 2015; Olivares & Piatak, 2022). This problem is partially rooted in the fact that the governing structures of cultural institutions, including both organizational executive leadership and the governing boards, lack diversity (Ostrower, 2020). Another persistent issue is the lack of museum staff diversity, which leads to insufficient representation of the various cultures and points of view in museum exhibitions and other programs (Acevedo, & Madara, 2015; Garibay, 2009). Despite some advances that have been made in recent years to increase these dimensions of diversity and improve cultural representation, the issue is still notable in many institutions (Olivares & Piatak, 2022; Sandell, & Nightingale, 2012).

Other barriers are more related to individuals, such as people's reluctance to visit a museum due to their lack of previous exposure and other social barriers, as well as physical-access barriers, such as the lack of transportation infrastructure. Access barriers are particularly prevalent in areas with significant income inequality and geographically vast metropolitan areas such as Detroit. Furthermore, as noted earlier, the local environment in which cultural institutions are embedded shapes what they do and how they do it. Therefore, structural and cultural change in organizations and their communities is needed to cope with operational as well as philosophical barriers to better enable their more inclusive public outreach. The manager of a suburban historical museum reflects on the barriers she experienced while trying to extend museum outreach to Detroit public schools and that were exacerbated by the evident suburban-urban divide in Metropolitan Detroit:

I did reach out to them [Detroit Public Schools], but a lot of it was about the cost of the busing, and also parents driving—there was a rule that third graders had to be in a car seat. I reached out to many schools—public, private, charter. We don't discriminate; we want everybody to able to come to this house, but it has sort of honed down to those that are local, and it serves them best, but it is the transportation issue. We don't have a bus. And the other thing is our mission and our charter. I mean, our mission is to serve the people who live here, and I know that sounds provincial, but that's who we have to serve first. (Personal Communication, 2015)

The matters of public access, however, become critical for the long-term sustainability of museums in these types of environments, particularly since most museums are tied to their geographical locations where they were established historically. This connection with particular locations also supports the increasing shift from displaying and communicating to cocreating the art with members of the local communities (Hadley, 2021; Olivares & Piatak, 2022).

Furthermore, while it is hard to overestimate the importance of the public outreach function in museums, this function is also most likely to suffer during a recession. Smaller museums, in particular, often react to the loss of funding by cutting subsidies for their art classes for children, charging higher fees, or suspending large-scale community outreach programs. For example, this was the case of the Natural History Museum at the University of Kansas. Once the budget for public education declined, the museum canceled popular community events, reduced the number of summer camps for children, and introduced summer-camp participation fees. Likewise, the Spencer Museum of Art at the University of Kansas ended up suspending its "It Starts with Art" classes after they lost state funding because of the elimination of the Kansas Arts Commission in 2011.

Similarly, many of the Detroit-based institutions had to substantially downsize or outright eliminate their public education function in the aftermath of the Great Recession. Such cuts result from seeing public education as less of a mission-critical function than preserving collections—the rationale that nevertheless contradicts the idea of sustainable thinking in intergenerational terms. There is also a recognition that public education outcomes are hard to measure in a meaningful way, and that it may take a while to see the actual effects on human lives. As described by a historical museum manager, "The issue there is that educational programs don't make any money. They're not profitable, but they're very central to your mission. You need to raise the money to support them, but they don't really bring anything measurable back" (Personal Communication, 2015).

Therefore, organizational commitment to community outreach is largely inspired by its intrinsic significance to museum managers who see it as a way of ensuring greater social relevance of museums as fundamentally public-serving institutions. Furthermore, museums' commitment to pursuing social equity, despite the budgetary and other types of restrictions, is also evidence of sustainable thinking—the managerial rationale that ensures the long-term continuity of museums.

## Institutional-Distinctiveness Narrative: Remembering the Purpose and Staying on Course

The second narrative of intergenerational sustainability is institutional distinctiveness. Conventionally speaking, institutional distinctiveness is about staying true to oneself and one's core beliefs. Likewise, institutional distinctiveness in organizations implies that they are capable of staying true to their missions as well as establishing their unique value in society without reducing it to a commodity or a mere source of economic capital (Table 2.1). In many cases, pursuing distinctiveness also means identifying a unique institutional niche and directing organizational focus toward occupying that niche. Organizations that excel at this narrative are focused on promoting and cultivating socially important values while capitalizing on the distinctiveness of museum-based learning. Thus, they complement the well-established conventional modes of social learning, such as learning as part of the traditional educational system. Although, similar to the resilience narrative, these types of strategies contribute to overall social and community relevance of museums as public-serving institutions, they are more introspective and internally driven than resilience-type strategies.

Furthermore, as compared to the institutional resilience narrative that is often voiced in museums' strategic plans, the institutional distinctiveness narrative is much less explicit. It is rooted in the interpretive institutional and managerial order, rather than in specific programmatic documents, statutes, or other formalized routines. Moreover, while the institutional resilience narrative is a common and widely recognized survival strategy in many public domains, the second narrative of intergenerational sustainability, institutional distinctiveness, is less common. Institutional distinctiveness, however, is particularly important for the long-term durability of cultural institutions, including museums.

**Staying true to the mission.** The commitment of managers to constantly keep institutional purpose in mind is key for the distinctiveness narrative, as missions allow developing the various operational strategies while keeping in mind the distinct positioning of a particular institution in a particular environment. Moreover, missions are important drivers of managerial intuition, and, while reviewing the mission may not be a daily occurrence, understanding the mission and living the mission enable museum managers to be forward-looking while considering and balancing the needs and interests of both current and future generations of the public that they serve. Missions, therefore, give museum managers a sense of optimism for the future (even if distant) and help guide their daily operational strategies, as described by managers of an art and science museum below:

> I think that the rooms [100 years from now] are different, the decision-making processes are different, the challenges are different, but it seems to me there is one thing that you can depend on, and that is the proximity to mission as you enact every moment. (Personal Communication, September 2011)

> Mission and vision that we state to people very clearly. You saw it right outside our door. I mean, we live it and breathe it every single day, and then it continues to build. (Personal Communication, 2016)

The commitment of managers to organizational missions is particularly important during times of stress, when it may be tempting to prioritize survival-type strategies over considerations of longer-term organizational sustainability. At those times, focusing on the mission itself—as the main element of institutional distinctiveness—serves as a form of sustainable thinking that enables managers to make appropriate operational decisions. Managers of two Detroit-based museums, both of which were significantly affected by the Great Recession, reflect on the importance of the mission in the following way:

First, it's our mission. We wanted to stick with our mission. Our mission does not say cut back when times are tough. Our mission says open minds and change lives . . . so we have to always honor our mission, regardless, and so that was our driving force: living up to our mission. (Personal Communication, 2015)

We have events here five days a week . . . but shifting to an earned-revenue model—which, you know, really is kind of a drift from your mission—is another thing that could be considered and one that we are not doing. (Personal Communication, 2015)

Museum missions, however, do not remain static over time, as is both appropriate for institutional distinctiveness and necessary for institutional resilience. The major historical shifts in the mission of museums are reflected in the various resilience-building strategies that museums pursue, including their transformation from elite to egalitarian institutions, greater focus on collective identity and community relationships as opposed to old-fashioned collections-based thinking, shifting to a more interdisciplinary focus rather than purely serving the humanities, and positioning the museum as an abiding catalyst for new ideas (Table 2.2). Evolving missions, however, guide the distinctiveness narrative as well, especially when it comes to values that museums promote to their current and future publics.

**Values promoted by museums to their current and future publics.** Museum scholarship long considered the moral effects of museums on their communities. The former director of the University of Nebraska Museum, Erwin H. Barbour, wrote in his 1912 essay that museums' impact on community is "invaluable, wholesome and good, and tends to high citizenship" (Genoways & Andrei, 2008, p. 112). Barbour believed that, since museum exhibits stimulate the desire to think and learn, the thoughts produced by looking at museum exhibits are taking visitors "from commonplaces to more ennobling themes" (Genoways, 2006, p. 112). This is true in modern times as well, as museums that aspire to achieve intergenerational sustainability increasingly position themselves as educational institutions promoting the connection between museum collections and the social discourses that shape our current and future world.

In particular, museums promote such socially important values as community citizenship, responsibility and sense of stewardship (Table 2.2). These values are not necessarily directly mentioned in museum missions; rather, they are embedded in museum practices and reflected in the museum managers' thinking. While community citizenship is more about the collective identity of people, sense of stewardship and responsibility is about taking personal responsibility for particular individual actions impacting common resources. These values are socially important, as they serve as building blocks for any sustainable community, but they also contribute to museums' organizational sustainability. As a natural science museum

Table 2.2. Evolving Missions, Managerial Roles, and Values Promoted to Current and Future Generations: Museums

| Evolving missions | Greater shift from an elite to an egalitarian institution |
|---|---|
| | Shift from serving the humanities to a more interdisciplinary focus |
| | Stewardship of collective identity and community relationships |
| | Museum as a social agent and a catalyst of new ideas |
| | Being up-to-date (reference to our time) |
| Evolving managerial roles | Stewardship (balancing preservation and sharing) |
| | Management as innovation |
| | Manager as an educator, illuminator |
| | Manager as facilitator of arts-inspired communication, conversation, debate |
| | Manager as "choreographer" of social relationships |
| Values promoted to current and future generations | Museum as an egalitarian educational institution |
| | Community citizenship: educating and fostering informed decision-making, cultivating virtuous attitudes toward community |
| | Responsibility and sense of stewardship of the common environmental, cultural, economic, and other resources |

director explained it, the true significance of museums is not about their economic value; it is rather about the broader set of societal values that they instill in their communities by capitalizing on the unique value of the arts and humanities. He further argued that promoting these values contributes to museums' own long-term sustainability:

> [. . .] I don't think we are here to add to their [citizens'] life economically; we are here to add to their sense of stewardship, sense of citizenship in a larger environment in which we are all part. And, if can reach the public with the sense of responsibility, whether through the beauty of nature, whether . . . through how nature makes their life possible—you know, puts the food on their table, puts the gas in their cars, puts the shirts and pants on their backs and legs, puts the medicines in their medicine chest—if they start appreciating that, then I think our chances are improved that they will be more responsible citizens, and, then, if they are more responsible citizens, they are going to vote for more responsible politicians. And, if that's the case, it increases the chances of museums having a longer life. I am not being prescriptive here; for some people, it might be short-term, for some people it might be long-term. We want to turn people on, whether it is to turn on a kid, or an adult, or a family. We want to turn them on to the basically why natural systems are, have never been more important in the history of humanity than they are today. [emphasis added] (Personal Communication, 2010)

Community citizenship implies an educational obligation of museums that entails their ability to influence both individual choices as well as collective decision-making in the form of public policies by promoting active and cognizant citizenship. Educating active citizens, who then are able to exercise their civil rights and capable of making wise policy choices, is part of the unwritten and often unspoken mission of modern museums. Having an impact on policy that is being enacted now implies having an impact 100 years from now, and by promoting the idea of community citizenship, museums assure the inclusion of future generations in the domain of their temporal public. Furthermore, in promoting the idea of community citizenship, museum managers do not see themselves as mere instructors handing out directions to people. Rather, they see museums disseminating ideas and educating the public, as described by a natural science museum manager:

> [. . .] Our role is to try and assemble the best minds. We are not going here to tell people what to do; we are not here to make policy, whether it is a personal policy or a government policy. We are here to provide the best information so that people can make their own decisions about the policies that they want to follow, the policies that are in their best interest, short-term or long-term, for themselves and their children. So, we can present exhibits and educational programs on how we use our collection and information to do predictive modeling and forecasting that will impact their lives. (Personal Communication, 2010)

Thus, museums' policy impact is being realized intuitively, and this impact, exercised by educating citizens, is intended to have both short- and long-term outcomes. The short-term outcome is about the immediate effects of personal and collective decisions on the well-being and prosperity of the community as a whole; and the long-term outcome is about how the choices made today would impact future generations and whether they are going to enjoy similar benefits as current generations do. An art museum director describes this kind of thinking:

> I want to know what art has to say to you about your life, about your environmental conditions . . . So, when your grandchildren come to the [museum], they will say, "That's very interesting; in 2011, the ice sheets were still melting, and here's the sense of loss and longing that human beings felt about that." What the art can do is say, "Why does it matter if they're melting even more? Why does it matter for human beings?" So, it's not really to solve the problems . . . but it is to cause a revelation in an artist, a scientist, a humanist, that will allow us to say, "This is a problem we need to work on; this is a problem we cannot fix; here's where I want to devote my life. (Personal Communication, 2011)

Museum exhibitions and experiences may inspire human curiosity and creativity and foster both informed decision-making and visitors' motivation to continue exploring socially meaningful issues after they leave a museum. Therefore, museums contribute to their communities by promoting more active citizenship. Furthermore, value impact is often achieved alongside regular educational programming that may be motivated by other, more practical types of goals. As an example, an art museum manager reflects upon the significance of their new program for teenagers that focuses on giving them practical life skills but also expanding their sense of community citizenship: "They realize that it may be an interest or hobby, or art could be a career. They learn it's something you can study and be proud of and make money and support yourself doing. They also learn the importance of giving back to the community. They learn not just capital—you know, soaking up all the assets and selling things to people and all of that; they learn that there is another way" (Personal Communication, 2016).

The idea of community citizenship is related to the idea of civic engagement, narrowly understood as citizens' participation in electoral politics and civic organizations (Skocpol & Fiorina, 1999), or broadly understood as an active participation of citizens in the life of their communities and individual and collective involvement in public affairs (Yang & Bergrud, 2008). However, community citizenship is different from civic engagement; community citizenship is a normative aspect of the citizens' engagement, a human virtue and the force driving such an engagement to happen in the first place. Community citizenship presupposes museums' ability to foster informed decision-making as well as virtuous attitudes toward community.

The other value that museums promote and cultivate in their local communities is the sense of stewardship and responsibility, which can be defined as a mindful attitude toward common environmental, cultural, economic, and other resources. This value is embedded in museums' core mission and their daily routines, as the practice of object preservation itself is an example of good stewardship. Museums promote the values of responsibility and stewardship by holding cultural objects in public trust. By interacting with museum collections and learning from museum practices directed toward preserving objects for future generations, visitors absorb the idea of stewardship, which is imperative for sustainable development.

Cultivating responsibility and stewardship often implies changing museums' attitude toward the value of their own collections, becoming more transparent, and equipping themselves with the proper technology that allows using collections in a way that best assures the sense of responsibility among the museum visitors. Needless to say, there is a strong sense of responsibility and stewardship within the museum community itself, which fosters the ability of museums to promote these ideas in a society. One of the art museum managers explains how museums' ability to steward their collections translates into their ability to be good partners and stewards in a community,

> Speaking of pragmatism, I would say accountability and stewardship. Our incredibly high values: putting the collection in the highest possible regard and being a very good steward of that resource, and a good steward of donated resources, a good steward of partnership, a good steward of community. So, in terms of values: stewardship and accountability in regard to management, and stewardship in regard to care. And transparency, wherever possible, and then imparting the role of the museum as a resource for all, and a resource that validates all aspects of the human experience. (Personal Communication, 2010)

As a result of their sense of stewardship, museums have become trusted sources of information, ahead of books and television news (Merritt, 2006). At the same time, a major source of public distrust arises when the value of stewardship is violated (Merritt, 2006). For example, the sense of museum stewardship may be diminished when museums are doing business with individual collectors and for-profit entities, such as loaning expensive artworks to private galleries or even permanently deaccessioning artworks from a museum (Anonymous, 1993; Nazarov, 2011; Pollock, 2009). Professional museum organizations, such as the American Alliance of Museums and American Association of Museum Directors, play an important role in setting the ethical standards for such practices and making sure that museum actions are "grounded in the traditions of public service" and "organized as public trusts holding their collections and information as a benefit for those they were established to serve" ("American Alliance of Museums, Code of Ethics for Museums," 2000).

**Shifting toward a semi-instrumental role.** Sustainable museums maintain their institutional distinctiveness by capitalizing on an important adaptive change in museums' purpose—the emphasis on the semi-instrumental role of the arts and humanities (i.e., their broader significance as a source of societal values), as opposed to preferring either a purely intrinsic (art as an idea and a value in and of itself) or a merely instrumental (art as a developmental tool) orientation (Moldavanova, 2013, 2014). The semi-instrumental role of museums, which has the capacity to shape community-level culture, is becoming increasingly important and likely to be more prevalent in the long term. "Art for the sake of art" as well as "art as a profitable industry" both appear too narrow and insufficient for addressing the growing sustainability concerns within and outside the domain of the arts and humanities.

Evidence of museums' inclination toward the semi-instrumental role is found in their evolving missions, which emphasize the use of arts and humanities as a means of fostering transformative thinking, dialogue, and communication in diverse communities of stakeholders. This means including museums in broader social discourses, including the discourse on sustainability. For example, the updated mission statement of the Colorado University Art Museum argues that part of the museum's mission is to explore the transformative power of art and inspire critical dialogue, and to promote greater understanding of art and societal issues within a global and historical context ("Strategic Plan 2010," 2010). Thus, it is clear that the museum sees itself as both a vital part of the community and a distinctive institution that offers something that no other public organization does.

These priorities are embodied in the kinds of exhibits that museums offer. An increasing number of museum exhibitions, for instance, are designed to educate people about environmental sustainability. These exhibitions cover such topics as global climate change, environmental awareness, sustainable clothing and food, and the preservation of natural resources. For example, an exhibition at the Spencer Art Museum (Lawrence, KS), entitled "An Introduction to Trees and Other Ramifications: Branches in Nature and Culture," encouraged visitors to rethink their answers to such questions as these: What is our responsibility to other species on our planet? What do "natural" and "unnatural" mean? And what does it mean to be ecologically aware (Goddard, 2010)? This exhibition indicates the potential for a unified aesthetics of natural and artistic beauty for stimulating critical thinking about long-term sustainability.

Increasingly, museums engage in exhibitions that highlight the relationship between culture and the socioeconomic dimensions of sustainability. Many museums are actively pursuing social justice agendas by raising public awareness about issues as diverse as economic inequities, racial disparities, immigration policy, and other important concerns in their local and global communities. For example, the Boulder Museum of Contemporary Art arranged an exhibition called "BIODOME: An Experiment in Diversity," which included the projects of four artists of various backgrounds who created a series of artworks addressing the concerns and hopes expressed by the local community. The idea behind the project was that "in a natural setting, a healthy ecosystem is characterized by considerable biodiversity, where a high level of varied life forms indicates greater health" ("BIODOME: An Experiment in Diversity," 2011). The exhibition implicitly argues that similar principles of diversity and tolerance are also critical in sustainable societies.

The engagement of museums in the semi-instrumental role is fostered via greater utilization of technology—one of the institutional resilience strategies described earlier in this chapter. Technology allows museums to appeal to universally important themes of social, economic, and environmental justice that are all embedded in the sustainable development narrative. By appealing to universal themes, museums are able to make connections between community-shaping experiences that happen in a particular cultural context with events worldwide. One example is a recent exhibition entitled "Landlord Colors: On Art, Economy, and Materiality," organized by the Cranbrook Art Museum located in Metro Detroit (Hooper, 2019). The exhibition connects multiple eras and art mediums to highlight 60 contemporary artists from Detroit and around the globe, all appealing to globally significant economic, social, environmental, and cultural themes, ranging from artistic reflections on the 1967 rebellion in Detroit to such globally significant topics as economic recessions, the material and infrastructural decay in postindustrial cities, the demise of economic and social systems, and climate change, among others.

In particular communities, these types of initiatives are important beyond sustainability, as they foster cultural learning, exchange, and understanding around the world, and arts and humanities institutions, including museums, are uniquely positioned to engage in such a role. An art museum manager describes this ability of museums to draw upon universal experiences:

> Museums are recognizing that art can be found anywhere. It can be found online. It can be found as copies—photocopies. People can see Monet anywhere. The question is, "Why is it important? Why is having seen the real thing relevant in the

community and important to people?" And I think connecting with people and having people come together around something that is about human creativity and about things that we all have in common [is what's important]. Every human, no matter what their race is, what religion they have—the arts is something that we all have in common. You might have a different take on it, and you might do things differently, but it's all about creativity. And so that's really important to us. (Personal Communication, 2015)

The overall significance of shifting toward the semi-instrumental role for organizational sustainability, therefore, lies in its appeal to universal aspects of the human condition and its ability to impact sustainable communities by instilling and promoting societal values, and thus justifying the important role of the arts and humanities as alternative, global, and uniquely forward-looking modes of thinking. Instilling values through the arts and humanities shapes current modes of thinking while also influencing the worldview of future generations.

**Distinct value of museum learning**. Museums' ability to promote knowledge and cultural and social values and to contribute to the multidimensional social discourse is the product of the distinct instrumental value of museum learning that has long been recognized in the literature (Falk & Dierking, 2000; Genoways, 2006; Packer, 2006; Packer & Ballantyne, 2002). However, aside from describing the particularities of free-choice learning in an object-based environment (Falk & Dierking, 2000), no serious connection has been made between unique, experience-based museum learning and museums' sustainability. Yet, unique museum learning is one key to the institutional distinctiveness of museums.

The distinctiveness of museum-based learning is often attributed to the power of museum objects. Although the emphasis on object-based epistemology has declined (Conn, 2010), most museum managers still regard objects as powerful contributors to museum learning, even as the role of objects has shifted from storage and exhibition to stimulating a dialogue between art and people. Therefore, a sustainable museum should be capable of finding a balance between object-based epistemology and communication. Objects also serve to distinguish museums from more popular institutions, thus enforcing the distinctiveness narrative.

The unique value of museum learning stems from the fact that museums are places where beauty and human aspirations can be learned through direct experience, rather than from books or in traditional lectures. Experience-based learning is particularly important for shaping underlying cultural assumptions and guiding and shaping human behavior now and in the long run, which is something that museums implicitly aspire to achieve. Unlike traditional learning, which is based on cognitive experience, logic, and rationality, the learning model offered by museums is based on emotional perception, experimentation, interaction, and the personal experience of creativity. The ability of the arts and humanities to evoke creativity, to teach people to look at their lives and societies in a critical way, and to reexamine social stereotypes, is particularly valuable for thinking about the future.

Moreover, the function of public education, which is the most institutionalized and direct form of museums' impact on future generations, is itself crucial for the long-term sustainability of museums themselves. Therefore, early outreach is becoming more of a signature approach in many museums, including both arts and science institutions, as there is a realization that early exposure to the arts and humanities is likely to bear fruit later in life on both individual and collective levels. For some of the managers, the value of early exposure resonates with personal experiences that they had earlier in their lives, and so they feel an ethical obligation to provide this type of experience to young generations now, as expressed by a science museum manager: "I still remember going to that science center when I was that age and coming home that night and telling my mom that one day my goal was to run one of those organizations. And I have been just blessed to have now run two of them. We want to provide that same opportunity to kids" (Personal Communication, 2016).

## Balancing the Resilience and Distinctiveness Narratives for the Long-Term Sustainability of Museums: Evolving Managerial Roles

While the distinctiveness narrative is critically important to the long-term sustainability of museums, organizations that rely too much on distinctiveness without balancing it with more broad-based resilience-type strategies appear to be in a particularly vulnerable position, especially during recessions. In fact, many organizations from the Detroit metropolitan area that suffered from high degrees of external stress during the Great Recession were also organizations that prioritized their distinctiveness over social relevance. One such example is the Belle Isle Aquarium—part of the last surviving Victorian combination of nature conservancy and aquarium—that remained closed throughout the recession and was reopened by a dedicated group of volunteers in 2015. Acknowledging its long history and uniqueness among other public aquariums, one of the interviewees described the Aquarium as "the last surviving unicorn"—a distinct kind of animal that "survived the Great Depression but failed to survive the Great Recession" (Personal Communication, 2016). As noted earlier, the demise of the Aquarium has been attributed to its overall lack of social connectedness and the inability to establish relevance to local political elites as well as the public at large. Subsequently, the lack of public awareness and support for the Aquarium led to its closure, as described by one of the volunteers responsible for eventually rebuilding and reopening the institution: "[. . .] it is dangerous to have an uninformed public because they just bought it. They just bought that, "Okay, you know, everything is tough. People are losing their jobs, and we just can't afford the aquarium." Well, in tough times this aquarium survived the Great Depression, two world wars, Prohibition, the Great Recession, and then another recession. So, the idea to take this away at a time when we needed it so badly was another counterintuitive terrible thing" (Personal Communication, 2014). In this case, the niche-type operational model played against the institution rather than in its favor. The path toward resurrecting and rebuilding the Aquarium in 2015 involved engaging in the various resilience strategies discussed earlier in this chapter, including capitalizing on its institutional structure and redefining its relationship with the patron organization—the Detroit Riverfront Conservancy, creating partnerships with educational institutions and civic groups, pursuing a more interdisciplinary focus, and actively utilizing technology and social media.

Another example of a Detroit-based institution that prioritized the distinctiveness path and was hard hit by the Great Recession is the Charles Wright Museum of African American History. As the name indicates, the Charles Wright Museum positioned itself as a primarily African American–serving institution, which created a problem for its financial viability when Detroit was hit hard by the Great Recession, and the three major automakers that financially supported local museums were no longer able to provide such support. As a result, the museum experienced what could be described as an identity crisis, as described by a museum official:

First, it's our mission. We wanted to stick with our mission. Our mission does not say cut back when times are tough. Our mission says open minds and change lives through African American history and culture, and so we have to always honor our mission, regardless, and so that was our driving force: living up to our mission. And then, secondly, perception. Being an African American institution, we oftentimes are seen in a different light than other institutions sometimes, and so we have to always maintain the highest standard and/or strive to maintain the highest standard. And any cut back could have resulted in a loss of confidence and support, and so we had to just go out of our way to make sure that we did everything we can to keep things going at the highest level so that we can maintain that support and that confidence, and that trust, and that impact. (Personal Communication, 2015)

For the Charles Wright Museum, getting back on track to delivering the mission continuously meant going through a new strategic-planning process, repositioning itself as a more broadly focused institution, and looking for ways of enhancing its overall social connectedness, from diversifying the board and funding sources to adapting programs and reinventing its public outreach function. The mission of the museum itself has evolved to reflect both its uniqueness and broader social relevance that collectively support the museum's path toward sustainability:

The wording of our mission has changed, and we adopted a new, much more succinct and powerful mission statement last year. It used to be a little bit more convoluted. It would say exactly everything that we're doing—that we are a learning institution focusing on exhibitions and collections and a library and programming. And now we've streamlined what it is that we are really all about. We are about opening minds and changing lives through African American history and culture. We're all about improving the quality of life for all people, and so our mission now reflects that. (Personal Communication, 2015)

Once again, as the two examples above illustrate, too much distinctiveness coupled with the lack of social relevance is likely to create a problem for the long-term sustainability of museums. Therefore, the final lesson about sustainability addressed in this chapter is the importance of balancing the two narratives of sustainability. The key to understanding how such balancing works lies in a special kind of institutional and managerial rationality that occurs in sustainable organizations. Managers of such organizations engage in sustainable thinking by making wise incremental decisions on a daily basis, which differs from the ability to engage in and stick with a formal strategic plan. This does not imply that strategic planning is an unimportant process in the name of organizational sustainability, but rather that strategic planning, management, and thinking, despite their undeniable utility in the short- and medium-term, have limited time horizons. Beyond those horizons, sustainable thinking steps in as a rationale that captures intergenerational thinking.

The ability of managers to engage in sustainable thinking and effectively reconcile various tensions among sustainability narratives is grounded in the evolving roles of museum managers. The two roles that particularly stand out in the managerial discourse include stewardship and innovation (Table 2.2). These roles enable museum managers to move their organizations on the path toward greater sustainability and reconcile tensions arising from the interplay of institutional distinctiveness and resilience, and they also foster museums' overall contributions to sustainable local communities.

The idea of management as stewardship has its roots in psychology and sociology, and explains the way in which managers as stewards are motivated to act in the best interests of their institutions and communities (Davis, Schoorman, & Donaldson, 1997). This model of managerial behavior is very relevant to the museum world, since many museum managers historically envision themselves as stewards of museum objects, collections, and other assets. However, the idea of traditional museum stewardship is being reconsidered and reconceptualized. The new model of stewardship implies greater emphasis on accountability and responsiveness to a broader group of stakeholders. Stewardship, therefore, goes beyond the museum itself and extends all the way to the community in which a museum exists, thus fostering its overall social connectedness. Subsequently, museum managers today serve as the stewards of collective identity and the stewards of museum relationships with the current and future publics:

> I think we've gone from a kind of lone idea of leadership and
> management to understanding that we all are part of an ecology,
> and we are an ecology that is focused on values, beliefs, meaning,

interpretation, social good, creating a better society—and that society then, now, has exploded. It's huge . . . So, I think that management is in a very interesting role. No longer is [it] the person at the top who knows everything. It seems more important—and maybe this is a little thing about resilience practice; I consider it more important for me—to understand the relationships among things than to understand the things. So, it's somehow re-conceptualizing the idea of an institution as a set of relationships, a constellation of people and ideas and, in our case, art. (Personal Communication, 2011)

The idea of management as stewardship is traditionally associated with the oldest museum functions—collecting and preserving—and is, therefore, reflective of museums' institutional distinctiveness. But management as innovation balances the focus on objects and collections with continuing evolution in museum practices in response to the demands of time. Managers' commitment to innovation fosters the role of museums as catalysts for social innovation, generating new ideas, looking into the future, and even engineering the future. The ability of museum managers to engage in innovation for more sustainable communities manifests itself in their ability to engage in intuitive intergenerational thinking despite the difficulty in predicting the future.

## Concluding Thoughts

This chapter has approached the idea of a museum as an institution of intergenerational memory. However, an examination of museum administration reveals that the significance of museums clearly goes beyond the idea of memory and preservation. By pursuing strategies that allow them to continue in their role as sustainable stewards of the cultural heritage, museums are, in essence, working today to protect the rights and interests of future generations. As an institutionalized form of cultural sustainability, they make the lineage between current and future generations possible by including future generations into the domain of their current public in a variety of ways that go beyond preservation and memory.

This chapter discussed two themes: the intergenerational significance of museums and the issue of museums' self-sustainability. The questions asked were, "What does it take for a museum to stand the test of time?

What makes museums sustainable?" As it turns out, long-term sustainability of museums results from the combination and balance between two narratives—institutional resilience and institutional distinctiveness. Combined, the two narratives lead to the formation of the capital for sustainability that ensures the long-term durability of museums.

First, museums achieve remarkable institutional resilience by being adaptable and responsive to various external and internal pressures: they are dynamic, rather than static, and innovative rather than conservative. Such structural adaptability is quite distinct from the path-dependency argument (Pierson, 2000) that might otherwise have been expected of museums as long-standing institutions focusing primarily on cultural preservation. The key to museums' resilience is the degree of their social connectedness and social and community relevance. Sustainable museums enhance their social and community relevance by building public-private partnerships, expanding and diversifying their public outreach, utilizing technology and social media, and engaging in interdisciplinary projects. Sustainable museums engage in both structural and cultural change that are necessary for institutional resilience, and they also capitalize on community-level culture that enables sustainability of the arts and humanities.

The choice of a particular adaptive strategy by museums is impacted by the institutional factors. However, regardless of institutional form, sustainable museums systematically seek ways to broaden the scope of their public, thus serving the needs of both current and future generations. A successful implementation of an adaptive strategy depends upon museums' operational and management capacity. A museum is more likely to have stronger capacity if it is relying on multiple funding sources, capable of building relationships with public and private supporters, able to engage in cross-disciplinary projects, open to the use of new technologies, and willing to adapt innovations that reach younger audiences. Organizations that pursue these strategies embed themselves within their communities and enhance their overall social connectedness. They engage in socially responsible behavior by becoming more inclusive and acting upon their commitment to serve a more diverse local and global public.

Second, museums safeguard their capital for sustainability by preserving and cultivating their institutional distinctiveness. This includes commitment to institutional missions, the inclusion of museums into broader societal sustainability discourses, and the promotion of particular values to their current and, by extension, future publics. The missions of sustainable museums continue to evolve, and a greater emphasis is placed on engaging in a more interactive dialogue within the museum community and with an increasingly diverse public; shifting from serving the humanities to a more interdisciplinary approach, and moving toward the emphasis on museums as cultivators of societal values and norms. While pursuing their own sustainability, museums contribute to communities and societies in many tangible and intangible ways, to include their contributions to environmentally, socially, and economically sustainable development. As a result of their integrity and overall significance, museums achieve the status of one of the most trusted public institutions, thus assuring them a long-term base of support.

The ability of museums to have a lasting intergenerational impact stems from the successful reconciliation of tensions that arise between the two narratives—the institutional distinctiveness embedded in museum missions and the willingness and ability of museums to change, adapt, and innovate. Sustainable museums are able to balance their distinctiveness with particular managerial responses to resilience pressures, and managers of sustainable museums are capable of balancing the traditional stewardship role with emerging emphasis on innovation. The key to the long-term sustainability of museums is the ability of their managers to act sustainably by making wise, incremental decisions on a day-to-day basis. This special kind of managerial rationality—what can be called sustainable thinking—allows for the reconciling of tensions between the two narratives (institutional resilience and institutional distinctiveness), as well as allowing for the two narratives to coexist. Sustainable thinking is present in museums with various institutional structures, so it is not a particular institutional arrangement that matters the most; what matters is how any arrangement could be used to enhance the museum capital for sustainability.

Chapter 3

# Literature and Its Institutions

## The Moral Language between Generations

Of all the arts and humanities, it is literature and its institutions that make possible the transmission of human experiences across borders and time. While cultural objects hosted in museums rarely travel, great literature is routinely published and republished, translated into many languages, and made available to people anywhere in the world. Hence, it is the wide accessibility of literature that makes it the possession of all of humanity rather than an object that belongs to a particular person or nation. And it is the timeless relevance of literature that makes it an asset and a universal language of communication between those currently living, the unborn, and the long dead. This chapter explores the relationship between these properties of literature and literary institutions and their intergenerational sustainability.

While working on this book, I came across a creative writing program at a county correctional facility that, for over 10 years, had been taught by a professor of English language and literature from a Midwestern university. When I first met the professor, he handed me several small poetry books written by the inmates and his own poems inspired by interactions with people at the jail. It was fascinating to discover that poetry would reach people in such a remote location. While I could see how teaching in jail could be inspirational for writing poetry, I wondered about the value of such a program for inmates and society, and why a university professor and his students would dedicate over a decade of their lives to teaching poetry writing in such a setting. As I learned later, there are quite a few similar programs in the United States, and even a nonprofit organization—the Justice Arts Coalition—which is a national network of people creating art in and around the American prison system that was established in 2008 in response to the growth in incarceration rates.

I had many questions about the program: What is its value for the inmates? Are they expected to develop practical skills that they can later use in their civil lives? Is it likely to transform their perceptions and make them law-abiding citizens? Is it going to impact their children and families? As I addressed these questions to the professor, I realized how remote they were from the truth. It turned out that the value of such a program is completely intrinsic yet extremely important: it gives people hope, brings them light, and helps them relate their life experiences to ours. It shows that inmates are people like everyone else, and it does so through the power of narrative or story being told through poetry. As the professor further explained, an amazing power of healing souls by enabling people to share their stories through poetry is especially valuable for people in exceptionally tough life situations, and, while he is not expecting immediate tangible payoffs from the inmates' ability to write poetry, he believes in the longer-term transformational effects of poetry writing on these individuals:

> When you do the same sort of class in a jail situation, you realize that the things that we do in class, like telling stories and talking about these things, writing and all of that, it can be really important and can be a kind of lifeline for people in desperate situations. When you see people who often have pretty much nothing, and they have found this way of making sense of their lives, and getting value to their lives in some way, then you just realize that the things that I do in English and with poetry are really important. I think it brings small benefits, and those benefits are extremely important. But I'm just always careful not to expect too much, not to think that this is going to save lives, change people completely. . . . [what] I would like it to be is a small good thing that they can then do more with, if possible, and, if not, then just have value for what it is at the time. (Personal Communication, 2012)

As this creative writing program illustrates, literature has important social meaning and significance because it tells us something about the human condition, and this knowledge impacts our future lives. Moreover, by preserving stories through literature, we are leaving a record of our society for future generations.

The instrumental value of reading literature has long been acknowledged (von Schlegel & Frost, 1878), and such value goes beyond the benefits of entertainment and education. The value of literature stems from its cultural significance, its ability to absorb and provide easy and quick access to cultural heritage from many civilizations—old and new, remote and near. Literature adds something intrinsically important and supplies something lacking to "materially successful, formally schooled, busy, highly organized lives," as the greatest literatures of different times and cultures are "the storehouses" of human values and aspirations (Blair, 2005, p. 9). The enduring significance of literature is rooted in its universal appeal to timeless human values. Even if some of the great books are resting on library shelves—written in the old long-gone languages (or even when those original literary works are not preserved)—these works have already influenced the development of literature and human intelligence over the course of history. And it is certainly possible to see their relevance to the modern world (Greenblatt, 2011).

Literature also serves as a catalyst of change in societal values, and the prominent role of poets and writers in helping societies recognize the faults of modernity and foresee the distant future has been widely recognized (Brooks, 2012; Ferris, 2011; Taylor, 2011). This ability of literature to challenge social stereotypes and alter human beliefs stems from the fact that literature exceeds the capacity of language: literature portrays gaps, silences, obstacles, and noise in language, and it often displays not only what can be said but also what cannot be said (Khair & Doubinsky, 2011). Therefore, by displaying, interpreting, and transmitting meanings, literature influences the deepest levels of individual and collective human consciousness, hence presenting an important setting for learning about intergenerational sustainability.

Formalized literature organizations, as well as less-formal literature institutions, have developed various instruments that enable the transmission of literary narratives across time and space, and have produced two outcomes with regard to intergenerational sustainability. First, by effectively serving as a language of communication between past, current, and future generations, literature has been contributing to the richness, continuity, and sustainability of human cultures. By including multiple generations in the domain of their public, literature institutions ensure their own timeless relevance and enhance their own sustainability, while also advancing sustainability in their communities.

Second, over the course of history, formalized literature organizations demonstrated their ability to adapt and successfully cope with external pressures by balancing the two narratives of intergenerational sustainability: institutional resilience, which ensures adaptation and change, and institutional distinctiveness, which is aimed at creating and sustaining the distinct value of literature and its institutions for individuals and societies. The resilience narrative is embedded in the missions, programs, and initiatives implemented by formalized literature organizations, while the distinctiveness narrative is more implicit and rooted in unique positioning and distinct values that literature institutions carry out in a society. The narratives are not always perfectly aligned, but reconciling tensions among them is, nevertheless, critical for the formation of institutional capital for sustainability, which ensures the long-term durability of literature and its institutions.

Although there is a wide array of formalized organizations that mediate the formation, promotion, and preservation of literature, as compared to the other arts and humanities, literature is much less institutionalized. Therefore, the key factors of the long-term sustainability of literature are both similar and distinct from other cultural institutions. This chapter first considers general institutions that are important for intergenerational sustainability of literature. It then interrogates experiences of formalized literature organizations, examining external pressures facing them, as well as adaptive institutional routines and logics and strategies that managers of literature organizations have developed over time to ensure their organizations' long-term sustainability.

## The Creation, Preservation, and Communication of Literature to Future Generations

The history of literature is commonly associated with the history of the book, which can be traced to the invention of alphabets and writing, which allowed people to keep a record of human life. The new technology of writing invented in the course of human history meant something really important for human civilization. Stories no longer had to be memorized collectively as musical verse, which was the earliest literary technology of storing stories in the mind (Epstein, 2002). With the invention of writing, stories about life and human nature could be recorded in book form and saved for future generations. The book, as it is understood today, is not just an artifact or a manufactured object; it is "a mind-to-mind transmission, which can cross all boundaries (except the sad border of illiteracy)" (Geiser, Dolin, & Topkis, 1985, p. 6). This transformation in the book's reach and impact, and its ability to exceed the boundaries of both space and time, is one key to understanding the intergenerational sustainability of literature.

The continuing significance of the book, as an intergenerationally sustainable form of cultural and public expression, is the result of specific institutions created by humans to ensure the long-term relevance of the book. Over the course of human history, three major institutions were developed in the domain of literature that ensured the creation, preservation, and communication of literature across generations: the literary canon, the libraries as institutions for book preservation and promotion, and the publishing industry as an instrument for literature dissemination. These institutions play important roles in preserving literature, books, and the written word, but they also adapt and change in order to respond to the various external pressures that the arts and humanities face. Moreover, as part of their own pursuit of sustainability, literature organizations become increasingly actively involved in their local communities, advancing sustainable development in many tangible and intangible ways.

## The Canon and the Intergenerational Significance of Literature

The earliest literature comprises religious books, and some of these books contain explicit reference to the idea and ethic of sustainability. In fact, one of the greatest examples of the ethic of sustainability can be found in the Book of Genesis in the Bible, when, in the face of a flood, Noah was instructed by God to build an ark to save himself, his family, and every kind of animal. This biblical episode could be interpreted as a metaphor that teaches a lesson about environmental sustainability and about preserving humans and nature as inseparable and interconnected elements of the same ecosystem. The Bible as a written work served and continues to serve as the foundation for Christian moral doctrine; its stories and narratives have been instrumental in helping to hold societies and cultures together through the shared system of meanings and interpretations (Hassan, 2011). The Bible, as well as other religious texts that became canonical, is the most direct example of the moral language between generations.

Likewise, the moral philosophy of India can be traced to the writings in Sanskrit that in literary form preserved information about the outward and inner lives of people from the past. The most ancient literature in China is contained in the Five Kings and Five Texts as well as in the Book of History compiled by Confucius from records as old as 720 BC, and the moral teachings of Confucius himself are the examples of moral literature that survived to this day (Blair, 2005). Many other great civilizations of the world—Egyptian, Greek, Persian, and Arabic—also managed to preserve some of their literary heritage since ancient times, and today we are still reading the legendary blind poet Homer—the earliest figure of Greek literature—of the ninth century BC.

The intergenerational significance of canonical literature stems from its ability to serve as the language between generations—not yet born, current, and long gone. Hence, each culture's system of values and beliefs is communicated to its young generations through the written tales and myths embedded in children's fables, and moral values are being absorbed by children through examples such as Robin Hood and the protagonists in Aesop's fables. Later on in their lives, when humans learn to read, they engage with serious literature written by people from earlier generations, and moral lessons from this literature become recognizable and unconsciously appreciated. The history of literature becomes the general history of culture and nation, and it reflects the system of values and beliefs as well as their transformation in particular cultural contexts.

The timeless value of canonical literature stems from its ability to appeal to universal human aspirations and fulfill the human search for deeper meanings of everyday routines. This becomes possible because great writers do not only report stories—consciously or unconsciously, they also reveal themselves in their works (Blair, 2005). Consequently, literature provides a space "in which the invisible relations between language and reality, between the symbolic and material" coexist in a form of art, which allows the reader "to dig into that space, to excavate it to her own depth and at her own pace" (Khair & Doubinsky, 2011, p. 27). Good literature allows for the uncovering of human potential and stimulation of moral growth; it emphasizes the unity of humans and nature and guards human values from being overshadowed by the speed of life, including unstoppable technological progress.

The literary canon is an institution that ensures the transmission of literature from one generation to another. Hence, works included in the literary canon are often described as universal, immortal, classic, timeless, and transcendent—words that are used as both the symbol of the universality of literature across time and space and as evaluative terms pertaining to the quality of literary works (Lindenberger, 1990). Literary canon reflects not only the history of literature but also the history of humanity as it is embedded in literature. It embeds the human inclination to share texts—texts dating back to the beginnings of culture—with the readers from the past and present, and these texts "exert a continuing power on those still unwritten texts that later generations will presumably assimilate" (Lindenberger 1990, p. 25).

The literary canon presents one of the most ancient examples of the human inclination to long-term sustainability. While systematic attempts to maintain a canon did not exist in the visual arts until the late Renaissance and the idea of a musical canon (with the exception of church music) arrived much later, at the end of the eighteenth century (Lindenberger, 1990), attempts to form and preserve the literary canon can be traced all the way from antiquity to the modern period. Due to this emphasis on preservation, the canon may appear rigid at first, but such an impression would be inaccurate since the canon is constantly evolving, which is key to its continuing relevance and intergenerational sustainability.

One reason for the canon's resilience is a historically established synergy formed between literature and other social institutions. For example, the major difference between a literary canon and canons within music or visual arts is that the literary canon always functioned as a central part of an educational system of a particular culture, especially for the young (Lindenberger, 1990, p. 146). Thus, by being an essential part of a common educational curriculum, literature became part of every educated person's life and a source of their cultural knowledge. The literary canon has also become more inclusive because of a greater appreciation for diversity and along with the development of informational technologies. Furthermore, unlike older works that disappeared when removed from the canon lists, the newer works, even if temporarily removed from the canon, are preserved in the libraries in their physical or digital forms, thus ensuring their access to future generations.

## The Role of Libraries as Intergenerationally Sustainable Institutions

The next important institution that ensures the preservation, access to, and transmission of literature from one generation to another is the library. While many libraries have been destroyed in the course of history, libraries remain among the most resilient institutions within the domain of arts and humanities, and their history in itself is an important lesson for sustainability. As Michael Harris claimed in his *History of Libraries of the Western World*, "The idea of the library, once established, was indestructible, and since the beginning of recorded history, it has served a vital purpose as the main communicative link in both time and space" (Harris, 1999, p. 13). Historically, the word "library" originated during the Roman book trade times, where there was a difference in roles between copyists (library) and scribes (scribae): the copyists were slaves or paid laborers who worked for booksellers, and scribae were free citizens working as archivists, government bureaucrats, and personal secretaries (Greenblatt, 2011). Librarianship was first defined as a legitimate profession around 4500–4000 BC in the ancient Sumerian civilization that existed in southern Mesopotamia (in the territory of modern Iraq) (Dunlap, 1972). Since early times, librarians were subjected to professional standards, including education, moral character, an intrinsic sense of order, and a natural love for books (Sapp, 2002).

The history of literature changed forever with the invention of libraries, which today serve as major institutions fulfilling social, educational, and cultural functions of literature, as well as serving as institutions responsible for the preservation and equitable access to literary heritage. Similar to museums, libraries started from personal collections of wealthy educated people, who either employed or owned librarians as slaves. Likewise, the "business" of book writing was originally controlled by wealthy patrons who commissioned the writings and retained the profits from book sales. In North America, institutions that became known later as public libraries first appeared in New England in the form of voluntary member-serving associations supported primarily via private philanthropy (Bobinski, 1969). Andrew Carnegie, in particular, became a patron for the libraries, and his corporation provided funding that was instrumental in establishing libraries in communities of various sizes across the United States (Bobinski, 1969). Gradually, libraries became symbols of civic pride and obtained public support via taxation.

The idea of a public library, as we know it today, can be traced back to the Renaissance. With the invention of printing and the expansion of universities, there came the recognition that, for libraries to have great cultural influence, they must be open to scholars, students, and the public (Harris, 1999). This historical transformation of the libraries' role and their accessibility to a larger public is what allows for their continuing relevance and sustainability. Although private libraries still exist in the modern world, most libraries are public, which makes them accessible to the community. What does this mean for literature? Simply put, public libraries can bring the best literature closer to every literate person—rich and poor, more educated and less educated.

In modern history, libraries have been the primary reason that published books and other materials have survived. Yet, for various reasons, including the impact of climate and pests, many great books did not manage to physically survive the "teeth of time," including those housed by some of the greatest libraries of the ancient world (Greenblatt, 2011). One such example is the library of Alexandria in Egypt—the largest and the most significant library of the ancient world, which covered the entire range of intellectual thought and was not associated with a particular philosophical school. According to Greenblatt, it represented "a global cosmopolitanism, a determination to assemble the accumulated knowledge of the whole world and to perfect and add to this knowledge" (Greenblatt, 2011, pp. 87–88). Scholars working for the library were famous for their rigor and the pursuit of textual accuracy, so the library contained a very large but also extremely significant collection of books. The library housed several systematically organized, labeled, and shelved collections—a number of which were accidentally burned in 48 B.C. during the Egyptian civil war between Cleopatra and her brother Ptolemy XIII, when Julius Caesar's actions caused the conflagration, and most of the rest were destroyed by the subsequent military interventions as well as part of the war against paganism (Greenblatt, 2011).

Similarly, an important challenge facing libraries today is the preservation of historical books and manuscripts—a task comparable with the idea of preserving cultural objects by museums. Indeed, many of the historical books cannot be as easily reproduced due to differences in printing technology and in how these books were created in the first place. Libraries with historical collections, therefore, are increasingly engaging in the book-digitization business, as there is a realization that some of their physical collections cannot be preserved in perpetuity. There are also grassroots efforts to restore and preserve historically significant literature that was created before the invention of print. One such example is the Hill Museum & Manuscript Library at Saint John's University in Minnesota, which holds the world's largest archive of handwritten and copied manuscripts photographed in microfilm and transferred to digital formats. The organization was founded in 1965 as the Monastic Microfilm Library to preserve manuscripts in Austria and

Germany, but, in the aftermath of the Cold War, preservation efforts have spread to other parts of the world, including Ethiopia, the Middle East, and India. The Hill Museum & Manuscript Library was able to preserve the classical and medieval handwritten culture of Western civilization for current and future generations. Due to the availability of private support, the mission of the library expanded in 2005 to include preservation of every kind of handwritten material that fits its mission.

Contemporary libraries face numerous sustainability issues. Among those are issues related to storage of the increasing number of published books, the need to cope with technological progress by reconciling traditional library roles with the new reality of digital informational technology, the problem of acquisition of new materials when economic resources are scarce, and the crisis of librarianship as a profession (Battles, 2003; Katz, 1995). Furthermore, the COVID-19 pandemic in 2020 demonstrated how vulnerable libraries and other institutions that rely on providing in-person services to their audiences are, and many institutions adapted appropriately by shifting to remote work and services (IPA, 2020). Sustainability of libraries also depends on their operational environment. Libraries tend to thrive in economically prosperous societies with literate and stable populations, strong public and governmental support, the presence of a creative class, the accessibility of technologies, and the availability of educational opportunities for library managers (Harris, 1999; Katz, 1995).

The Great Recession and economic downturn have added fuel to the fire of the problems libraries face; and despite their community embeddedness and seeming stability, some libraries ended up closing in the aftermath of the recession. For example, the Detroit metropolitan area—one of the hardest-hit urban areas during the Great Recession—has seen several of its public libraries close due to budget cuts (Abbey-Lambertz, 2011). This happened despite the fact that the Detroit Public Library system is one of the oldest (and the fourth-largest) library systems in the United States. Therefore, even libraries—the most durable of the arts and humanities institutions—are not immune to external pressures. Despite these challenges, scholars of libraries are generally optimistic regarding the future of these institutions, and there is a strong belief that libraries of the future will thrive and will continue providing highly valued service, and librarians, as champions of information rights, will be recognized as the ultimate information professionals (Sapp, 2002). The history of libraries, however, has been intertwined with the history of the publishing industry.

## From Traditional Publishing to Electronic World: The Emergence of New Challenges and Opportunities for Literature

The history of the book is the history of communication, and the nature of this communication keeps changing as the means of communication evolve and become more complex. The earliest writing is dated to approximately 3500 B.C.; it originated as the result of collective urbanization, a formal religion, and active trade, all of which required written communication (Katz, 1995). At its earliest beginnings, literacy was limited to a select few who had been taught to read and write, and who thus gained power over information and an elite status. The invention of printing in the mid-fifteenth century changed the nature of communication, which then became mass communication, and gained its momentum in the 19th century with widespread literacy and printing technology (Katz, 1995). Published works became accessible to many people who could read, and, historically, it was the institution of publishing that fostered the transformation of the written word from elitist to egalitarian.

Since the invention of publishing during the Renaissance, many things have changed. First and foremost, as a result of the technological revolution and the advent of the Internet in the late 1980s, the way in which people obtain, transmit, and process information has changed. While, in the age of print, words often remained fixed in time and space, information and communication technologies "have accelerated time and how society lives in it" (Hassan, 2011). These changes have resulted in the invention and spread of electronic literature, which in many respects is different from traditional print.

First, traditional and electronic book publishing models produce different kinds of products that satisfy different types of demands in the literature marketplace. Electronic publications are seen as something that fulfills current needs for up-to-date information and can be accessed relatively quickly, but they are also more transient, as many electronic publications may get lost in the sea of the World Wide Web. At the same time, published literature treats a book as an object that has unique value, something to be held and appreciated, and something that has long-term significance. Because of this distinctiveness, there is a sense in the publishing community that print literature will persist, as expressed by the managers from an independent and a university-affiliated press:

Publishing will always exist in one form or another; people are going to be creating literature no matter what happens—TV, or the Internet, or anything. There is probably going to be a shift toward more digital things, but there will still be print books 100 years from now . . . (Personal Communication, 2012)

There is a handful of organizations, member organizations that are creating a lot of tools, webinars and seminars, to keep print relevant . . . it is just really true that not only people are going to continue to print, but there is no academic institution or society that has truly gone online only. . . . but the market is really exploding because it is so inexpensive to print in lower quantities. Now we are seeing a lot of people printing books that never would have gotten into print before . . . So, it is pretty exciting! You know, people say, "Printing is dead," and I usually just say, "Really? You are just not figuring out where print is relevant and who wants to still print." (Personal Communication, 2012)

Second, the advent of electronic literature three decades ago changed our understanding of what literature is, and it created new long-term challenges. With the movement into digital media, literature today has become a complex web of activities that, along with conventional reading and writing, includes technologies, cultural and economic mechanisms, reading habits and predispositions, networks of producers and consumers, professional societies, and many other components (Hayles, 2008; Schober, 2023). Electronic literature is dependent upon networked and program-mable media, and it is influenced by computer games, films, animations, digital arts, graphic design, and electronic visual culture (Schober, 2023). E-literature is also not as coherent as most of the published literature. At the same time, there are many works of high literary merit in the form of electronic literature, and paying close attention to these works requires new modes of analysis—so-called digital thinking (Hayles, 2008, p. 30).

Third, in terms of long-term sustainability, both forms of literature face their own preservation concerns. While there are many mechanisms, institutions, and entire professions dealing with the preservation of books and other print forms of literature for future generations, books and monographs, much like any cultural objects, are not infinite. Therefore, many rare books and manuscripts are being digitized for future preservation.

Electronic literature, on the other hand, is vulnerable to the fluid nature of digital media, as it can become unreadable after a decade or even less due to outdated software and hardware (Hayles, 2008). The Electronic Literature Organization, a nonprofit agency, has started developing solutions to this problem; however, reservations regarding the future of e-literature remain valid.

An alternative point of view, however, suggests that the electronic model is not as flawed. If anything, it creates an opportunity with great potential to contribute to the long-term relevance and sustainability of all literature. In fact, technology can be seen as a guarantor of the bottom line for literature, something that will help it thrive in the long run, rather than something that will compete with traditional print. One expression of such thinking is the emergence and expansion of the digital humanities movement (Berry & Fagerjord, 2017), which is an area of scholarship that exists at the intersection between computing or digital technologies and the disciplines of the humanities (Grigar & O'Sullivan, 2021). Scholars relying on the digital approach to humanities recognize the limitations of the printed word and no longer view it as the main medium for knowledge production (Grigar & O'Sullivan, 2021); they work in collaborative and interdisciplinary ways to employ digital tools as a means of producing and communicating their work to the increasingly digital public (Berry & Fagerjord, 2017).

Likewise, we have come to appreciate the electronic model and digital thinking more with the onset of the COVID-19 pandemic in 2020, which created both challenges and opportunities for literature and the other areas of the arts and humanities. The pandemic caused cancellations of book fairs and major industry events, lockdowns, and substantial declines in book sales due to its effects on the entire publishing supply chain, to include both authors and readers (IPA, 2020). Governments also provided subsidies to other social sectors, while neglecting publishing and other creative industries. In response to such stressors, many in the industry put the distancing measures in place that forced traditional publishers to work remotely and in virtual settings and have engaged in various innovative endeavors, such as launching online member marketplaces and book fairs (IPA, 2020). The pandemic has also affected workplace cultures and fostered the growth of self-publishing and independent publishing.

Therefore, when thinking about long-term sustainability of literature, it is important to envision a balanced model that includes both traditional and electronic publishing modes and appeals appropriately to future generations. The manager of an online literature publishing platform reflects on the importance of e-literature and its promise of wider access as follows:

> Literature will always be a part of our culture. And I think that the challenges and the opportunities that the electronic model provides are going to be crucial in what we can do to promote literature. I think at this point again we are accessible to everyone who has access to a computer, and, I think also, because we are free, we are entirely grant-supported, and we have major funders and smaller funders. We have some private donors, but we are run entirely on grant money, and that is what allows us to be free online and to make us available online free of charge, and they want very much to continue this mission—again—to find this new generation of leaders and install the habit of reading and the interest in the sense of adventure in exploring other cultures through literature. (Personal Communication, 2012)

As is clear from the quotation above, literature as an idea itself is much more resilient than any of its institutionalized forms, and it will continue transforming, adapting, and changing to accommodate societal reality and the demands of ever-evolving markets. As Jason Epstein said, "Technologies change the world, but human nature remains the same," hence "the defining human act of storytelling will survive the evolution of cultures and their institutions as it always has" (Epstein, 2002, pp. 11–12).

The preservation and promotion of literature is important for its own sake, but literature also plays an important role in the long-term sustainability of societies. The literary canon—whether electronic or printed—performs and will continue performing a very important normative function. For instance, in his book *The Age of Distraction*, Robert Hassan argues that we live in an extremely destabilized networked world, where the digital representation of meaning is being transmitted at an extremely high speed, and writing itself has become digital and highly unstable (2011). Hassan further claims that the literary canon serves to safeguard important human values and defend against digital distractions. According to Hassan, "It is the stabilization of the written word, both printed and electronic, that we must look to as the source of cognitive recuperation and relief from the informational stimuli of our post-modern condition" (Hassan, 2011, pp. 146–147).

Hopes for the future of literature are high, although there has definitely been a realization that sustainability of literature depends upon the successful modification and adaptation of its institutions. In Epstein's words, book publishing in the future "may therefore become once more a cottage industry of diverse, creative, autonomous units" (Epstein, 2002, p. 79). This vision of the future of publishing reflects the aspirations and preferences of future readers—an increasingly diverse and multicultural group of people who would rather find themselves seeking uniqueness, individualism, and diversity than uniformity. The promise of the long-term sustainability of literature is assured through the work of formalized organizations that keep literature relevant for both current and future generations. This chapter further considers the long-term sustainability of literature through the prism of its formal organizations.

## Intergenerational Sustainability of Literature: Common Pressures and Responses

Current pressures on literature are many, and its institutions are facing an increasing need to adjust in response to these pressures. Furthermore, they are part of a broader economy, social environment, and culture (Thompson, 2012), and their sustainability depends on a combination of cultural, economic, political, technological, and other societal issues. The most significant concerns with the long-term implications for literature include unstable reading patterns, especially among younger generations; the declining value of the book as a cultural object; the crisis of the publishing industry; lower visibility of literature as compared to other cultural industries; and the increasing dynamism and fragmentation within the literature market.

Among other factors, reading habits of various population groups, as evidenced by how much and how well people read, are among the most critical indicators of the long-term sustainability of literature. According to the former chairman of the NEA, Dana Gioia, "Reading is not a timeless, universal capacity"; it requires "a specific intellectual skill and social habit that depends on a great many educational, cultural, and economic factors," and, in the absence of such a capacity, "the nation becomes less informed, active, and independent minded" (NEA, 2004). Thus, the decline in reading may, in the long run, not only question the sustainability of literature and its institutions but also lead to broader societal consequences (Gifford, 2007).

In 2004, the National Endowment for the Arts released a survey titled "Reading at Risk: A Survey of Literary Reading in America," which determined that literary reading was in dramatic decline (NEA, 2004). From 1982 to 2002, literary reading declined by 10 percent (a loss of about 20 million potential readers) in all population groups, but the decline was especially significant for the youngest age group. However, the newest report issued by the NEA in 2018, which analyzed data covering the period between 2002 and 2017, showed that some forms of reading have seen an upward trend. For example, in 2017, 11.7 percent of U.S. adults read poetry, which is a 76 percent increase since 2012 (NEA, 2018). Although the most recent study showed that literary reading may rise among different population groups, concerns regarding a population's reading habits remain valid. For example, while 52.7 percent of adults read any book not required for work or school in 2017, this rate has not changed since 2012, and the rate for reading novels and short stories has actually declined by 7.6 percent.

On the positive side, however, there is also evidence of the emergence of the so-called reading class (mainly book readers) that is restricted in size but disproportionate in influence (Fuller & Sedo, 2013; Griswold, McDonnell, & Wright, 2005). Griswold et al. (2005) discovered a certain "pile-on effect" that is important for the future of reading. This effect shows that "reading practices, once they reach some critical mass, generate their own support structure," and in the long run this means that "the reading class will flourish even if overall reading by the general public declines" (Griswold, et al. 2005). Likewise, mass reading events have successfully boosted renewed interest in reading and the overall popularity of the reading culture, both of which have been helped along by televised book clubs, various film adaptations of literary works, big-box book stores, online bookselling, and face-to-face and online book groups (Fuller and Sedo, 2013).

Modern reading is increasingly envisioned as a network of practices, conditioned by the social, historical, and cultural context (Fuller & Sedo, 2013; Griswold et al., 2005; Olave, 2020). It is an important social activity, as people often engage in reading and related activities with families, social groups, and organizations. Furthermore, the reading capacity of the population, especially young people, is an important indicator of their general level of participation in the arts as well as their civic engagement and active participation in the life of a community. For example, studies of literary reading have established that literary readers are nearly three times as likely to attend a performing arts event, almost four times as likely to visit an art museum, and more than 2.5 times as likely to do volunteer and charity work (NEA, 2006, 2007). Although it is hard to infer causality, there is clearly a strong association between reading habits and engagement in other social activities.

To that extent, managers of formalized literature organizations are tasked with tackling all the above macro-level challenges that the field of literature is facing, while simultaneously looking for ways to sustain their own organizations. They do so by engaging in structural modifications and program adaptations that support a path toward greater institutional resilience, as well as by emphasizing the unique value their organizations offer to a society via the institutional distinctiveness narrative (Table 3.1).

Table 3.1. Two Narratives of Intergenerational Sustainability: Literature

| Institutional Resilience Narrative | • Structural adaptability<br>• Social and community relevance | • Capitalizing on institutional structure<br>• Institutional change<br>• Institutional hybrids<br>• Public-private partnerships<br>• Interdisciplinary focus<br>• Utilizing technology and social media<br>• Diversifying and expanding community outreach |
|---|---|---|
| Institutional Distinctiveness Narrative | Capitalizing on institutional uniqueness and distinctiveness | • Staying true to the core mission<br>• Occupying unique institutional niche<br>• Promoting and cultivating socially important values<br>• Shifting towards semi-instrumental role<br>• Placing a distinct value on arts-based learning |

By pursuing the two narratives of sustainability and reconciling the various tensions that may arise along the way, literature organizations build their own capital for sustainability, upon which they are able to rely in hard times. Furthermore, the pursuit of long-term organizational sustainability involves making a variety of instrumental and intrinsic contributions to sustainability in local communities and the global world.

### Institutional Resilience Narrative: An Adaptive Path for Literature

The first narrative of organizational sustainability—institutional resilience— implies the ability of institutions to withstand various environmental shocks, which is contingent upon their successful adaptation and change rather than maintaining a status quo. The process of adaptation itself involves undergoing changes in both cultural assumptions and organizational structure, as both types of changes are necessary for enabling sustainable thinking and decisions favorable to both current and future generations. However, the logic of institutional resilience also unfolds differently within different organizational forms, as adaptive responses to external shocks are shaped by organizational structure, and it is critically important for managers to be able to navigate the advantages and disadvantages of particular structures.

**Capitalizing on institutional structure and moving toward hybrids.** Similar to the other arts and humanities, the vast majority of literature organizations could be structurally divided into two groups: freestanding and university affiliated. The first group is primarily formed by organizations registered as nonprofits, such as friends of the library organizations, literary magazines, online presses, literature-advocacy groups, community writing programs, book clubs, etc. There is also a number of privately owned literature businesses, such as private publishing houses and literary magazines, private and personal libraries and rare-book collections, bookstores, and bookstore chains. The second group is university-affiliated organizations, which include university presses, university research libraries, and special collections maintained by university libraries. In recent years, there has also been a growth of university departments or schools that provide education in the domain of literatures, languages, and cultures. Such departments typically result from a merger of several university units.

It is important to examine the differences between freestanding and university-based structural models since a particular structural arrangement has important implications for institutional resilience (and these two configurations are most common). For example, being part of a university has a number of advantages for literature organizations (Appendix B). First, being part of a larger organization provides a buffer from external shocks and ensures baseline funding. Second, being part of a university ensures direct access to intellectual elites and quality human resources. Third, being part of a rich, intellectually engaging, experimental, and multidisciplinary environment ensures the connectedness of literature institutions with a broader group of stakeholders. Finally, being part of a university opens up opportunities for cross-disciplinary collaboration and synergy.

However, being part of a university also has some disadvantages, which are mainly associated with reduced autonomy in making financial and other strategic decisions, issues of succession, staff retention, and professionalization. For example, university-affiliated literature organizations often rely on student workers, who may lack skills and/or require extensive training. University students also graduate and move on, which creates a constant need for recruiting new personnel. There are also challenges with retaining full-time professional staff who are able to focus on both creative pursuits and daily operations, such as management and fundraising. A manager of a university-affiliated literary magazine describes these issues in the following way:

> That seems to be a problem with some literary journals: sometimes these organizations are very tied to the university, so the folks who are doing the journal are the graduate students, but there's no continuity, so the success of the journal depends on the students who are doing it at the time. One year it could be great, and one year it couldn't be, and often the students are focused on the content—a lot of them are working on their own writing and editing. You don't have someone necessarily focused on the financial part of it or fundraising . . . to keep it sustainable. There's oftentimes the faculty member behind it, but often there are students who are staff, and there should be some sort of staff that makes the organization sustainable year after year. (Personal Communication, 2012)

The other disadvantage of a university affiliation is the dependence of university-based literature organizations on a university's institutional and financial support, which may or may not be available, depending on the condition of that university. Additionally, much like on-campus museums, literature organizations at universities are often criticized for being "elitist" by targeting primarily university-related stakeholders, sometimes at the expense of the public at large. Managers of forward-looking university-affiliated organizations, however, recognize the importance of balancing academic focus with wider outreach as a condition for their organizations' sustainability. They reach out and work with their wider community, as expressed by the manager of a university-affiliated historical library:

> I have very much realized that as a professional commitment to myself that we are collecting these things [not only] for the future but also for the present. We cannot just assume, by having something, that we are doing our job because there is this other part of our job. I think this is borne out by what I have seen in the literature—I think people get excited about it; librarians get excited about it because it gives us sort of a push to really feel passionate, connected to our communities, and there has always been a perception in the library world that special collections, whether they are university special collections or something like the American Antiquarian Society, anything like that . . . they are different . . . I think these ideas of stewardship, and accountability, and responsibility helps people of my generation and younger feel like we can fight against that stereotype. (Personal Communication, 2012)

Likewise, the freestanding model, whether nonprofit or commercial, has its upsides and downsides. One obvious disadvantage, as compared to university-affiliated institutions, is the absence of an external buffer. At the same time, freestanding organizations tend to be more effective in responding quickly and adaptively to the changing market, and they (especially the nonprofits) are able to provide more individualized support to their authors and more tailored services to their readers. Additionally, mission-driven nonprofit literature organizations often tend to pursue niche-type operational models, which affords them greater flexibility and offers opportunities to experiment and take risks—both of which are necessary conditions for institutional resilience. The trade-off in this greater agility of a freestanding model is that it requires managers of literature organizations to spend a lot of time on marketing, sales, and fundraising, often at the expense of their creative work. A representative of a governmental agency reflects on the challenges and advantages of a nonprofit model in the following way:

Writers with big publishers are getting lost in the shuffle, and they're going back to the nonprofits because they take care of them, help them with editing, and keep their books in print. Really give them personal attention, whereas the commercial publishers, they are so busy keeping up and making money, they can't do that. The nonprofits have a tough time finding money to keep up on digital rights, but, on the other hand, they could figure out that a strategy works and quickly do it, and respond. And a larger publisher would not be able to respond as quickly . . .

What I'm saying is that I haven't heard from the non-profits that it's all bad. I think, perhaps, the fundraising in the nonprofit model is struggling these days. I can speak to the fact that nonprofits are struggling to get money, and, on the other hand, I don't see a lot of nonprofits necessarily taking risks, and there's not a lot of funding. And, without a lot of funding, they're just trying to keep their heads above water, and they are stabilizing and not necessarily moving ahead. But some of them are taking risks because that's what you have to do to stay alive. But I do hear that there is more accessibility . . . it helps nonprofit publishers. The fact that bloggers are out there helps nonprofits. Whatever you can use to compete with the traditional marketers, commercial houses . . . and they are seeing more authors come back to them, and there is more self-publishing too. (Personal Communication, 2012)

Having a nonprofit status also allows literature organizations to capitalize on their unique missions, build networks of clients and sup-porters, seek project-based funding, and implement various educational projects that promote literature for young generations. One example of such a model is the Center for the Art of Translation—a 501(c)(3) non-profit organization based in San Francisco. The goal of the organization is to make international literature more accessible to English-speaking audiences and to represent often overlooked international voices in the U.S. Additionally, responding to the needs of its culturally and socially diverse local community, the Center for the Art of Translation is also an important civic organization that conducts various events to connect readers with international authors and translators and provides educational programs for local schools that teach students to appreciate literature and understand other cultures ("The Center for the Art of Translation," 2000).

As this example shows, a nonprofit model allows for a greater connectedness of literature organizations and society, and it serves as a vehicle for literature organizations' own contributions to sustainable development in their local communities.

Unlike their commercial counterparts, nonprofit literature organizations are typically smaller in size, but their form and that size are welcomed by the changing literature market, especially as large literature publishing and literature distribution chains gradually dissolve in favor of smaller and more agile organizations. Furthermore, the future of literature likely lies with small personable organizations existing in close proximity to the centers of education and enlightenment (such as universities), rather than with big impersonal publishing corporations and uniform bookstore chains. Managers of a nonprofit literary magazine and a small press reflect on this tendency in the following ways:

> I suspect that, moving forward, there may be a few very large organizations but many, many small ones. (Personal Communication, 2012)

> I think that something that will happen in the midterm, a press of our size will become more prominent, and the huge publishing corporate structures are not going to work as well anymore. That seems to be happening a lot recently, and places that are not doing only market-based publishing are going to be more powerful in the future. In 50 years, publishing will exist not only in New York City; I think that a lot of publishing houses will be affiliated with the university nonprofit community structures. There will be more of a combination between publishers and booksellers working together than there is right now, but it will be more about literature than about publishing as a whole. Kind of a flawed model, and there are things that purely do not work, and, as things go forward, those flaws will become more exposed . . . and some commercial stuff . . . and a lot of smaller things doing kind of unique niche products. (Personal Communication, 2012)

Along with this, smaller and larger organizations are responding to environmental and market pressures in different ways, and their success is more dependent upon the effectiveness of their adaptive strategy rather than the organizational size itself. A representative of a governmental agency offers an analogy to describe how organizations of different sizes handle external stress:

> The analogy that I can maybe give . . . is like a very large tanker ship versus a kayak that is in a big storm. The tanker ship can survive, and the kayak will get blown all over; on the other hand, once the tanker ship goes off course, it's hard to shift, whereas the kayak is very shifty and could make turns easily and survive because it is small and can shift to the trends and be more innovative, change more quickly, and keep up. (Personal Communication, 2012)

Furthermore, literature is a fluid and dynamic field, and it is prone to develop institutional hybrids—an institutional form that combines elements of several forms into a single, more adaptable structure. A hybrid institutional form is an example of a structural adaptation to the ongoing changes in the literature market. It results in greater institutional flexibility and stronger institutional capacity, both of which increase overall institutional resilience. One example of such a hybrid is Open Letter Books—a literary press that publishes mostly novels, collections of short stories, and literary essays; it is based on a hybrid model, in which the University of Rochester's literary publishing house is combined with an independent nonprofit organization. According to its manager, Open Letter Books utilizes advantages of both of these structural forms by reaching out to young generations of writers and editors who are under-represented by commercial industry, as well as by ensuring the high-quality independent review process that nonprofit organizations may lack:

> . . . .[s]o we are publishing books that we want everyone to read. Those books are selected by an editor and not by the academic-review process, mostly promoted in the normal marketplace, trade marketplace. To function like that, it's sort of unusual because most university presses I have seen that fit that university model . . . we have a very much . . . we have a nonprofit business model . . .
>
> In addition, I think that what we were trying to come up with was a perfect place, a perfect way, a perfect scheme for accomplishing two goals: one being that we wanted to provide students at the university with background in literature, translation, and how publishing works. We also wanted to

promote, to publicize the international literature, and get more readers for it. The university is a good haven in some sense for a project like this; it is not going to make a lot of money, but it has the potential for doing a lot of good for the world, and it makes sense, it fits the university model, although it is kind of different. (Personal Communication, 2012)

Another example of a hybrid-type structure is *The Iowa Review* (TIR)—a literary magazine founded in 1970 in affiliation with the University of Iowa that publishes fiction, poetry, essays, and reviews. As a university-affiliated organization with a nonprofit status, *The Iowa Review* is able to leverage the strengths of the two institutional forms by drawing support from the University of Iowa as well as from external donors, such as the National Endowment for the Arts. The other factor contributing to *The Iowa Review*'s institutional resilience is its integration with the extensive writing program at the University of Iowa—the Writer's Workshop. The Workshop is part of a long tradition, beginning in 1897, as the first creative writing class at Iowa University, which was gradually transformed into a degree program.

Another example of a successful strategy aimed at enhancing institutional resilience via structural adaptation is the creation of symbiotic organizational forms, which ensure that literature is kept vital long after it is published. For example, considering unstable reading patterns, it becomes important to incorporate literature into other art forms, into something that is potentially more appealing to both active readers and those who do not read much. There are numerous examples of people discovering classic literature through movies and other forms of popular entertainment and performing arts (Temple, 2019). Live performance has the ability to bring literature alive, and in many cases a literary work gains its second life through a play. Moreover, embedding literary heritage in a performing arts form makes it more accessible and attractive to the population as a whole.

There are also examples of adaptive institutional changes that happen in a university context, as the survival and long-term sustainability of literature, as well as other arts and humanities, are conditioned upon the sustainability of relevant departments that produce scholarship and talent to support these fields. In a public university context, in particular, the decline of state support for higher education, rising tuition costs, and shift away from social sciences and humanities toward greater emphasis on grant-generating "hard" science fields—as well as applied-type schools, such as business, law, and medicine—have created severe pressures for the arts and humanities. Although their primary purpose lies in their intrinsic significance and broader role as beacons of knowledge and human values, the humanities and related fields are nowadays tasked with demonstrating their continuing relevance in tangible and quantitatively convincing ways, such as via tuition dollars and evidence of humanities majors' employability and subsequent contributions to the economy, as well as how they can help advance the STEM fields. In many cases, this type of logic is hard to grasp for humanities professors and administrators, who see their universities as homes of holistic educational models that value both hard sciences and humanities. Nevertheless, the ability to demonstrate their tangible impact is critical to both the immediate survival and intergenerational sustainability of these departments.

In an effort to tackle this complex task, and partially as a means to reduce their operational expenses, several public universities have merged multiple departments under the auspices of new schools focusing on languages, literatures, and intercultural learning. Examples of such newly created entities include the School of Global Languages, Literatures, and Cultures at Penn State; the Schools of Languages, Literatures, and Cultures at the University of Kansas and the University of Maryland College Park; and the Departments of Literatures, Languages, and Cultures at the University of South Carolina and the University of Delaware, to name a few. Missions of these institutions focus on a holistic educational model that promotes global cultural awareness and elevates the importance of language, literature, and intercultural learning as valuable universal competencies. Their vision embodies broader philosophical goals that are relevant to the long-term sustainability of literature and the humanities, as described by the inaugural Director of the School of Languages, Literatures, and Cultures at the University of Kansas that was created in 2014: "As a teacher and administrator, there is a limit to what I can do about it, but I am concerned about preserving the best parts of education so that present and future generations can live in a rich, well-informed, and thoughtful society" (Greenberg, 2015). Implicitly, therefore, these institutions pursue an ethic of intergenerational sustainability by thinking about both current and future generations and providing institutional framework for the survival of a broader field that allows humanities to flourish.

These new institutional forms are examples of multiple levels of institutional adaptation. On a programmatic level, in addition to granting traditional graduate and undergraduate degrees, they offer certificates, study-abroad programs, and student-research opportunities and internships, as well as nondegree programs. These newly created entities also focus on achieving both global and local relevance by appealing to international students as well as plugging themselves into the lives of their domestic communities. They have also been taking a more strategic approach to their own management by focusing on strategic planning, marketing, and fundraising, as well as investing in their capacity by creating institutional advisory boards comprising successful alumni, business leaders, and intellectuals who support their missions. There is a hope that this new institutional form will lead to the advancement of the role of humanities in a society and improve chances for their intergenerational sustainability.

**Achieving greater social and community relevance.** Another strategy employed to enhance institutional resilience of literature organizations is their movement toward greater social and community relevance. Being socially relevant has become an important goal for contemporary literature organizations alongside producing and promoting high-quality literature. From a strategic point of view, seeking greater social and community relevance represents an adaptive organizational response to the challenges in the literature market itself, as well as to external pressures that literature organizations share with other arts and humanities, such as technology and capacity-building pressures, changing reader preferences, public recognition concerns, and competition for resources, among others (Appendix A). This adaptive response to environmental pressures is important for literature organizations regardless of their structural form and affiliation, and both university-affiliated institutions as well as nonprofits and businesses seek to achieve greater social and community relevance.

Furthermore, the strive for greater social and community relevance is also motivated by an organizational intent to foster sustainable development locally and globally. Such motivation reflects an overall expansion of the literature organizations' missions that encompass a variety of roles that they play in a society beyond pursuing their core purpose of producing and promoting literature. A manager of a private publishing company reflects upon the drivers behind a gradual evolution of his company's mission in the following way:

> Our mission over the last five-six years has gotten much more community oriented than it was in the past, socially and

community oriented, which I think, particularly in [name of a city], is a mission well-served in that people truly understand and believe it. It has not changed our whole company, but the goals have changed to be more community oriented and globally conscious in terms of what we have done, both locally to the community—charitable events, charitable donations, activities—and in making our plant more environmentally friendly: more sustainable manufacturing processes, you know, environmentally sustainable. (Personal Communication, 2012)

The reflection above signifies a larger organizational shift toward greater social responsibility, in this case illustrated as the commitment of a private corporation to the advancement of social and environmental sustainability in its local community. In the case of a business, this type of rationale exceeds the mere financial bottom-line considerations and thus resembles the idea of the Triple Bottom Line that signifies the importance of economy, society, and environment as the three related facets of sustainable development (Elkington, 1994).

Pursuing a path toward greater social and community relevance requires an expansion of overall social connectedness between literature institutions and their local and global communities. Literature organizations enhance such connectedness in a variety of ways, including by engaging in audience development and public outreach, forming partnerships with a variety of other social institutions, becoming more interdisciplinary, shifting toward performing a broader range of societal roles, and adopting technology and social media (Table 3.1). Employing these innovative strategies involves structural and cultural shifts in organizational routines, as well as the development of a holistic operational model that reflects current thinking in the field, incorporates best practices, and attempts to forecast future developments. In return, organizations that adopt these innovations become more resilient, as described by the representative of a governmental agency:

I think organizations are resilient when they're focused on current trends, so now a publisher of a journal, if they're not into all of the social media, then I don't think they're going to stick around. They're going to have to keep up. They are going to have to think about e-books, podcasting, Facebook and Twitter and whatever social media exist; they're going to have to pay attention to the trends and try to keep up in order to not lose audience members and readers . . . new genre perhaps. They are going to have to think about partnerships in the community—particularly if it's a literary center or a reader series, they should be reaching out community members. And they should be thinking about their long-range financial stability, thinking about what they're going to do in the coming years; they should be doing three-year strategic plans—where they are headed? And what's most important is *assessment*. An organization should effectively assess their projects in qualitative and quantitative ways. An organization that doesn't do this is probably not going to be resilient because it has to know how well it is doing, so it knows which direction to take. (Personal Communication, 2012)

Although the above strategies do not focus on the core mission of producing and promoting literature per se, they are nevertheless important for enhancing overall institutional resilience of literature organizations. They result in more stable funding, an increased number of readers and book buyers, and a loyal group of patrons—all of which helps to keep literature organizations afloat in the short and medium term. In the long run, achieving greater social and community relevance via these strategies also leads to the formation of institutional capital for sustainability that serves to safeguard the long-term future of literature organizations.

**Audience development and public outreach.** The first strategy employed by organizations in the field of literature to enhance their social and community relevance is their engagement in audience development programs. Yet, while many museums and performing arts institutions have a formal public outreach department, outreach function in the field of literature is much less institutionalized. Furthermore, extensive public outreach programs, such as poetry- or fiction-writing contests, are mainly organized by large national nonprofit organizations rather than local actors. One explanation of the less institutionalized public outreach function in literature organizations is the fact that they are more accustomed to relying on the public education system to instill reading habits in younger generations, as compared to the other arts and humanities, and therefore may be taking their "audience" for granted.

While literary magazines and book publishers in the past cared mostly about ensuring quality literary products and their proper marking, with the decline in readership, literature organizations have faced new demands for relevancy. Many of them have responded accordingly by implementing programs aimed at audience development, with some supporting such programs institutionally by enhancing their public outreach functions. Public libraries, for example, engage in relatively extensive outreach work in their communities, and many have a formalized public outreach department. The public education function also tends to be more prominent in hybrid institutional forms that are based on the combination of literature and performing arts, such as literary festivals. Many festivals have formally established public education departments that work with different age groups and have a particularly significant number of programs for young people.

Another explanation of a less extensive and institutionalized outreach function lies in the design of the outreach programs for literature. Many organizations, such as literary magazines and certain book publishers, primarily target mature adult readers; the lack of programs for younger people is explained by the belief that serious literature is of little interest to public school students because it is not age appropriate. However, not everyone shares this point of view, and managers of forward-looking organizations engage in various strategies aimed at breaking these stereotypical views by emphasizing the importance of earlier and more diverse outreach. The manager of one such organization—a literary magazine—describes the importance of an early exposure to literature in the following way:

> There aren't any people doing this particular project. There are attempts by other literature magazines to get their magazines used in classrooms, usually in college classrooms. The emphasis on younger readers, especially tenth to twelfth grade readers—I think that is not something that other people have explored. Maybe because they feel like the product they are producing is not really appropriate for those audiences. I think that's wrong. If they're really thinking that, they are absolutely wrong. And some of the time it might not be appropriate because it couldn't get approved by the school board, because of the language, or it might have sexual situations, or something like that. But there is plenty of material that those students will find really

interesting and will want to read, and they will want to read it more than the things they are being given. And what are you doing when you give them that material? You're actively developing an audience for your work later. And some of them might really get interested, and you hope they get excited. I don't know exactly what happens when you put [name of the publication] into the hands of a bunch of tenth graders, but I think that it is really exciting. (Personal Communication, 2012)

Increasingly, unstable reading patterns have fostered the interest of both national and local literature organizations in searching for both more effective and equitable audience development programs. Many organizations no longer take their audiences for granted, realizing that the decline in reading often results from the absence of reading habits. And if such habits are developed early on in life, readers would also be more likely to continue appreciating literature during their lifetime; they would also be more likely to hand down this passion for literature on to future generations. The manager of a literary magazine reflects on this tendency:

A lot of people don't like reading. I think that many times they don't like reading because they are not given things that are appropriate for them. And so that's one of the things that you'd hope to encourage. Lifelong attraction to reading, it's something that we value at the mag. That is, and we hope to make a difference for some of these students who haven't picked it up for some reason, and it might be too late, we don't know, but we're pushing. Besides that, the things that come through in the reading are part of the values that we think are important. I mentioned some of those in the selection process—those are diversity . . . so that's all wrapped up in the set of things that we hope will come through in reading this material. (Personal Communication, 2012)

Furthermore, programs exposing people to literature early on in their lives serve as the evidence of literature organizations' commitment to both current and future generations, thus representing important investment in the institutional capital for sustainability. Such programs assume that to be sustainable in the long term, literature organizations need to establish connections with people from different generations. One example of these programs are the two initiatives developed by *The Iowa Review* for public school students—"Enhanced Access Project" and "Open Book Project." The goal of these programs is to incorporate the literary content into the high school language classes by using a variety of new web-based resources that will make the issues of *The Iowa Review* available for students and teachers in a digital form, which is attractive to younger generations. These programs also include an aural- and video-essay gallery of the digitized readings and an application for mobile devices. These programs seek to both connect with existing readers and create new readership by cultivating reading habits and developing an appreciation for literature among young people.

Instilling early reading habits, however, could be particularly tough in geographical areas with challenged public school systems (public school systems being the traditional anchor of literature organizations), and it may require such organizations reaching out to young people in nonstandard ways. For example, recognizing the benefits of early exposure in forming healthy reading habits, Detroit groups have developed early reading outreach efforts tackling age groups as young as two years. Since 2008, the Detroit Riverfront Conservancy has been running a "Reading & Rhythm on the Riverfront" program, which is a unique, interactive, early literacy program that provides children with an opportunity to hear a story read by a local community leader and receive a free book. The program also features a special family lending library with more than two hundred selections. Serving over forty-five hundred children a year, the program relies on a public-private partnership with the General Motors Corporation and the Detroit Public Library's "Library on Wheels" program.

These types of programs embrace the value of social equity by providing access to literature to everyone regardless of their financial means, as well as targeting historically disadvantaged populations. An example of a program that targets underserved youth in Detroit is the InsideOut Literary Arts organization, so named after one of its participants observed that writing literature has a transformational effect on one's worldview and self-perception. Since 1995, InsideOut Literary Arts has engaged nearly 60,000 Detroit youth and helped them to build their literary and academic skills through creative writing (InsideOut, 2019). Its mission has been to transform lives through the written and spoken word by broadening horizons and giving young people valuable writing skills. Once started on a public school teacher's own initiative, today InsideOut Literary Arts is Detroit's largest and oldest literary nonprofit, serving a hundred classrooms and community sites annually. Aside from enhancing students' creative writing skills and fostering their appreciation for literature, the program has contributed to their overall academic success and therefore has had an overall positive impact on local community.

**Engaging in partnerships.** The next important element of literature organizations' institutional resilience is their engagement in various forms of networking behavior, including interorganizational and cross-sectoral partnerships. For example, many of the new audience-development initiatives discussed above depend on literature organizations' partnerships with businesses, media, the National Endowment for the Arts (NEA) and local arts councils, and the public schools, to name a few of their typical partners. One such example is the Poetry Out Loud competition, which has been implemented annually since 2005 as a partnership between the NEA, the Poetry Foundation, state arts agencies, and local schools. This arts education program addresses the problem of declining interest in poetry by encouraging high school students to memorize and perform poems (Poetry Out Loud, 2012).

Furthermore, for all its relative "fluidity," the domain of literature is an interconnected world of institutions and formalized organizations that often engage in developing collective strategies that enhance overall institutional resilience of the sector. Developing these strategies requires greater networking and collaboration, and there are organizations that serve as platforms for such collaboration by providing a framework for the exchange of ideas among writers, publishers, literary magazines, and other actors. Professional nonprofit literature organizations, often working at the national level, serve as infrastructure for such collaborations.

One such example is the Community of Literary Magazines and Presses—a nonprofit organization founded in 1967 to support literary magazines and publishers by "discovering new writers; supporting mid-career writers; publishing the creative voices of communities underrepresented in the mainstream commercial culture; and preserving literature for future readers by keeping books in print" ("Community of Literary Magazines and Presses," 2012). The organization is supported by public and private donors and is based on the premise that a literary organization is a unique balance of art and business. Since 2000, following the digitization movement, it has launched an online resource providing support services for literary publishers as well as an online information center for readers, writers, media, and the general public. This collaborative platform connects various organizations as well as the two sides of the literature market—providers and consumers.

Another example is Poets & Writers—one of the largest nonprofit literary organizations in the United States; it serves poets, fiction writers, and creative nonfiction writers. It was founded in 1970 on the premise that writers are important agents for social change making significant contributions to the national culture. Today Poets & Writers plays a crucial role in building and maintaining the bridge between the professional community and public at large. Its mission is "to foster the professional development of poets and writers, to promote communication throughout the literary community, and to help create an environment in which literature can be appreciated by [the] widest possible public" ("Poets & Writers, Inc.," 2012). Through their public outreach programs, often implemented in partnership with other actors, Poets & Writers fosters overall social and community relevance of literature.

One such example of a socially meaningful program organized in partnership with other actors is a series of writing workshops at the Veterans Hospital in Manhattan arranged by the Poets & Writers group in collaboration with the Mental Health Association. Another program implemented in partnership with public schools and retiree organizations—the Annual Intergenerational Reading Program—seeks to specifically bridge the generational gap by bringing together people of various ages—from seniors to public school students—in their common passion for poetry. Such partnerships seek to create valuable social capital within local communities, which is important for advancing community sustainability.

**Embracing interdisciplinarity.** In their path toward greater social and community relevance, literature organizations often search for ways to engage in a variety of actions outside their own domain. One of the best examples of this approach is the broader societal role that public libraries came to play over time. Modern public libraries perform a wide array of functions aside from their main purpose of book storage and preservation. These functions include, but are not limited to, providing various public services to the population, such as computer training, access to community meeting rooms, preschool programs and book clubs for adults, book presentations, and community events, among others. By performing these functions, libraries become integral parts of community life, and their various contributions to sustainable local communities are some of the major factors that make libraries themselves sustainable.

In their desire to become more socially relevant, libraries seek ways to meet the diverse needs of their communities, and they rely on both pull-type strategies that attract people to libraries and push-type strategies that ensure libraries' presence in the community at large. One example of a latter strategy is the "Wash and Learn" program by the Detroit Public Library, which brings the resources of a library to children whose parents may not have the time or means to access their local library branches (Community Foundation for Southeast Michigan, 2019). Library staff holds reading lessons and engages in arts projects with children who are waiting for their parents to finish the laundry. This program is also an example of cultural institutions realizing that their main value is not about buildings or collections per se; rather, it is about what those tangible assets mean to their communities and how they help to meet their communities' needs.

The expansion of the libraries' missions and their greater engagement in community affairs is often credited to the work of the Library Friends' Foundations. These are grassroots organizations that were often initially created informally by like-minded individuals and later registered as 501(c)(3) nonprofits to support libraries via volunteering and fundraising. The Detroit Public Library Friends Foundation, for example, was created as early as 1943, and has since been able to continually pursue its mission of providing enrichment programming to library patrons and preserving a space in Detroit where everyone can work, study, learn, and create. The work of this organization has been instrumental in helping the library meet the changing needs of Detroit's population by responding to the various postrecession challenges and opportunities, including those brought in by Detroit's revitalization agenda. In that sense, the role of the library as an institution becomes increasingly more interdisciplinary, where its ability to facilitate dialogue and community action across multiple domains becomes mission critical.

**Adopting digital technology.** As was discussed earlier in this chapter, the invention of the electronic publishing model has had a dual effect on the literature market. On the one hand, shifting to a greater reliance on e-publishing and web platforms has created competitive pressures for traditional institutions; on the other hand, the success of many contemporary initiatives by the traditional publishing industry depends on the effective use of technology. Furthermore, adopting digital technology becomes essential for pursuing other resilience strategies. As many of the examples above show, contemporary literature organizations are embracing technological tools in order to expand their public outreach; they rely on technology in their interdisciplinary initiatives and to enable their partnerships. However, digital technology is also used as a standalone strategy for establishing the social and community relevance of literature, especially for keeping it a vital part of younger generations' life.

Greater adoption of technology and social media is increasingly seen as a way of making literature more socially relevant and appealing to people from multiple generations. One example of an innovative and highly technological way to encourage the reading of classic literature is the InstaNovel program initiated in 2018 by the New York Public Library, with the goal being to reach beyond the library's walls. The program, implemented in partnership with an advertising agency, transforms classic novels into animated Instagram stories, thus converting books into a more tech-savvy and digitally appealing format that could draw busy adults as well as younger readers (FastCompany, 2019). This unconventional approach to the use of technology, however, has provoked a debate about whether this mode of delivery is the proper way to communicate literature, especially in a public library setting. Nevertheless, within a year since the launch of the program, it has proven successful, with an estimated three hundred thousand people reading the library's books this way. The program has won one of the Fast Company's 2019 Innovation by Design Awards, and some commentators even call this program "the future" of literature (FastCompany, 2019).

Furthermore, the use of digital technology is even more prevalent in the world of literature, as compared to the realms of museums and performing arts. More and more publishers and literary magazines develop online versions of their publications and design digital applications to make literature easily accessible to the public through electronic devices. There is a realization that "the world of literary magazines, and the world of print publishing as a whole, is changing rapidly and dramatically," and, although "publishers have not yet figured out how exactly to respond to digitization . . . it is clear that "greater access, more readers, and more readers of diverse background and ages will increase the potential impact" ("The Iowa Review Enhanced Access Project," 2011). More so than other cultural industries, literature depends upon rapid technological advances and, therefore, it is important for literature institutions to speed up so as to stay up to date, as described by the manager of a university-affiliated literary magazine: "Publishing used to be a very slow industry. To now have a greater social impact—especially with nonfiction, political . . . whatever— the ability to reach readership so quickly after something is done is really advantageous for doing social good, like cultural good. I do think that digital technology will play a larger role in the future" (Personal Communication, 2012).

The tendency to rely on technology to both widen and broaden the impact of literature provides an example of sustainable thinking—an intuitive rationality resulting in particular strategies, programs, and actions aimed at enhancing organizational capital for sustainability. Overall, the dynamic and fluid nature of literature markets creates multiple opportunities for institutional adaptation and flexibility, and many organizations in the domain of literature achieve their institutional resilience by taking advantage of these opportunities. However, the ability to translate immediate survival into longer-term organizational sustainability requires balancing the above-discussed resilience strategies with the considerations of institutional distinctiveness.

## Institutional Distinctiveness Narrative: Capitalizing on Uniqueness and Staying on Course

While the resilience narrative focuses on responding to external pressures and is, therefore, naturally outward looking, the distinctiveness narrative is more inward looking, as it capitalizes on the distinct nature of institutions and the sector itself. Specific elements of the distinctiveness narrative include staying true to the core mission, promoting and cultivating socially important values, offering unique learning experiences, and shifting toward a broader (semi-instrumental) role of the arts and humanities in a society (Table 3.1).

**Staying true to the mission.** The first element of the distinctiveness narrative is the ability of institutions to stay true to their core missions and maintain their unique institutional niches. As discussed earlier, the literature market is highly dynamic; it combines multiple organizational structures and accommodates two distinct but complementary models—traditional publishing and electronic publishing. Subsequently, organizational missions and institutional niches embedded in these two models are distinct as well.

Organizations pursuing traditional print, for example, derive much of their capital for sustainability from the value of the book itself as a culturally significant object. Books are viewed as a unique art form, whose inner value is not easily replicated by technology. The uniqueness of books, as compared to other forms of popular media, is also expected to rise in importance. This assertion is based upon the recognition that books possess the capacity to generate both economic and symbolic capital due to their intrinsic quality (Thompson, 2012). To that extent, editors and publishers often value a literary work because they believe in its significance, sometimes despite its projected sales. They also dedicate their time and capital to curating published books to the reader, which goes beyond mere marketing and is similar to curating objects in a museum, as reflected upon by the manager of a publishing company:

[. . .] the big chain stores and the big publishers treat literature like an object to be disposable, like they are for reading at the beach . . . I think that is one thing that is going to have to shift for people to take more interest in literature and books. You can't look at these things as the same as watching a YouTube video; it is different in a good way. I think there is going to be more of a shift toward being selective, things being curated in some sense. If people will start paying attention to books as objects, if that starts to happen, people will become more interested in books because they will treat them as a unique thing. (Personal Communication, 2012)

At the same time, the electronic model has its own niche as well, as it caters to broader and more global audiences, thus making literature nearly universally accessible and widely transmittable within a relatively short period. Electronic publishing organizations, therefore, derive their sustainability capital from the promise of accessibility and global impact. A growing number of hybrid and online-only publishing platforms, as well as literary translation projects, are examples of how this particular niche is expanding. These differences between the traditional publishing and e-publishing models, however, create room for the two publishing models to coexist in the same market, complementing rather than contradicting each other, as described by another publisher:

As far as where the publishing is going, I have no idea. I know that print is not dead; print is still extremely relevant, and it's got a generational thing; it's really a very personal thing about how people want to connect with information that they are getting, how their brains [are] processing the information. People are either screen readers or not screen readers. I used to be able to find something really fast on the screen, but, if I really want to dig deeper into the content and what it means, I can't sit and read it on the screen. I need to print it and take it somewhere where I can sit and read it, think about it, make some notes on it. So, I use blended technology, and, until I am completely out of this world, I am going to need something in my hands that tactile, and I can get my hand around it, my fingers around it. (Personal Communication, 2012)

Furthermore, the dynamic tendencies within the literature market discussed in the previous section call on both publishing models to adopt new philosophies capable of guiding sustainable literature organizations into the future. Therefore, many literature organizations, both traditional print and e-publishing, have responded to these pressures by modifying their missions, especially to stress the importance of access and accessibility. These organizations emphasize such values as inclusiveness, multiplicity of viewpoints and the richness of human experience grasped through the interpretation of literature; recognizing and promoting the global impact of literature; and integrating literature into wider community development (Table 3.2).

Table 3.2. Evolving Missions, Managerial Roles, and Values Promoted to Current and Future Generations: Literature

| Evolving missions | Increasing importance of access and accessibility |
|---|---|
| | Emphasis on multiplicity of viewpoints and cultures, richness of human experience |
| | Recognizing and promoting global impact |
| | Integrating literature in community development |
| | Being up-to-date (timeliness and timelessness) |
| Evolving managerial roles | Stewardship of the book as an art object (for print literature) |
| | Management as innovation |
| | Managing opportunities rather than organizations |
| | Management as facilitation of art-inspired communication, conversation, debate |
| Values promoted to current and future generations | Literature as a language of communication among generations and cultures |
| | Broad access and universal accessibility |
| | Transcending the boundaries of time: connecting past to present and to future |
| | Transmission of cultural capital and global impact: raising global cultural awareness, contributing to world diplomacy, fostering creativity and openness to new ideas |

Another mission-critical element for literature is, in many ways, its unique disposition toward the factor of time. Literature institutions, in their path to long-term sustainability, accommodate ideas of continuity and change by ensuring both the transmission of human heritage to future generations and the successful timely adaptation to the changing realities of the day. In fact, the greatest works of literature in the world possess two properties: timeliness—understood as the ability to be relevant today, and timelessness—understood as the ability to remain relevant to many generations ahead. Focusing on timeliness and timelessness requires the presence of sustainable thinking, which allows managers to choose timely strategies that also support their organizations' legacy and intergenerational trajectories.

On a substantive level it means ensuring the relevance of classical literature to particular personal experiences and the universal human values of our time, while also appealing to multiple generations at once. Reflecting upon the dynamic nature of the literature field and its ability to be both current and timeless, managers of a publishing house and a Shakespeare festival describe this type of thinking in the following way:

> You know it really comes down to creating a value proposition in front of the potential market place, whether you view a market place as a potential student, a potential author, a potential member, a potential reader, or someone who is going to buy a bag of chips out of the wending machine. *You know it is do the right things at the right place at the right time, and that's been the fundamental law of being in business, being sustainable for millennia.* [emphasis added] (Personal Communication, 2012)

> And certainly, [we want to foster in people] an appreciation for Shakespeare as a living, and not a historical artifact, text. We try to help them understand how much the situations, the characters, the themes, the relationships in Shakespeare, how current they still are, which is why he's still the most produced playwright in the world. Human beings have not changed—our fundamental desires, our lusts, our passions, our hopes, our dreams—and Shakespeare articulated those, perhaps, better than anyone else ever has . . . And not only that, but we also try to give them an appreciation for how much Shakespeare continues to influence popular culture. So, when I give talks, I'm always talking about the TV shows, the films, the songs by

popular artists that are inspired by and draw from the canon of Shakespeare. [emphasis added] (Personal Communication, 2011)

Finally, the importance of the factor of time for literature is also explained by the fact that some literature, regardless of the publishing model, gains momentum and relevancy long after its initial publication date. Therefore, recognizing good literature is important, and it is often the responsibility of managers to distinguish between meaningful and meaningless literature, transient and timeless literature.

**Values promoted by literature institutions to their current and future publics.** Another important element of the institutional distinctiveness narrative is the broader set of values that literature organizations promote in a society beyond the appreciation for the written word (Table 3.2). Literature serves as a language of communication among multiple cultures and generations by transmitting cultural capital globally and across time. In doing so, literature institutions increasingly emphasize the importance of broad access and universal accessibility to human heritage embedded in literary works. They also emphasize multiplicity of viewpoints and cultures embedded in literary texts and that allows for grasping the richness of human experiences by fostering global cultural awareness. The value impact of literature organizations is rooted in their story-telling power, upon which many of them capitalize by engaging in public outreach and education activities that offer modes of learning uniquely attributable to them.

Providing broader access to cultural heritage embedded in literary works is particularly essential for enhancing sustainability of literature and its institutions, as the greater and the broader the readership is—in terms of type of audience, geography, and time—the greater the overall chances for literature to endure over time. In fact, the accessibility of literature has greatly expanded with the spread of online literary platforms. Many literary magazines today exist in both printed and online forms, and some are functioning as online publications only. Anyone with Internet access has an opportunity to read literature published online. Furthermore, online literature publications are accessible to younger generations since the technology is already an inseparable part of young people's lives and is "the language" they speak fluently. Therefore, going online is at least a partially effective strategy for those literature providers that desire to remain relevant.

However, despite the capacity of the online format to provide broad access to literature and ensure the preservation of the written word, e-publishing is experiencing its own unique accessibility concerns. These concerns arise due to a fast-changing technology and the need to keep electronic archives up-to-date and accessible, which requires a certain degree of innovation and sustainable thinking more generally, as described by the manager of an independent publishing organization:

> Staying plugged in, keeping an eye toward your backlist or archiving video, so you can access it . . . Accessibility is important. People get a lot of stuff for free online. Organizations should be thinking about what content they are making accessible and how. Innovation for sure speaks to how they are keeping up with social media and being innovative. These are all buzzwords now. Diversity seemed to be the buzzword years ago, but now it seems to not be so important. Now the buzzwords are accessibility, and innovation, and sustainability. (Personal Communication, 2012)

Another concern with e-publishing models has to do with the price of accessing electronic publications in the first place, which is designed to keep these models financially sustainable. This concern is widespread outside of the world of literary fiction as well, and it presents an example of a tension that arises between the considerations of broader access and organizational-survival motivation.

One example of this is the question of access to academic scholarship published in commercial online depositories that are typically not open to the public. The open-access movement that emerged in the 1990s within the scholarly publishing community seeks to alleviate the problem (Antelman, 2004). To date, the open-access movement has resulted in the adoption of formal open-access policies by several major universities, as well as the creation of the Coalition of Open Access Policy Institutions—an advocacy organization attempting to promote the spread of open access. Open-access policies reflect the idea of a broader public interest; however, the paradox of the open-access model is that, while modern technology provides the necessary preconditions for global information accessibility, economic factors are often cited among the major barriers that prevent wider adoption of open-access publishing models. This problem is described by an open-access coordinator in a university-based library: "When the costs were going up, and up, and up, actually, the technology and the costs were at odds with each other. Technology would say, 'We can share with everybody, and the economics were saying, 'But now we are out of money on this on the commercial side; we don't want everybody to have access, open-public access reduces our profits'" (Personal Communication, 2012).

Libraries, in particular, have assumed an active role in establishing and promoting open-access policies, which is not surprising, as providing broader access to information is part of the libraries' core institutional missions and one of their major ethical principles, as expressed below by the same person:

> . . . .[a]nd then you have the libraries providing a support because they do, as an ethical principle of their mission, provide access to materials. Although, in the past, access meant preserve it over time, so the people can physically walk in and have access to it, and it needs to be preserved for hundreds of years; it needs to be controlled and managed, kept in certain ways, so that people can access it. But what access means has shifted, now that the technology has made it available in different ways, so the libraries began playing a supportive role. And the libraries decided to establish [an] open-access publishing arm, so that we have services in [name of a university]. (Personal Communication, 2012)

Although open-access policy was developed within the realm of academic publishing, it has important implications for the dissemination of all written works created in the electronic format, including classic literature. While the adoption of open-access policies is likely to be a slow process, in the long run it will have significant public benefit, and publishers committed to sustainability are going to have to adjust their business models to effectively balance considerations of the financial bottom line with the broader equity of access concerns.

Another important value that literature organizations promote in a society is global cultural awareness. The prominent role of literature in spreading knowledge about different cultures and influencing world diplomacy is hard to overestimate. According to Jameson and Miyoshi, globalization is "a communicational concept, which alternately masks and transmits cultural or economic meanings" (Jameson & Miyoshi, 1998, p. 55). If globalization is about communication, then literary communication, regardless of whether it exists in the form of published books or digital archives, is a key factor in raising global cultural awareness. In fact, as compared to visual and performing arts organizations, literature institutions ensure the transmission and exchange of cultural heritage in a much broader way. A painting on display in a prominent art museum rarely leaves the building to travel somewhere else in the country and almost never anywhere else in the world. Music and performing arts festivals do travel; however, to reproduce the same kind of experience, they often need to be staged in a specific venue. Literature, on the other hand, is being translated into many languages; it is being published in book form and online, and it is much easier transmittable to any part of the world, as compared to the other arts and humanities.

Some examples of globally important U.S. literary magazines that pursue global cultural awareness as part of their unique mission include *A Public Space*—an independent quarterly English-language literary magazine established in 2005 in New York; Words Without Borders—an international literary magazine that translates, publishes, and promotes eight to ten literary works online and also releases print anthologies in partnership with publishing houses; and Open Letter Books—the University of Rochester's literary publishing house that runs an online literary website called Three Percent, dedicated to cultivating an appreciation for international literature.

By fostering the transmission and exchange of cultural capital around the world, literature organizations not only raise global cultural awareness and help global diplomacy, but they also foster overall creativity by encouraging people to look for ideas outside of their familiar mental schemes grounded in a particular cultural context. In these ways, literature organizations contribute to overall societal progress, which, in the long run, leads to greater sustainability of literature and its institutions. Managers of two online publishing platforms describe the goals of their organizations in this regard in the following way:

> What we are doing is filling out and providing a much fuller sense of the rest of the world. Our first three issues, for example,

presented writings from Iraq, Iran, and North Korea. These are three of the many countries that the US came to know strictly from a political prism, and the US has very little sense of full global culture. Of course, the best insight to country's culture is obtained through literature, and we are interested in promoting knowledge and making the rest of the world available to English-language readers who have only had a limited, and often politically driven, exposure. (Personal Communication, 2012)

One thing I would like to do is to raise people's awareness of literature from around the world and to help them appreciate the values that are not that far out of line with other social movements. Encouraging readers to pay attention to things—to open their minds, to read things that may not fit the exact model that you are expecting it to—broadens people's horizons to the work of art. Because it is international, there is a certain focus on cultural awareness, but, if we were doing American books, it would be the same thing: trying to come up with new forms, demonstrate new forms for how something can be relayed, created, and help people understand that. (Personal Communication, 2012)

Literature, as we know it today, is capable of transcending the boundaries of time and space, and such invention as an institution of literary translation makes this property even more powerful. Although the literary canon has always facilitated the global impact of the world's greatest literature, the institution of literary translation has significantly increased the scope, extent, and quality of such impact. Nowadays, there are specific formalized organizations whose sole mission is to support literary translation. One example is the Center for the Art of Translation—a nonprofit organization based in San Francisco that translates and publishes fiction and poetry in over 50 languages. The mission of the center is "to promote a truly global community, creating a world where writers and readers can cross both boundaries of borders and of language" ("Center for the Art of Translation," 2012). As this statement illustrates, the organization seeks to overcome both geographical and cultural barriers with the power of translated literary works.

Another example of an organization that relies on literary translation to foster global cultural awareness is Words Without Borders—a fully online platform that runs an educational program for high school and college students in order to expose them to a broad spectrum of contemporary international literature. In the words of one of its managers, Words Without Borders is "an organization devoted to the promotion of literature and translation in the interest of global understanding." Its goal in reaching out to students is to "create a passion for international literature, a curiosity about other cultures, and help cultivate true world citizens" (Personal Communication, 2012). This function of literature is especially important in monolingual societies, where literature opens doors "to the multiplicity of viewpoints, the richness of experience, and the literary perspective of world events" (Personal Communication, 2012).

The universal accessibility of literature combined with its global impact resonates with idea of cultural mobility understood as "the capacity to navigate between or across cultural realms, a freedom to choose or select one's position in the cultural landscape" (Emmison, 2003). It results in a cultural competence—the possession of various forms of cultural capital existing both inside and outside of one's immediate culture of origin. Furthermore, cultural mobility is a multidirectional concept that essentially implies that the culture of the future is impossible without the culture of the past; and, in the modern world, the culture of the East is no longer opposite to the culture of the West (Greenblatt et al., 2009). As Stephen Greenblatt further argues, we are living in the multicultural world where local and global processes and identities coexist within the boundaries of the same culture (Greenblatt et al., 2009). In this regard, the role of literature as an institution is invaluable because of its ability to ensure both the continuity and the transmission of human culture both globally and across generations. Through stories and narratives about human life and human condition, literature organizations foster creativity and openness to new ideas across social groups, geographies, and times, thus advancing sustainable thinking within their communities and globally.

**Shifting toward the semi-instrumental role.** The final element of the distinctiveness narrative is the greater involvement of literature organizations in community affairs, which is also referred to here as the semi-instrumental role. Engagement in this role implies broadening the scope of organizational missions beyond serving the domain of the arts and humanities by pursuing initiatives that advance social, economic, and environmental progress. Organizations engaged in the semi-instrumental role are acting as socially responsible actors committed to the well-being of their communities as well as their own long-term sustainability. Oftentimes, the two motivations occur simultaneously, as creating opportunities for the organizational staff to actively engage in the lives of their local communities also means advancing more sustainable organizational cultures. The manager of a publishing house reflects upon the effects of such engagement on internal organizational culture in the following way:

> I think it gives people the sense of belonging and involvement, and it makes them feel, as employees, pride in the workplace that they are working for, that it is good for the community, and it also makes them feel like they are not just working a job but working for [a] purpose that helps not only them but where they live, and people they live around. And it creates the opportunity for some extra-curricular activity—whether it is a fundraising event or going out to the community activities and being involved in whatever this is. It creates a lot of community involvement for employees inside and outside the building walls where they work that are not just related to getting the job done. (Personal Communication, 2012)

Engagement in the semi-instrumental role can therefore emerge organically as an organizational strategy and be driven by internal institutional logic that aspires to broaden organizational missions beyond their main focus on the arts. However, organizations could also pursue the semi-instrumental role as a form of socially responsible behavior in response to the needs of local communities. For example, the Detroit revitalization agenda and postrecession recovery brought a number of opportunities for local literature organizations to advance sustainability in their communities. Some cultural organizations took advantage of these opportunities by tackling the numerous economic, social, and environmental challenges in the city.

One of the most urgent problems in Detroit, for example, is the deterioration of the housing stock. In the U.S., the Detroit metropolitan area has the largest per capita number of single homes located within an urban core. As a long-term consequence of the population migrations, as well as the result of the housing market collapse in the aftermath of the Great Recession, many Detroit homes, including some of the most beautiful historical mansions, sit empty on acres of semioccupied land. Moreover, since 2008, more than 125,000 housing properties in Detroit have been foreclosed for property tax issues (MacDonald, 2019). The city proper, as well as many of its nearby suburbs, suffers from blight, infrastructure deterioration, and crime problems: having empty homes in these areas further contributes to its decline.

While a clearer policy solution to the problem of urban blight in Detroit is yet to be proposed, arts and culture institutions contribute to the revitalization of these neighborhoods, frequently working collaboratively with other industries spanning both public and private sectors. One example is a literature-driven initiative "Write a House" that has been running since 2012 with the goal of fixing up derelict homes in Detroit while providing creative residencies to writers, many of whom are looking to relocate to the city (Woods, 2017). The program tackles two problems at once—the issue of housing affordability for people in creative professions and the problem of urban blight in Detroit. Aside from the benefit of occupying a house that otherwise may be destined to demolition or malicious fire, the writers who participate in the program create literary works about Detroit and the city's comeback efforts, thus raising public awareness and drawing the attention of local and global communities to Detroit's long-term future.

Another problem in Metropolitan Detroit, especially the city proper, is the high unemployment rate that leads to a variety of negative socioeconomic outcomes. Many factors have contributed over time to the problem of unemployment, including the state of the economy, the decline of manufacturing, and the diminishing quality of public education. Some of these factors are harder to control, but there are aspects of the problem that local organizations, including those in the literature field, are attempting to tackle. For example, an issue that limits the population's access to jobs and other types of economic opportunities is the low literacy rate. As the Detroit Regional Workforce Fund reported in 2011, 47% of Detroit's adults were functionally illiterate (The Week, 2011).

In response to this problem, Reading Works, a nonprofit organization that aims to improve adult literacy in Detroit, has been offering learning and tutoring classes to nearly 4,000 people a year on topics ranging from reading and math to employment skills and English as a second language (Zaniewski, 2017). The program is the result of a collaborative action by community leaders, civic organizations, and a major local newspaper, the *Detroit Free Press*. Since 2012, Reading Works has been a registered nonprofit pursuing the mission of bolstering adult literacy in Detroit and the wider metropolitan area, so that more adults will be able to qualify for sustainable jobs and provide a better learning environment for their children (Zaniewski, 2017). This program is known for bolstering school graduation rates, but it has also proven to be successful in helping older adults, many of whom have dependent children or even grandchildren and who have nearly lost their hope of regaining the reading skills necessary for moving into sustainable jobs. The program, therefore, has been a source of economic, social, and psychological empowerment for the most disadvantaged city residents. It is an example of contributions that literature organizations can make toward sustainability in their local communities.

The programs discussed above illustrate the shift toward the semi-instrumental role of the arts and humanities and their greater emphasis on impacting societal values and agendas, as opposed to pursuing purely intrinsic roles or focusing solely on economic development and other instrumental contributions of the arts to local communities. These types of efforts are highly beneficial to local communities to some extent, but they also represent an important long-term investment in the well-being of future generations by shaping societal values and attitudes. Therefore, by pursuing these roles, arts and humanities organizations establish themselves as important pillars of sustainable development.

Balancing the Resilience and Distinctiveness Narratives
for the Long-Term Sustainability of Literature:
Evolving Managerial Roles

Many tensions are embedded in the idea of organizational sustainability. Yet it is these tensions that allow institutions to learn and grow by capitalizing on their institutional structure and increasing their social and community relevance, as well as maintaining the distinctiveness of their missions and their unique societal impacts. Organizational sustainability at its heart is a concept that requires various kinds of balancing—first and foremost, between the two narratives of sustainability. But balancing also occurs while pursuing specific organizational strategies, such as, for example, pursuing electronic publication models while also advancing print and valuing books as historically and socially significant objects.

One of the most important tasks for managers of literature organizations is to reconcile the various tensions embedded in multiple organizational logics, and there is a set of roles that managers of literature organizations came to pursue over time to support such a balance: management as stewardship, management as innovation, and management as facilitation of art-inspired communication, conversation, debate (Table 3.1). Managers that pursue these roles engage in a special kind of rationality—sustainable thinking—that allows them to effectively combine various responses to external shocks with the fundamental nature of the institutions that they are tasked to safeguard for future generations. What enables managers to reconcile the various tensions embedded in the idea of sustainability, and to serve their institutions in this regard, is their own deep understanding of and commitment to organizational missions, as described by one of the managers: "I think that, in terms of management of any kind of arts organization, you need both the abstract devotion and the very concrete devotion to the mission. It works to have a clear idea of what the mission is and what the organization promotes, and then also a very strong sense of how to effect that, how to make that happen, how to embody the mission" (Personal Communication, 2012).

Furthermore, the various roles that managers of literature organizations came to pursue over time have evolved to accommodate the dynamic nature of the environment in which literature organizations exist. One such change is the rediscovery of the traditional role of management as stewardship, which is especially relevant to organizations that publish, promote, and store printed literature, as well as to libraries that hold historic and special book collections and treat books as intrinsically valuable objects. Much like in the world of museums, the idea of management as stewardship for literature organizations today accommodates the ideas of sharing, community outreach, and partnership alongside the core focus on preservation. Increasingly, the role of stewardship implies an emphasis on openness, inclusion, and access, as described by the manager of a publishing house:

> It was started approximately 14 or 15 years ago, and it really started as [the] technology and dynamics of the industry—academic publishing—started to change in the late 1990s. As the way to provide a very low-cost way for people in the industry

to come together and talk, and hear where the industry is going in the future, and also put together at least some of the basic strategies, or at least to share what other people in the industry are thinking in terms of how to respond to it. Obviously, this is something that we believe as a corporation—that, without our customers, there are no means to be in business, so it is important to shepherd organizations through the difficult times and build those long-term partnerships. So, it was really the rationale behind it. [emphasis added] (Personal Communication, 2012)

The idea of management as stewardship is both an internally and externally oriented institutional assumption. On the one hand, managers of literature organizations emphasize the importance of guiding literature organizations through challenging times, protecting them from the impacts of recession and other external shocks, as evidenced by the metaphor "shepherd" used by the manager above. On the other hand, management as stewardship is also an externally oriented idea, which implies that organizations would treat resources in their external environment with as much care as they would treat their own internal assets. This type of externally oriented stewardship often requires working through and with other actors, including those outside the literature market itself. For example, a university-affiliated publisher describes an approach to publishing practices that his organization has adopted in the name of stewarding community resources:

In business for more than 75 years, [name of the organization] not only strives to be a high-quality printing company and the provider of services to the scholarly publishing community— we also pride ourselves on being a good citizen of the global community. In partnership with our suppliers, vendors, clients, and employees, we have worked to find sustainable resources and more efficient technology, developed new processes and procedures, participated in a variety of environmental initiatives, and promoted and supported sustainability in the publishing and printing industry. (Personal Communication, 2012)

Although management as stewardship is an important role, to be able to fully guide institutions toward intergenerational sustainability, this role needs to be balanced with others such as management as innovation and management as facilitation. The first of these roles—management as innovation—reflects the dynamic nature and fluidity of the literature market as well as its increasing dependence on technology. Additionally, the literature market is a highly networked environment of authors, publishers, distributors, and readers, which is also conducive to innovation. Therefore, greater innovativeness and attention to opportunities that constantly arise inside and outside of the literature market are critically important managerial frames that contribute to long-term organizational thriving. A manager of a nonprofit literature magazine describes the importance of management as innovation in the following way:

> Being in publishing for 27 years now, and the first 17 of those in book publishing, of course, I have seen the industry itself has changed so much in that time, and management has evolved, particularly in nonprofits, to include not only managing staff and managing mission, but also managing the enormous opportunities provided by the electronic model. Certainly, the concerns of online magazines are in some ways similar, and in some ways quite different, from what they were in book publishing. Of course, some things no longer matter, and other things matter still a great deal. (Personal Communication, 2012)

Furthermore, due to the dynamic nature of the literature market, literature organizations are frequently experiencing leadership transitions and succession-type pressures. In some cases, organizational founders and previous managers might not be fully aware of the challenges that their organizations will face in the future. Therefore, the ability of literature organizations and their managers to innovate is critically important for both organizational survival and long-term sustainability, as described by the managers of an online nonprofit literary magazine and a publishing house:

> I think, too, that every nonprofit organization reaches a point where the transition from the founders to the next generation must happen, and that is certainly something that we saw at [name of the organization]. That is a crucial transition, *a crucial time* . . . that, I think, is something that needs to be very carefully monitored and managed. [emphasis added] (Personal Communication, 2012)

Yes, maybe you've heard of the founders' syndrome that can be a problem for any organization. There are a lot of organizations in literature where someone started a press or a reading series decades ago, but things have changed so much, and that person [needs to be] keeping up and hiring new staff that can keep up, and changing the management style from the top down, hierarchical style, to be more collaborative and innovative—that's a very big buzzword in literature. (Personal Communication, 2012)

Furthermore, management as innovation is viewed as an important role regardless of the type of institutional structure. For example, nonprofit literature organizations can take advantage of their agility and flexibility, expertise gained through their board of directors, and close ties with their local communities. University-affiliated literature organizations, likewise, can capitalize on universities as intellectual hubs that play a prominent role in the production of new technologies and new ideas. Being able to manage innovation is not a given, however, and it requires time, commitment, and personal dedication on the part of literature managers. It is also especially valuable when literature managers have an intuitive sense of where the field is going.

The final role, management as facilitation, positions literature organizations in a special place among other cultural enterprises. Management as facilitation is associated with the idea of greater collaboration and building sustainable partnerships with other institutions within and outside of the domain of literature, resulting in greater institutional resilience for the entire field. Facilitative management also involves raising global cultural awareness by facilitating the spread of culture, knowledge, ideas, and values through literature, which reflects the distinctiveness narrative. As an internally oriented management practice, it is associated with the shared leadership style and engaging many actors in the decision-making process. Both of these elements of facilitative management are important for ensuring long-term sustainability of literature organizations, as described by the manager of a literary press:

Probably I would think in terms of being a manager of a press . . . hmmm, my role is almost cheerleading and facilitating, raising awareness of literature. My focus is more on getting everyone to be on the same page with the press and making the work the best it can be. It is a bit of a tricky situation because here the three of us came simultaneously, so it's like I'm their boss but at the same time a manager. We have worked together for such a long time; we have similar roles, so it is a bit tricky. I think it is more promotional and forward-looking . . . (Personal Communication, 2012)

The dynamism of the literature market often results in uncertainty regarding the effectiveness of particular management strategies, and it requires managers to take risks. However, taking risks also requires ethical judgment and high levels of intrinsic motivation based on a truly benevolent attitude toward one's work. The importance of intrinsic motivation particularly stands out in the field of literature, as compared to the more institutionalized and less fluid fields of museum and performing arts management. In literature, whether it is an informal creative writing program for people in jail or an incorporated literary magazine, intrinsic motivation is a very important element of good management. As one manager explained it, "Nobody works in publishing for the money, and people work in publishing for the love of the ideas . . . I think organizations need very strong structures and strong, very good, planning . . . the ability to operate on both short-term and long-term visions, but I also think most organizations were started by people out of love, and out of conviction and devotion" (Personal Communication, 2012). To ensure organizational sustainability now and in the long term, it is important that managers have a sense of pride in their work and love for their field, and that they pursue both inward- and outward-focusing roles. It is also important that they follow timely trends while constantly keeping missions of their organizations in mind.

## Concluding Thoughts

This chapter argued that one key to understanding the sustainability of literature lies in its ability to serve as the moral language among generations by ensuring the continuous transmission of cultural heritage from one generation to another. This ability of literature is based on two main factors: first, the ability of major literature institutions (the literary canons, the libraries, and the publishing institutions) to preserve, promote, and ensure access to literature created at different times in human history for current and future generations; and second, the ability of formal organizations within the domain of literature to sustain themselves and make sure that literature remains relevant and socially important for local and global communities.

Similar to the other arts and humanities, literature organizations developed a number of resilience strategies in response to the changing environment and the ever-dynamic literature market, while also maintaining their institutional distinctiveness. While some of the strategies aimed at enhancing institutional capital for sustainability in literature are similar to the other arts and humanities, this field is also distinct in several respects. Firstly, in the face of unstable reading patterns, literature organizations have been developing public outreach programs and establishing educational initiatives for the young. Although many literature organizations generally do not have institutionalized public education departments, there is a clear move in that direction. Moreover, following the COVID-19 pandemic, many in the industry have increased their reliance on information technology and initiated digital events and programs, which ensured their continuing adaptation and resilience.

Secondly, literature organizations tend to be highly dynamic and open to innovation, including the use of digital technologies and the adoption of open-access policies. As a matter of their long-term survival, literature organizations tend to be more responsive to the factor of time, as compared to the other arts and humanities. Thirdly, in addition to engaging in greater partnerships with other institutions, literature organizations have developed hybrid and synergetic institutional forms to a greater extent than other arts and humanities. The future of literature is also likely to be associated with smaller, more intimate organizations existing either in physical, hybrid, or online forms.

The most prominent recent development in the literature field is the spread of e-publishing. However, this development does not mean that prominent publishers with reputations spanning several generations will all go out of business, but it does signify an important change in the readership market, which is likely to reshape the future of the field. A symbiosis of online and traditional publishing, where two forms reinforce each other by pursuing different goals and reaching different audiences, is likely to become more common in the future. While the traditional publishing model will continue ensuring the appreciation of the book as a valuable object, promoting literature through online literary platforms will allow for literature's greater accessibility and an increasingly global impact.

The most distinct lesson about the long-term sustainability of literature stems from its ability to serve as an egalitarian intergenerational institution to a much greater degree than other institutions in the domain of arts and humanities. Over the course of their history, literature institutions have evolved from serving the interests of a narrow class of the powerful and wealthy to being universally and globally accessible. The invention of publishing forever changed literature and its societal impact by making books reproducible and transferable across geography and time. The literary canons were gradually embedded into the educational curriculum of schools, thus making human literary heritage available to any literate person. Libraries transformed from private book storages to important social institutions by providing wide public access to literature along with performing many other socially important functions. By being universally accessible and globally important, literature institutions have built up capital for sustainability that will help to sustain them for generations to come.

The balancing nature of organizational sustainability is reflected in the institutional structures' adaptability as well as evolving organizational cultures and missions. Sustainable thinking and evolving managerial roles have been guiding managers of literature organizations in their path toward adaptation and reconciliation of the various tensions that arise between the two sustainability narratives, thus preserving their organizations now and for the future. While engaging in such strategies, literature organizations have been making contributions to sustainability in their local and global communities by transferring cultural capital from one generation to another, ensuring wider and more universal access to cultural heritage embedded in literary works and fostering global cultural awareness.

Chapter 4

# The Boundaries of Art and Society

## Sustainability Lessons from the Performing Arts

Music and performing arts organizations represent another fruitful context in which the idea of intergenerational sustainability can be explored. The nature of music and performing arts experiences is quite distinct from that of the mostly solitary appreciation of viewing objects at museums or reading books. Performing arts experiences typically unfold in a specific community context and are shaped by that context. A show one sees in a Broadway theater in New York is a different kind of experience than a show seen in a small-town theater or a college performing arts center. The plays may be the same, but the actors and the settings are very different, as are the environment and surroundings. As described by the CEO of a music organization, experience offered by live performing arts to their audiences is a communal kind of experience; it has a very strong emotional appeal, is very dynamic, more unpredictable and surprising, and is definitely much less still, compared to experiences offered by many other arts and humanities experiences:

> I would say that the art museum experience is by and large a solitary experience, and performing arts experience is a communal experience. When you go to art museums, you don't do it with a group of hundreds of people, and you do not all move to a gallery at the same time . . . So it is a very different kind of experience that you can get every time that the place is open, and it is created by the individual. And these

are wonderful works of art, but they are frozen in time; they never change: once the last brush stroke is on that painting, it will never change—unless it is damaged. Now, the work of music—no matter how hard you try—it is never exactly the same when you perform it. And, every night, every performance is slightly different; there is a live component to it; in its own way, there is almost an athletic component to it because the precision that is required of a symphony orchestra far exceeds the precision that is required in virtually every sport that you can imagine . . . I have never seen anyone stand up in the middle of an art gallery and give a standing ovation, but last weekend, when we finished Beethoven's ninth symphony, you had sixteen hundred people standing up and screaming—they were very happy. (Personal Communication, 2012)

This collective kind of experience, where artists and audiences share not only spaces but also emotions, perceptions, and aspirations, serves as an enabling condition for developing symbiotic connections between music and performing arts organizations and their communities, including by drawing in and connecting with increasingly diverse groups of people—both performers and audiences. This chapter, therefore, argues that the long-term sustainability of orchestras and other music and performing arts organizations is a product of a "co-play" or connectedness that they establish with their local communities. In order to deepen their community connectedness, organizations engage in a variety of strategies that advance local sustainable development goals through the arts. This ability of organizations to simultaneously contribute to their own sustainability while actively engaging in community affairs, as well as the reciprocal relationship that obtains between organizations and their communities, is key to understanding intergenerational sustainability of the music and performing arts sector.

This chapter argues that long-term sustainability of music and performing arts organizations lies in their ability to constantly adapt to external shocks, justify their vital significance, and connect with their communities in coherent, inclusive, and comprehensive ways. The symbiosis that obtains between music and performing arts organizations and their communities embodies the two dynamic narratives of intergenerational sustainability—institutional resilience narrative that reflects the adaptive nature of institutions and institutional distinctiveness narrative that upholds institutional identity. Collectively, the two narratives result in the institutional capital for sustainability that allows organizations to sustain themselves in hard times and for the generations to come.

In order to illustrate these institutional logics, this chapter utilizes examples of sustainability practices found in organizations of various genres and institutional forms, including music festivals and symphony orchestras, opera and ballet companies, university-affiliated and freestanding nonprofit arts organizations, and producing and presenting organizations. The examination of historical adaptations of the sector along with the analysis of managerial interviews, organizational practices, mission statements, and programmatic documents, provides insight regarding the long-term sustainability of music and performing arts organizations and how such sustainability is achieved.

## History and Context: Institutional Adaptations of the Performing Arts

History of the music and performing arts field provides many examples of successful institutional adaptations leading to the long-term sustainability of the sector. The most significant of these adaptations include the changing nature of performing arts production and delivery after the invention of broadcasting and digital media; the evolution of institutional forms after the invention of the nonprofit-organizational model; and changes in the funding structure, including the development of philanthropic support for the performing arts. These historical developments reflect adaptive institutional responses to both the various changes in the external environment and the evolving public views regarding the broader role and significance of the arts.

In the 19th-century United States, music and performing arts were represented by either commercial or amateur artists and organizations, which were typically managed by individual owners, offering a mix of high and popular arts (McCarthy, 2001). Most performances took place in large cities, presented by local groups or by touring artists (who also took their talents to smaller towns). These performances were typically produced for mixed audiences, and few distinctions existed between high and popular arts. However, with the invention of technology in the 20th century—recorded music, film, radio, and television—those earlier commercial organizations began to disappear, and the world of music and performing arts underwent a major transformation. For example, while there were 327 theater companies in the U.S. at the end of the nineteenth century, in 1915 there were fewer than 100 (Baumol & Bowen, 1993).

In the beginning of the 20th century, the sector adopted "a new model of arts organization: the subsidized nonprofit organization" (McCarthy, 2001, p. 12). This model had been recognized as a natural solution to technical and financial problems that many performing arts were experiencing, as it effectively allowed cultural organizations to rely on a combination of earned and contributed income to support their operations (Hansmann, 1981). According to Paul DiMaggio (1986), the nonprofit model had five benefits: (1) offering the familiarity of a corporate-like structure to elites that served as a useful instrument for communal governance; (2) providing partial insulation of organizations from market pressures via the fundraising activity of their board of trustees; (3) enabling governors to rule without interference from the state and other social classes; (4) allowing organizations to insulate high-cultural from popular-cultural work; and (5) accommodating the plurality of conflicting purposes and changing ends.

Subsequently, nonprofit organizations presenting primarily live "high" arts replaced old-style commercial performing arts organizations, and commercial organizations came to focus on more popular arts (Baumol & Bowen, 1993; DiMaggio, 1986). The divisions within the performing arts sector and the spread of the nonprofit model signified a major shift not only in terms of the division of labor between live performers and broadcasters but also in terms of audience segmentation. While performing arts organizations of the 19th century accommodated various audiences— rich and poor, urban and rural—in the 20th century there was a major division between audiences of popular, folk, and high arts (McCarthy, 2001). Within that segmentation, the technological advantages that were more accessible to the commercial sector exacerbated the divide between high-art attendees and consumers of entertainment from commercial sources (McCarthy, 2001).

The introduction of the nonprofit model had changed the system of organizational governance by allowing the establishment of a musical, theatrical, or dance group by either an artistic or general director, or by patrons and community leaders themselves (DiMaggio, 1986; Lowry, 1978; Peterson, 1986). Subsequently, the proliferation in the number and expanding scope of nonprofit performing arts organizations resulted in increasing arts participation and the strengthening of the social significance of this art form. On the other hand, the expansion of the sector increased competition for audiences and funding, which posed serious questions for organizational managers, donors, and other policymakers (RockefellerBrothersFund, 1965). It also produced an emphasis on the utilitarian use of the arts as means to some other end, often at the expense of their intrinsic significance (DiMaggio, 1986). For instance, organizations were expected to contribute to the formation of a positive image of American society abroad, provide support for liberal education, offer a meaningful occupation for the youth, suggest ways to grasp one's history and modernity, and enhance the business environment, among other goals (Lowry, 1978). In many respects, this view regarding the value of the performing arts as a means to some other end—a heritage of earlier times—is present today as well.

Another crucial aspect of the performing arts' institutional evolution was the change in their funding structure. Professional music and performing arts in the 19th century were provided by a few elite organizations located in major metropolitan areas and supported by a select few patrons (McCarthy, 2001). Moreover, as compared to many European models, the U.S. system of public support for culture was always more fragmented, and federal levels of funding for the arts were smaller relative to those provided for nonprofit activity in other social realms (DiMaggio, 1986). While indirect public support for the arts was available early on via various fiscal-policy tools, such as individual income-tax deductions and federal, state, and local tax preferences (e.g., property tax exemptions), most of this support depended on fluctuations in the tax code (Feld, O'Hare, & Shuster, 1983). As described by Feld et al. (1983), this support system flowed "like an underground river through the tax system" (p. 2). Furthermore, subsidies channeled through the tax system tend to have equity issues, as they ensure the flow "from the very wealthy to the moderately wealthy and well-educated" (Feld et al., 1983, p. 71), thus raising the question of who benefits from such subsidies and who provides them.

The nonprofit operational model, on the other hand, came with a tax-exempt status applied to federal income tax and state income tax on investments and admissions (Feld et al., 1983). Tax-exempt status (coupled with the qualification to receive deductible contributions and such privileges as special bulk mail) allowed nonprofit performing organizations to serve as funnels of support for artistic production in the form of both direct grants and tax incentives. Subsequently, in the late 1950s and early 1960s, the structure of financial support for the arts changed by shifting toward reliance on multiple sources of support (Baumol & Bowen,

1993; DiMaggio, 1986; Feld et al., 1983; Lowry, 1978; McCarthy, 2001). Furthermore, organizational financial health became the responsibility of the institutionalized boards of directors who began seeking diversified funds. Overall, organizational professionalization via the nonprofit model led to both more sustainable financial practices and enhanced quality control (Hansmann, 1981; Peterson, 1986). At the same time, the engagement of broader stakeholders in supporting the performing arts also came with conflicts in institutional priorities, where the realities of the economic marketplace, aesthetic goals, and educational visions often clashed (DiMaggio, 1986).

## The Diverse Funding Model and Financial Sustainability of the Music and Performing Arts

One of the most important institutions that sustained the performing arts over the course of their history is the institution of private patronage that, particularly in the American context, has been very influential as compared to governmental patronage (DiMaggio, 1986; Lowry, 1978). Private patronage had existed since the early years of the American Republic, long before the income and inheritance taxes were legislated and a nonprofit model was adopted. The system of deductions for charitable giving, as an incentive for encouraging individual patronage, was fully adopted only after the Second World War, and, by the time systematic public support for culture and arts was introduced, private and foundation-based patronage had already legitimized the performing arts sector (Lowry, 1978). Like many other social phenomena, however, private patronage had undergone periods of relative strength and decline (Grønbjerg, 1993; Young, 2007). Since the late 1970s, several trends have been prominent in the financial landscape of music and performing arts organizations, including the changing funding practices and corporate donors' shifting from unrestricted grants to targeted support (McCarthy, 2001).

The rise and further professionalization of private philanthropy in the 20th century had contributed to greater overall sustainability of the social sectors that it supported, including the arts. In this regard, while private foundations received less attention as sources of contributed income as compared to corporations and governments, they nevertheless played a very important role in supporting the performing arts (DiMaggio, 1986). The Ford Foundation is considered the first national patron of the music and performing arts (Lowry, 1978). The leveraged-funding technique initiated by the foundation produced massive growth in the diversity of arts funders. According to McCarthy, the idea of leveraged funding as a fundraising strategy "was the most significant evolution of the arts infrastructure in America, leading to complex public-private partnerships" (McCarthy, 2001, p. 13). The model's intention was to stimulate a great number of private institutions to render their support for the arts. Another important initiative fostered by the Ford Foundation was a scholarship program for all music and performing arts areas directed at increasing the diversity of arts participation, enhancing the prestige of the artistic profession, and providing early exposure to young people from racial and economic minorities (Lowry, 1978). The Ford Foundation's programs have influenced the subsequent allocation of governmental funds for arts education programs through Titles I and III of the National Defense Education Act, administered through the public school system.

Despite substantial philanthropic support, the vast majority of live music and performing arts organizations were unable to raise revenues sufficient to sustain their operations, and such acknowledgment led to the recognition of the crucial importance of public funding for the live arts, in contrast with the recorded popular arts that did not suffer from the same issues (Baumol & Bowen, 1993). Since the 1960s, governmental organizations started playing a more active role in supporting music and performing arts organizations, as evidenced by the establishment of a State Council for the Arts in New York and the National Endowment for the Arts in Washington, D.C. in 1965. The combination of public and private support helped the music and performing arts sector cope with existing issues and strengthened its financial sustainability. On the other hand, as more public funding for the performing arts became available, recipients focused on documenting the various tangible outcomes of the arts on local communities, such as their economic impact or service delivery function, which effectively framed the arts as "industry" (DiMaggio, 1986, p. 6).

However, the economic recession of the 1990s created serious problems for the leveraged-funding paradigm, causing the decline in both public and private funding for the arts. The performing arts' typical responses to these financial pressures included attempts to diversify funding sources, cut administrative costs, increase the number of performances of the same successful production, produce more familiar programs starring celebrity artists, hire less-expensive artists, maximize the audience per production by performing in larger venues, and arrange joint for-profit and nonprofit productions, among others (McCarthy, 2001). Nonprofit organizations also engaged in professionalization and businesslike approaches to their management (Dart, 2004; Grønbjerg, 1993; McCarthy, 2001; McCarthy, Ondaatje & Novak, 2007). These approaches resulted in the blurring of boundaries between the sectors and the emergence of organizational hybrids that combine nonprofit governance structure with business-management techniques (McCarthy, 2001). Many organizations also shifted toward greater reliance on local donors; focused more on the demand side of the market; and divided institutional niches, with larger organizations providing programs aimed at a wider public and smaller organizations targeting their production to local needs (McCarthy, 2001).

While the recession of the 1990s incentivized (mostly large) organizations to create institutional endowments (Young, 2007), during the 2008 Great Recession, organizations that depended on their endowments were among the most vulnerable (Foster, 2010). As the values of their endowments declined, many organizations were forced to downsize. Additionally, the average gift amount given by wealthy patrons for the arts declined, priorities of individual donors were shifting, and there was also a decline in ticket and merchandise sale (DiMento, 2012; Foster, 2010). At the same time, realizing the detrimental effects of the Great Recession on organizational capacity, some donors provided support for nonprofit organizations' general operations (DiMento, 2012).

Both economic recessions, in the 1990s and in 2008, demonstrated that, for small and medium-sized organizations, governmental support remains especially critical, as it can allow leveraging private and public support through a system of matching grants (Bekkers & Wiepking, 2011; DiMaggio, 1986; McCarthy, 2001). There is, however, evidence that under certain conditions public funding may crowd out private support (Borgonovi, 2006; Dokko, 2008). For instance, Borgonovi found that, while at low levels public support attracts more private donations, at higher levels it actually displaces them (Borgonovi, 2006). Others, however, found that private donors' motivation is not contingent upon the institutional ability to get governmental grants (Brooks, 1999; Horne, Johnson, & Van Slyke, 2005). Some have also discovered that public funding may affect programmatic decisions, such as making choices between experimental and conventional programming (Neligan, 2006; O'Hagan & Neligan, 2005; Pierce, 2000).

Contemporary music and performing arts organizations rely on diversified sources of funding, including earned income, individual and corporate donations, foundations' contributions, and public funding (DiMaggio, 1986). As compared to the other arts and humanities, music and performing arts are more reliant on earned income, which is considered to be a relatively stable revenue source (DiMaggio, 1986; Hughes & Luksetich, 2004). In this sense, music and performing arts most closely resemble the entertainment industry, where ticket sales define most of the organizational bottom line. Contributions from individuals, however, remain the second-largest source of funding, approximately twice the size of contributions from foundations and businesses (DiMaggio, 1986; McCarthy, 2001). Some people have reservations about whether the music and performing arts rely too heavily on the private-funding model, particularly since it decreases the emphasis on programs and services and increases the emphasis on fundraising (Hughes & Luksetich, 2004). At the same time, greater emphasis on fundraising by itself does not produce mission drift, and most organizations are still capable of staying true to their core objectives, as long as they are selective in working with donors who support those objectives (Hughes & Luksetich, 2004).

The focus on individual donors explains the proliferation of marketing studies, including assessments of sociodemographic profiles and the psychological characteristics of patrons. For instance, on the eve of the 2008 recession, 14 major university presenters commissioned a series of self-funded survey-based assessments of performing arts stakeholders—their tastes and preferences with regard to the arts' production—as well as the key determinants of their ticket-buying and giving behavior (Brown, 2007a, 2007b). Such studies, while useful, are also expensive and time consuming. Many music and performing arts organizations have also institutionalized their marketing function by hiring at least one part-time employee who focuses chiefly on marketing. However, an overemphasis on marketing has its downsides. As described by the public outreach director of a university-affiliated performing arts center, too much marketing also means more commercialized institutions:

> . . . .[t]here has been so much more pressure, I think, on selling tickets more, on marketing. Sometimes I joke that this should be called the [Name] Marketing Center instead of [Name] Performing Arts Center. Marketing seems to be what we all talk about all the time. When we sit around this table with our staff, we tend to talk more about marketing than we do about the arts that we are bringing in, but that's part of

the pressure we are under. It's not just the recession. It's that whole value thing about performing arts centers. (Personal Communication, 2012)

Hence, when performing arts institutions focus too much on marketing aimed at their donors and ticket buyers, it may distract them from the supply side of production and impede their focus on quality. Furthermore, considering that more familiar and well-advertised productions are more likely to generate greater revenues, performing arts organizations sometimes tend to rely on safer production choices and abstain from producing and performing more contemporary and experimental works. In the long run, this may result in subpar production quality and increasing organizational proximity to the entertainment industry. Hence, for the performing arts organizations of the future, it will be particularly important to balance the demand and supply sides of the market, while seeking opportunities to invest in the development of innovations that highlight the distinctiveness of the sector and its individual organizations.

## Performing Arts Sector of Today and Tomorrow: Common Pressures and Responses

McNeil Lowry (1978) concluded that the future of the performing arts depends upon the answer to one question: What is the importance of the arts to American society? Four decades later, this question remains relevant. Successful institutional adaptations, including the nonprofit business model as well as the institution of philanthropy, helped to establish and sustain the music and performing arts sector to this day. However, contemporary organizations are still struggling with issues that pose threats to their long-term sustainability. Among the most important long-term pressures are ongoing financial concerns and changes in giving behavior; generational shifts and changing audience preferences; technological, capacity-building, and professionalization pressures; increasing competition with the entertainment industry; and identity crises, among others (Appendix A).

In recent years, the challenge of sustainability affected many music and performing arts organizations, posing threats unknown to them in the past and going beyond the preferences of changing audiences. External events, such as, for example, the Great Recession of 2007–2009, have threatened the very survival of many music and performing arts organizations that lost substantial portions of their private and public funding as well as subscriptions, which many of them used to rely on for their financial health. Several organizations, such as Florida Philharmonic Orchestra, San Jose Repertory Theatre and San Jose Symphony, the Tulsa Philharmonic, the Colorado Springs Symphony, and the San Antonio Symphony, to name a few, ceased to exist. Many organizations are still recovering from the consequences of that recession.

The Detroit music and performing arts sector was hit hard by the Great Recession, and many organizations (especially major nonprofits, such as Michigan Opera Theater), which used to derive a substantial portion of their budget from the three automaking companies located in Detroit, lost portions of that support. Two of these companies, Chrysler and General Motors, filed for bankruptcy, while Ford Motor Company underwent substantial downsizing. A few years later, in 2013, the City of Detroit itself became the first major U.S. city of that size to file for bankruptcy protection, leaving its publicly supported arts dry. Furthermore, the recession didn't affect all organizations in the same way. Many large organizations in Detroit, for example, were undercapitalized and lacked the endowments needed to sustain their substantial size and scope of operations. This partially resulted from the nearsightedness of their boards and management, and partially from organizational overreliance on support from the auto industry and the city itself. On the other hand, smaller Detroit organizations, which already lacked human and organizational capacity and ability to attract and retain top talent, saw this capacity further depleted; as a result, many had to reduce hours and cut staff and programs. As it was unclear how things would develop in the future, some of these organizations stuck to a "nimble" approach and avoided the kinds of growth strategies that might have worked for their larger counterparts.

Additionally, both public and private donors responded to the Great Recession by shifting their priorities away from the arts and toward essential social and human services, as well as taking a more consolidated approach to funding that prioritized larger organizations. Smaller music and performing arts organizations, for example, met with the unwillingness of private philanthropic institutions to sustain their commitment to organizations of smaller sizes and more diverse varieties, especially niche organizations. Additionally, many foundations and other private donors favored supporting new programs as opposed to providing support for ongoing programs. This problem was one in addition to the already known issue that many donors had with providing general operational support to organizations. Another concern was the tendency of both private and public donors to spread their funding further by incentivizing and, in some cases, requiring organizations to establish partnerships in order to qualify for a grant. Engaging in partnerships, however, requires operational capacity and poses a collaboration challenge for small organizations (Moldavanova & Akbulut-Gok, 2022).

Issues that the sector continues to struggle with are not limited to economic recessions. According to Foster, arts organizations are experiencing a moment of potential cultural shift, as evidenced by the gradual deterioration in the methodologies of cultural production and dissemination that has been occurring since the 1980s and by the widespread view of art as a commodity (Foster, 2010). What contributed to this problem is the nonprofit-governance-model crisis caused by the increasing competition with for-profit and entertainment industries and by too much reliance on business-like management strategies (Dart, 2004; Eikenberry, 2009; Salamon, 2015). These strategies include adopting business organizational practices, onboarding businesspeople to serve on the boards of directors, and adopting quantitative quality assessment tools that focus on measurable outputs at the expense of artistic quality (Dart, 2004; Salamon, 2015). By adopting a mindset that a nonprofit should act like a business, organizations risk deviating from their core missions—addressing a public need that cannot be supported in the marketplace (Eikenberry, 2009; Foster, 2010).

Furthermore, music and performing arts organizations are increasingly affected by global events and larger societal shifts. One example of an external shock that affected cultural organizations is the global spread of the COVID-19 pandemic in early 2020. This global health emergency questioned the common ways through which people interact with each other, forcing entire countries to declare quarantines and businesses to shut down. Many industries, including the entire social sphere, had no choice but to close their doors and rapidly transition to remote modes of operation. Arts and culture establishments, from libraries to symphonies, had to confront the alternative operational reality in which they could no longer bring people in the door. In no dream would symphonies, orchestras, theaters, and other performing arts institutions envision a future in which they were unable to conduct the live performances that allow them to capitalize on the distinctiveness of their art form. But that future came, and this new reality affected their internal operations as well as how they interact with their audiences.

As a result of the pandemic, some organizations, for example the Nashville Symphony, experienced major financial shocks that forced them to close their doors until further notice. The symphony had to furlough its 79 musicians and 49 full-time staff members, as a result of having to cancel or reschedule more than 65 concerts and after suffering financial losses of $8 million (Valentine & Peacock, 2020). Other organizations considered reopening but had to scale those plans back. For example, the Broadway League opted against reopening its shows on the New York stage and also decided to delay productions previously scheduled to play during the 2019–2020 season (Sullivan, 2020). These types of decisions involved the input of public health experts as well as negotiations with the theatrical unions, which reflect the broader political environment in which performing arts operate. To be sure, the pandemic has threatened the existence of organizations operating in a variety of formats, including media. For example, a popular American radio show featuring folk and traditional musicians, *Live from Here* (formerly known as *A Prairie Home Companion*), suspended its programs in June 2020, reporting dramatic monetary shortfalls and numerous cuts in both programming and personnel (Lawless, 2020). The show had been broadcast by Minnesota Public Radio on nearly six hundred Public Broadcasting Stations in the U.S. and was widely popular, which still did not make it immune from the crisis and suspension.

In order to address many of these increasingly unexpected issues, music and performing arts organizations have been developing a variety of responses, including seeking new modes of governance, reconsidering some of the currently dominant management ideas, and searching for ways to bring their paradigm back to the arts and community service. Sustainability discourse itself for the music and performing arts has become less about growth and more about sustainability itself, which means rethinking values and focusing on the impact and quality of experiences (Foster, 2010). It has become crucial for the long-term sustainability of music and performing arts organizations to address the dire consequences of external pressures and respond to broader cultural and societal shifts while also adhering to their core institutional ethos. Successful implementation of these goals requires achieving a careful balance between the two narratives of intergenerational sustainability.

The first narrative—institutional resilience—reflects a special kind of adaptive rationality that allows institutions to be flexible, adaptable, and reinvent themselves while learning from their successes and mistakes, and the second narrative—institutional distinctiveness—makes sure that, in the process of adaptation, organizations preserve their legacies and remain true to their core missions for the generations to come. Sustainable thinking and sustainable acting help reconcile tensions between the two narratives of organizational sustainability. This chapter further unpacks the idea of a sustainable organization through the prism of music and performing arts organizations by focusing on the interplay of the two sustainability narratives and discussing specific strategies that support such narratives (Table 4.1). Many examples will highlight the balancing nature of organizational sustainability as well as the importance of developing symbiotic relationships between organizations and their communities, as important elements of the intergenerational sustainability of music and performing arts organizations.

Table 4.1. Two Narratives of Intergenerational Sustainability: Music and Performing Arts

| Institutional Resilience Narrative | • Structural adaptability<br>• Social and community relevance | • Capitalizing on institutional structure<br>• Institutional change<br>• Institutional hybrids<br>• Public-private partnerships<br>• Interdisciplinary focus<br>• Utilizing technology and social media<br>• Diversifying and expanding community outreach |
|---|---|---|
| Institutional Distinctiveness Narrative | Capitalizing on institutional uniqueness and distinctiveness | • Staying true to the core mission<br>• Occupying unique institutional niche<br>• Promoting and cultivating socially important values<br>• Shifting towards semi-instrumental role<br>• Placing a distinct value on arts-based learning |

## Institutional Resilience Narrative:
## Adaptive Responses by the Performing Arts

The first narrative of intergenerational sustainability—institutional resilience—resembles adaptive responses found in natural systems to changes in environmental, economic, and social systems, allowing them to sustain external shocks and cope in productive ways (Gallopín, 2006; Holling, 2000; Walker, Holling, Carpenter, & Kinzig, 2004; Walker & Salt, 2006). The language of resilience entered the cultural world in the first decade of the new millennium. For example, in 2010, the Arts Council of England released a report by Mark Robinson, wherein he applies the idea of "resilience thinking," borrowed from the environmental context to the arts. Robinson claims that "adaptive resilience," defined as the capacity to remain productive and true to core purpose and identity while coping with changing circumstances, is one key to understanding why arts organizations thrive despite significant external shocks (Robinson, 2010). From a management point of view, increasing institutional resilience means being adaptable, responsive to change, innovative, and open to new opportunities. This type of institutional adaptation unfolds via institutional change that occurs both structurally (via modified programs and changes in institutional structure) and culturally (via modified organizational assumptions and belief systems).

While organizations can plan some of their adaptive responses in advance, there are also times when they must come up with an urgent response to a totally unforeseen event, such as, for example, in the case of the COVID-19 pandemic that unfolded in 2020. Therefore, a critically important element of the institutional resilience narrative is the ability of organizations to be open and responsive to shocks and stressors coming from the external environment. Conventionally speaking, stress has a negative connotation; however, external shocks are important for long-term sustainability, as previous experiences of coping with such shocks provide opportunities for continuing organizational learning. For example, Foster argues that, contrary to conventional assumptions, environmental uncertainty and unpredictability actually improve the resilience of performing arts organizations by pushing them to discover new solutions to old problems and adapt to the changing reality (Foster, 2010).

Likewise, many organizational managers interviewed for this book in the aftermath of the Great Recession of 2007–2009 have reflected on the importance of recession-induced shocks for pushing their organizations to reconsider their conventional cultural assumptions and modify existing structures. External shocks that organizations experienced during the recession have highlighted the inevitability and importance of adaptive organizational responses. They have enacted a "do or die" kind of mindset, which provided opportunities to shake the convention and reconsider old ways of doing business, even if those ways were deeply ingrained. The CEO of a Detroit-based performing arts center describes this type of situation as ground shifting under one's feet:

> Everybody's business models are falling apart before their eyes, and they're desperately trying to be sustainable, but the ground is shifting under their feet since the bankruptcy and the auto meltdown. And what's interesting is that the bankruptcy gave Detroit this kind of unparalleled American opportunity to reinvent itself with state-of-the-art systems and missions and business models, and the cultural community really needs to respond to this opportunity because I think they're scratching and trying to hold on to their funders who are 82 years old. Seize this moment to create a new business model—I mean, all the way. Emerge from bankruptcy with a new business model; that's what the cultural community needs to do. (Personal Communication, 2016)

Organizational adaptive responses in the aftermath of the Great Recession were associated with administrative professionalization and adopting business-like operational strategies, especially more aggressive marketing and audience growing. Enacting these strategies, however, called for multiple acts of balancing, such as, for example, balancing earned-revenue considerations with ticket affordability and balancing greater emphasis on professional management with high-quality artistic productions. Adaptive responses were also conditioned by particular organizational conditions. For example, while some (especially large) organizations engaged in growth strategies that included developing new programs and mastering new markets, others, especially small organizations, stayed nimble and frugal. The art of adaptation, therefore, needed to be tailored to what made sense at the time in light of the organizational and environmental conditions. Moreover, adaptive responses in which organizations engage reflect their broader environment, and such an environment can present itself as an opportunity or a hindrance, or both.

**The role of external environment in shaping institutional adaptive potential.** The case of Detroit serves as an example of the dual nature that such operational environment plays for arts and culture organizations recovering from economic recessions and coping with ongoing pressures. On the one hand, the Detroit metropolitan area has a vibrant, diverse, and long-standing cultural ecosystem created over time by multiple generations of creative people and arts patrons. This ecosystem capitalizes on the uniquely rich cultural traditions grounded in the diversity of ethnic groups populating the area, its proximity to the international border (with Canada), and its connections to a variety of industries. Of all places in the U.S., Detroit represents an example of how the arts-and-culture kind of creativity flourishes alongside industrial and technology-based kinds of creativity. Although distinct from the Silicon Valley types of environments, Detroit's cultural ecosystem has fundamentally benefitted from early American innovations in many areas of science and technology, creating various opportunities for the arts and humanities.

At the same time, Detroit has been one of the national centers of many controversies and a multitude of socioeconomic issues ranging from bankruptcy and blight to environmental deterioration, social neglect, and high crime. All these issues date back generations. Therefore, "going forward" for Detroit, as well as "going forward" in the context of Detroit, involves dealing with many problems, whether you are a tech entrepreneur or a performing arts organization. One example of how operational environment hinders the ability of arts-and-culture organizations to adapt and bounce back is the issue of structural racism that affects organizations and those whom they serve. Minority-serving arts organizations, for example, are not always recognized for the work that they do, particularly since many of them are located in marginalized communities. This makes it harder for them to get recognition, achieve legitimacy in different social circles, and obtain funding and institutional support. The manager of a professional urban theater located in a low-income and predominantly minority-populated area describes the recognition issues from multiple stakeholders that their organization has experienced while trying to bounce back from the effects of the Great Recession:

> That's a question that society has to decide. Is whether we're worth it. And that's what we've been talking about: the whole thing here is to what degree are we worth it? And we have a substantial group of individuals who think we're worth it.

They don't have the kind of money that would be the sign of [the] kind of sustaining money that would be necessary. There aren't enough of them to march down Woodward—even the 25,000 on our mailing list to march down Woodward and say, "The arts matter." We have a cultural legacy worth preserving, whether or not we have enough people out there who would recognize the name [name]. Last week, we just read articles about diversity in the arts. We weren't even mentioned in it. Well, Mr. [name] just doesn't know us; *The Detroit Free Press* doesn't get out there, I guess . . . We still get "[name] *who?*" The people that we need for the kind of sustained income [we need] don't even know we exist. (Personal Communication, 2015)

In addition to the lack of recognition and increasing marginalization by all types of donors, small and medium-sized organizations located in areas devastated by blight, crime, and other problems of urban decline were unable to rely on earned-income strategies as much as larger and more capitalized suburban organizations could. The neighborhoods in which they operate simply do not have affluent residents capable of supporting them, while suburban ticket buyers avoid these areas altogether in favor of patronizing organizations close to home or located in the gentrified Detroit downtown and midtown areas. Moreover, many Detroit-based organizations are still coping with the consequences of "white flight" that took off in the 1960s. Detroit's past and controversial historical legacy, as well as the multiple path dependencies that come with it, affect other organizations located in more affluent and gentrified downtown and midtown areas. Organizations located in historical population centers still have a hard time getting people to attend performances in Detroit, while their financial sustainability greatly depends on suburban audiences.

The Detroit downtown revitalization agenda has also created additional pressures for music and performing arts organizations. One recent development has been the creation of the District Detroit in 2017. This public-private partnership is a 50-block plan tasked with transforming parts of Detroit's downtown by creating a new business-development district. While the District Detroit brought in some immediate economic benefits, some commentators called the project a "failure to deliver," questioning its sustainability and citing both financial and developmental problems. Controversial aspects of the district include the demolishing of historical buildings, the displacement of elderly residents from their apartments, and the underutilization of empty spaces (Pinho & Shea, 2019). In this context, the new stadium, alongside the already existing sports facilities, has reshaped downtown Detroit's image into something more like a "sports capital," creating competitive pressures for local music and performing arts organizations.

The new development has also exacerbated the fragmentation of the downtown ecosystem, forcing some organizations to consider consolidation; it also increased the land and rent prices, pushing some long-standing organizations, such as the PuppetArt Theater, which operated in Detroit for almost 20 years, to leave their downtown locations (Rahal, 2017). What these developments in Detroit illustrate is a familiar tendency of this particular city that highlights both the importance of an operational environment in shaping institutional adaptive potential and the value of being able to anticipate the dynamics that can affect organizational trajectories and their longer-term sustainability.

**Structural adaptation: University-affiliation versus a freestanding model.** Similar to the museums and literature organizations, adaptive strategies developed by music and performing arts organizations center around two themes—structural aspects that have the ability to both frame and constrain the choice of an adaptive path, and strategies aimed at increasing the social and community relevance of the music and performing arts organizations (Appendix B). Institutional structure shapes the institutional resilience of music and performing arts organizations, and it also has the capacity to define some of the organizational cultural assumptions that frame how organizations operate and make decisions. However, while a particular institutional structure is important, what is even more critical for institutional resilience is how organizational managers are able to navigate the strengths and weaknesses of a particular structural arrangement.

The music and performing arts ecosystem comprises commercial, nonprofit, and university-affiliated organizations, and each of these forms has developed its own niche in the process of historical evolution. Nonprofit and university-affiliated organizations, however, share more similarities in terms of the type of artistic product that they produce and the demands placed on them by society, as compared to commercial industries. For example, nonprofit and university-affiliated organizations typically pursue classical repertoire and are seen as "protectors" of the canon; they are often referred to as the classic arts. Nonprofits also tend to either serve "highbrow" audiences or pursue community-based models that reflect the needs of their local communities, while commercial organizations are driven by market demand.

University-affiliated organizational models are commonly adopted by university theater and music departments as part of their required instructional curriculum, and they offer either year-round programs or summer-season programming, such as Shakespeare or Bach festivals. There is also a "hybrid" structural model, where an organization keeps its university affiliation while also being incorporated as a nonprofit (for example, the Oregon Bach Festival, a nonprofit established in affiliation with the University of Oregon, and the Lied Center of Kansas, a nonprofit performing arts center established in affiliation with the University of Kansas). These types of institutional hybrids in and of themselves are examples of institutional adaptation where organizations seek to capitalize on the strengths of both nonprofit and university-affiliated models.

The university affiliation and the freestanding nonprofit model both have their advantages and disadvantages (Appendix B). While the nonprofit model is generally perceived as a structure with greater flexibility that allows organizations less-constrained paths to connect externally, gain access to more diverse funding sources, and achieve better representation via a board of directors, the university-based model is generally perceived as a safer choice that comes with baseline support from a "parent" organization. The baseline support is foundational for the institutional resilience of university-based organizations, as it may guarantee a certain degree of stability and predictability by mitigating the impacts of an otherwise very competitive institutional environment.

The presence of this baseline support is a chief factor that prevents many university-affiliated organizations from considering a freestanding nonprofit model. Many artistic directors are wary of the constant fundraising pressures that nonprofits face to sustain their operations and unwilling to trade the artistic functions of their jobs for the fundraising roles that may be expected of them. If a university is supportive of an arts organization, then its managers gain an opportunity to focus more on the creative part of their work while worrying less about the cash flow. However, the baseline support that university presenters get from their "parent" institutions typically covers only a small part of the organizational expenses and is rarely sufficient for supporting organizational growth. Furthermore, universities themselves experience financial shortfalls and struggle to maintain public funding, which is reflective of a broader contemporary political and social context—in particular, the growing suspicion with regard to public spending that prompts universities to search for the justification of their funding allocations, including those to the arts organizations affiliated with them. Additionally, while in some geographic areas, nonprofit music and performing arts organizations can gain direct access to public funding through the so-called cultural-district model that produces tax revenues to support the arts, university-affiliated organizations are excluded from this support.

When it comes to accessing private funding, a university affiliation tends to obstruct the ability of organizations to work directly with donors. While nonprofit music and performing arts organizations typically have more diverse funding sources and are also more reliant on earned income through ticket sales and other commercialized types of services, some of these strategies are neither "culturally acceptable" nor otherwise accessible to university-affiliated institutions. This problem is described by the director of a university-affiliated theater:

> Unfortunately, it's very expensive to produce, so the University supports us through all of our teaching, but not through our laboratory, so the balance there is we have to have an income large enough to continue to produce. Production income, production costs. Those production costs include stipends for a number of graduate students, undergraduate assistantships, travel to recruit students. There's a whole lot that comes out of that, not just longer canvas and fabric and lighting equipment. I think that's—it's an odd way that this department works differently than perhaps any other department on campus, in that we run a business. We receive grants here, of course; like many members of the faculty, we apply for grants, although, in the arts, it's difficult to get grants. Not because they're not out there. There are a lot of granting organizations, but they see the "university" on it and go with people with greater need. (Personal Communication, 2015)

These issues are exacerbated at times of economic downturn when the lack of alternative funding may limit the overall capacity of university-affiliated organizations to run their programs full-scale. Therefore, at times of crisis, university-affiliated music and performing arts organizations tend to follow the nonprofit example by increasing reliance on earned income via ticket sales and seeking alternative funding. This is yet another example of institutional hybridity, where organizations adopt strategies that mimic those used by other institutional forms.

When it comes to university affiliation, there is a variety of nonfinancial resources that music and performing arts organizations can gain from their "parent" institutions, ranging from access to professionally trained musicians and performers to quality physical spaces and technology. Universities also offer opportunities for cross-departmental collaboration and access to intellectual capital and highly educated audiences. Importantly, they often serve as a catalyst for new ideas and development that stem from a university's research mission. There are many examples of cutting-edge experimental and innovative projects that university-affiliated organizations can pursue collaboratively with other units on campus. One such example is the Performing Arts Medicine initiative developed as a partnership between university-affiliated music and performing arts organizations and medical schools (McDermott, 2021). The first program of this kind was established by Washington University in St. Louis in 1988. The so-called performing arts medicine movement focuses on the unique health needs of music and performing arts as a vocation; it expands clinical-care options for performing artists and develops educational and research efforts that connect medicine and the arts. Another example is a growing number of university-led programs that rely on music, dance, and theater as forms of physical and mental therapy and that often serve vulnerable populations.

In a more philosophical sense, being part of a university impacts organizational identity by implying sophistication and allowing access to a special kind of intellectual environment, where faculty and students themselves directly engage with and patronize music and performing arts. Moreover, the advantages of university affiliation are mutual, as both universities and their cultural institutions can benefit from the symbiosis. Universities can leverage their cultural resources to increase their own recognition and standing—both locally and globally, and they can provide students, faculty, and staff with easier access to the arts. Therefore, university-affiliated organizations commonly see it as an integral part of their missions to serve the university's community, as expressed by the managers of university-affiliated theater and music organizations:

> I believe, fundamentally, we have a responsibility to the university to provide culture for the people who work and study here. Part of the college experience is not just a football game on Saturday; part of the college experience is also being introduced to culture. It's the basis of liberal arts education, and it's

found in culture, and we need to be more present and more accessible. (Personal Communication, 2015)

The university is a big part of us—maybe not the biggest, but it is a big one—so that gives us some advantages in that way . . . But, for us, it is a major advantage that we have. You have stability, you have other resources, and you have the university as an audience because you have a lot of highly educated, highly cultured people that have musical training that is important in their life, so, you know, that helps to make a stronger foundation. (Personal Communication, 2012)

However, being a part of a university has its limitations as well. The most widely perceived limitation of a university-affiliated structure is its general disconnectedness from the community at large, which results from a public perception of a university as an "elite" institution. Institutional structure also shapes organizational decisions when it comes to forming collaborations. Nonprofit organizations tend to develop more diverse, bridging types of networks by connecting with a variety of community actors as well as forming cross-sectoral partnerships. University-affiliated organizations tend to rely more on internal ties within the university itself. This limitation is particularly important for the sustainability of music and performing arts organizations, considering their "mass" character and inherent reliance on community as a source of both artistic talent and patronage. Their perceived distance from the general public produces two major effects: limiting the audience and devaluing the quality of an artistic product to the extent that it is being associated with student rather than professional actors.

The impact of the university affiliation on audiences could be even more limiting for organizations that perform seasonally, such as summer Shakespeare theaters or classical music festivals. Although during the summer recess, organizations can take better advantage of the university resources that would otherwise be used for educational purposes, summers on college campuses tend to be empty. Additionally, summer recess is not a particularly favorable time for partnering with public schools—a strategy that is routinely used by nonprofit music and performing arts organizations to increase arts participation. Other commonly acknowledged disadvantages of a university-affiliated model include pressures to engage in university-related projects that might take a lot of time and resources;

lack of managerial autonomy, including over financial decisions; and slower rates of making adaptive changes as a consequence of the more hierarchical structure of a university-based arrangement.

Managers of university-affiliated organizations also note the inclination of university administrators to use their organizations primarily for public relations or funding-generating purposes, as opposed to treating them as valuable institutions in their own right. University affiliation also implies adopting broader educational goals, which in some cases means going out of the comfort zone and engaging in university-related agendas with no direct reference to the art. Some arts organizations go so far as to modify their missions in order to justify their importance and fit. This can, however, make a university-affiliated organization more susceptible to mission drift by subordinating its mission and priorities to a mission of its "parent" institution. What becomes critical here in avoiding a subordination to a "parent" organization, is for organizations to develop and constantly keep in mind a clear view of their own mission, as reflected upon by the public education director of a university-affiliated performing arts center:

> It is incredibly important to have a really strong opinion and feeling about what you think the role of the performing arts center is at a university, and then what you are willing to do to make sure that that really happens. That's really important to know who you are—to know the art, and to know where you want to take it because you are going to be bombarded from all different sides, to not go down that road because of financial pressures, and community pressures. . . . You know, all the other stuff is learned . . . but, to me, that's the most important thing—to know where you really want to go . . . (Personal Communication, 2012)

Finally, as compared to their university-affiliated counterparts, freestanding nonprofit organizations not only have the advantage of accessing more diverse funding and connecting with their local communities in more direct ways, but they also tend to be more focused on experimentation, innovation, and mixed repertoire, as their institutional status allows for that kind of freedom and flexibility (McCarthy, 2001). University-affiliated organizations, on the other hand, are often constrained by the hierarchy. In order to respond to this limitation, some organizations have gradually started producing more contemporary and more popular performances, following the example of their nonprofit counterparts. Many have also expanded their public outreach programs and marketing and audience-development efforts, taking a hybrid-like approach where multiple institutional tendencies mix and mingle, thus producing qualitatively different outcomes.

**Social and community relevance: Cultivating a sense of community ownership.** In recent years, music and performing arts organizations have focused on strategies aimed at increasing their social and community relevance as a path toward greater social connectedness. These strategies help in creating a sense of community ownership over cultural institutions, which is critical for safeguarding institutions now and in the long run. Furthermore, as music and performing arts organizations continue embracing greater community involvement, their strategies for long-term sustainability increasingly focus on communities and their needs, which in and of itself represents a form of socially responsible behavior that leads to both more sustainable communities and more sustainable organizations.

Pursuing strategies of greater social and community relevance requires changing how organizations do things and why they do them, meaning that it affects both organizational structure and cultural norms. One such example is the reconsideration of a deeply ingrained assumption about the value of the arts for society. While arts and humanities organizations themselves appreciate intrinsic significance embedded in their missions, this aspect of their work is not always visible to their key stakeholders and ordinary community members. Therefore, organizations end up risking their long-term sustainability if they fail to change their own underlying assumptions and do not move beyond intangible intrinsic value to establish broader social and community relevance. Moreover, if a cultural organization dies or fails to achieve its full potential, it is a loss for the community as well. Therefore, it becomes critically important for cultural managers to balance the intrinsic value of their organizations with a more tangible vision of what those organizations can add to their local communities.

When it comes to choosing specific strategies of increasing social and community relevance, music and performing arts represent a unique context, as organizations within this subsector offer a collective experience and are capable of connecting with many people at once. This type of "power of scale" gives them an opportunity to establish their social and community relevance broadly and widely. Specific organizational strategies associated with greater social and community relevance include engaging in public-private partnerships, expanding and diversifying community outreach, adopting an interdisciplinary mindset, and utilizing more technology and social media (Appendix B). These strategies help organizations establish themselves as indispensable elements of larger social and cultural ecosystems that exist in their local and global communities.

**Engaging in partnerships.** The strategy of developing partnerships has only grown in importance in recent years, and it is increasingly seen as a productive way of enhancing collective institutional resilience of the sector. Reliance on interorganizational as well as cross-sectoral partnerships provides opportunities to share resources, such as administrative staff and services, information, and even spaces; it is especially useful for small and medium-sized organizations as a way of stretching their already scarce resources. Importantly, engaging in partnerships with other actors allows music and performing arts organizations to enhance and broaden their missions, expand their stakeholder base, and diversify their outreach. Communities greatly benefit from such partnerships as well, as partnerships between arts organizations and other community actors facilitate local economic development and offer access to the arts to underserved individuals, thus fostering more sustainable community development.

In the music and performing arts sector, partnerships may also take the form of consolidating various organizations located in the same geographical area in the same physical space, all while preserving organizational identities. This typically happens in urban environments where multiple music and performing arts organizations exist in separate buildings. These organizations may have aging infrastructure or may have outgrown the capacity of their current spaces. The strategy involves the construction of a new, centrally located performing arts center that has the capacity to physically host many organizations, offering them updated infrastructure and technology and offering their audiences "one-stop shopping." Philosophically, the idea of a unified space is grounded in the vision of a city center as a center of public life where multiple actors converge. However, the main driving force for this consolidation and building movement is the broader urban revitalization agenda that seeks to incorporate the arts.

One example of a collective institutional resilience strategy that is based on collaboration and partnership is the Kauffman Center for the Performing Arts in downtown Kansas City, Missouri. It was originally begun in 1995 as a civic initiative of philanthropist Muriel McBrien Kauffman and was constructed in 2011 with no taxpayer funds. The center was later incorporated as a 501(c)(3) nonprofit. In addition to its two unique performance venues—Muriel Kauffman Theatre and Helzberg Hall—the center serves as the home to the Kansas City Symphony, the Lyric Opera of Kansas City, and the Kansas City Ballet. Aside from hosting these organizations, the Kauffman Center serves as the hub for many related institutions, such as the Heartland Men's Chorus, Kansas City Broadway Series, Kansas City Friends of Chamber Music, University of Missouri Conservatory of Music and Dance, Kansas City Jazz Orchestra, Youth Symphony of Kansas City, and Starlight Children's Theatre.

Today, the Kaufmann Center serves several important purposes. First, having an excellent venue and worrying less about infrastructure and technology allows music and performing arts organizations in the area to dedicate more attention to their programming and audience-development goals. Additionally, organizations have better production opportunities, greater access to performers and producers, and better marketing and promotion, which all have positive effects on institutional resilience. This consolidated model fills gaps in program offerings by bringing in repertoire that complements existing organizations, and, in many respects, makes performances more accessible to the public, as expressed by the center's representative:

> Often, people think that performing arts centers are elitist, and we really did not want to fall into that trap, so the easiest thing to do that was to provide a diverse genre, range of genres, range of performances. We do our own "preventing" and offer performances that try to complement what the Symphony, the Opera, Ballet, and other presenters in the community are doing. We do not want to duplicate; we just try to go the other direction, to provide the greater breadth of performances for the community, so there will be something available for everyone. Our mission is to bring in a diverse range of constituents representing all walks of life and all levels of income . . . And success for us . . . I can walk out to the lobby and see the attendees, and, if I do not recognize them, that's one of the greatest successes to me. If I do not know them, this is an opportunity to get to know them; they aren't one standard audience. (Personal Communication, 2012)

Importantly, the center has broadened the scope of and created additional opportunities for partnerships between music and performing arts organizations and other community actors, such as, for example, public schools. Therefore, the center's main value for the community stems not from its advanced technical design and architectural appeal, but rather from its broader reach and a greater sense of inclusion and community ownership. In these various ways, the Kauffman Center plays an important role in enhancing the global image and reputation of the Kansas City area, thus attracting more businesses and the creative class. At the same time, the consolidation of many performing arts institutions in one space has its downsides. First, shared facilities imply shared spaces and shared audiences, and they also imply that a particular institution is associated less with its own peculiar space. In this sense, an organization moving out of its original space and into a consolidated venue may sacrifice part of its long-established identity, which was linked to the old building. Second, more often than not, improved performing arts facilities imply increased production costs and, subsequently, increased ticket prices, which could limit accessibility to some population groups, as expressed by a CEO of a smaller performing arts organization from the area:

> One thing that has happened in moving to the new Kauffman Center is that it's hard to maintain expenses for us. And we did raise ticket prices, and we continued selling tickets even though it was more expensive. But we have always had a certain number of inexpensive tickets, and we kept those seats when we moved it to the Kauffman. We would like to feel that nobody who would like to attend the Lyric Opera wouldn't be able to because it is too expensive. (Personal Communication, 2012)

In theory, while this type of consolidating partnership could allow opportunities for cross-promotion and solve some urgent infrastructure needs, individual organizations are often concerned about the effects of the space merger on their visibility and distinctiveness, and many are also concerned about competition. An example of this is the downtown Detroit ecosystem that hosts multiple performing arts organizations—large and small, nonprofits and businesses—an environment where discussions about physical-space mergers have been challenging. While some of these organizations see physical consolidation as an opportunity to leverage the sector's collective capacity and improve institutional resilience, others are being threatened by the growing sports infrastructure and the resulting competition, which complicates talks about creating a common performing space. Hence, moving a "natural" ecosystem into a new space is often a difficult undertaking that involves a lot of resistance, and it may not work everywhere, especially in the absence of preexisting partnerships and consensus among the arts leaders.

**Embracing interdisciplinarity.** The next strategy that helps elevate the social and community relevance of music and performing arts organizations is their ability to take more of an interdisciplinary focus by looking beyond the boundaries of not only a particular art form but also those of the arts sector itself. Organizations increasingly adopt interdisciplinary approaches to their programming, which Kenneth J. Foster calls a "mixtape narrative"—that is, a hybrid of aesthetic expressions united by the same idea: it looks like theater; it sounds like music; it draws some of its ideas from popular culture and creates a new experience (Foster, 2010). Embracing interdisciplinarity is a way of creating synergies among multiple art forms by merging their creative capacities into a more powerful unified experience and, as explained by the CEO of a performing arts center, the various synergies are going to become more common in the future:

> I am guessing that there will be greater community involvement, and it will be across disciplines, and gone are the days when a single art form, a single art genre, will be by itself, but it will partner with all kinds of other artistic genres, visual and performing arts movements together. In terms of creating a separate product—it would not be just visual arts on one side and performing arts on the other side; different types of instruments will join with other types, like music making and dance, so the arts will start becoming more synthesized than they will be separate. (Personal Communication, 2012)

Being more interdisciplinary and more synergistic also involves broadening and expanding the mission by establishing the value of the arts outside of the concert halls, once again emphasizing the same message that comes across all the arts and humanities: it is not the quality of the building that defines institutional resilience but rather how organizations are able to connect with their communities located outside of that building. An example of an innovative way of getting music and performing arts outside their performing halls and connected with the wider community is the so-called community-music movement, which has been developing for over 50 years and gaining more popularity in the 21st century with the greater access to technology and increasing globalization (Bartleet & Higgins, 2018). The main goal of this movement is to establish social and community relevance of music in the lives of ordinary people from multiple generations by demolishing stereotypes associated with traditional music instruction.

An example of an organization that specifically pursues the mission of empowering community members to lead happier and healthier lives by participating in music is Musical Connections, which was created in 2008 in the U.K. and later incorporated as a nonprofit in 2016. The organization seeks to challenge age-related stereotypes by not making assumptions about the types of music that participants will enjoy. Higher education institutions, likewise, have capitalized on these grassroots initiatives by including community music instruction in their curriculum. For example, York University in Great Britain first introduced a community music module to its undergraduate courses and then became the first university to establish a full graduate program—Master of Arts in Community Music designed for a range of community settings, including education and disability arts, world music, theater, and technology. The goal of this interdisciplinary program, which targets artists working outside traditional concert-hall settings—in schools, prisons, hospitals, and other social institutions—is to stimulate the growth of new careers where music and performing arts are considered essential for the economy and society rather than merely viewed as a form of entertainment. The program also keeps music education relevant by enabling young musicians to develop a multiskilled interdisciplinary "portfolio" supporting a range of careers that could be pursued in diverse settings.

The many programs that emerged worldwide from the community-music movement have been empowering ordinary older adults as well as young people to pursue their passion for music. Some of these programs facilitate connections between nursing homes and other elder-care institutions and early childhood centers, thus contributing to a sense of community connectedness and more sustainable communities overall. For example, the Calhoun Intermediate School District in Battle Creek, Michigan, has tasked its Early Childhood Connections program that serves families with children (newborns to kindergartners) with programs that connect children with elderly adults from nursing homes and assisted-living facilities. Its programs, such as "Connecting Generations: Creative Arts Playgroup," include playgroups, home visits, developmental screenings, and special events. In many cases, these programs also have therapeutic effects, as they exert positive cognitive, social, and emotional benefits for their participants. These programs, however, are also highly beneficial for organizations that facilitate them, as they elevate the social and community relevance of such organizations, improve their social connectedness, and increase overall chances for their long-term sustainability.

**Expanding and diversifying public outreach.** Building and sustaining audiences is one of the most critical challenges for modern-day music and performing arts organizations, all of which these days have a formal public outreach department. For music and performing arts organizations, regular audiences represent their lifeline, as they rely on ticket sales and subscriptions as their main revenue source. Engaged community programming and institutionalized public outreach are, therefore, very important for enhancing institutional resilience of music and performing arts organizations. The executive director of a dance organization uses the metaphor of the "third leg" of a stool to describe how institutionalized public outreach supports organizational strategy:

> Our community programming is very fundamental to our mission; it is sort of the third leg of our stool: you've got the company performances; you've got the school; and you've got the community programming. I have to say that almost every ballet company in America . . . has community programs as a vital part of their mission . . . They certainly not only have commitment and obligation to a community program, but it is an essential part of being in their communities and being successful in their community . . . For any sustainable arts organization that depends on fundraising as a good part of their budget, you have to be able to understand how to speak to all the different varieties and variances, and it makes your organization important to the community. (Personal Communication, 2012)

Institutionalized public outreach allows organizations to appropriately respond to urgent challenges that the sectors are facing. The most critical of these issues is the downward trend in attendance at traditional performing arts events: the lowest participation is in opera (4.8 percent), ballet (6.6 percent), nonmusical plays (21.2 percent), and classical music (20.9 percent), and the highest participation is in musical plays (37.6 percent) (Hager & Winkler, 2012). Several performing arts forms, such as ballet or classic opera, are suffering from audience decline more than others, and their performances are often perceived as "expensive, elitist, and stuffy events for men in tuxedos and women in pearls and not much fun" (Wan, Ludwig & Boyle, 2018, p. 4). Additionally, many organizations also suffer from the phenomenon of audience "graying" (aging) and are also struggling with fewer regular subscriptions, as members of younger generations tend to participate more sporadically and buy cheaper tickets in comparison to previous generations. This problem has been metaphorically termed as a "leaky-bucket," indicating a slow and steady decline in audience numbers (Wan, Ludwig, & Boyle, 2018). In part, it is a product of generational differences, but it is also a consequence of the changing economy, an increasingly unstable job market, and loosening of the social safety net that younger generations are experiencing. Organizations also struggle with building more diverse audiences, in terms of both race and ethnicity as well as social status.

Many music and performing arts organizations have responded to these problems by diversifying their repertoire and designing generation-appropriate marketing campaigns that rely a lot more on digital content and social media than in the past. There have also been integrated national efforts supported both by the National Endowment for the Arts and the philanthropic community aimed at understanding the dynamics of audience decline and how the situation can be improved. One example is the $64 million Building Audiences for Sustainability Initiative launched by the Wallace Foundation to support several major art forms (Wan, Ludwig, & Boyle, 2018). The initiative commissioned multiple studies to better understand the various audience groups. Findings from these studies show that new audiences often prefer a more relaxed atmosphere than is currently offered by most classical music organizations and theaters and, regardless of their own race, prefer seeing a more diverse cast on stage.

In order to engage their audiences in more interactive ways, organizations arrange direct interactions with artists inside and outside of the performance halls; organize audience workshops and lectures about the history of a particular play, opera, or other kind of performance; communicate information through websites; and arrange dialogues between artists and audiences on social media. Many organizations also arrange postperformance activities to provide an opportunity for their audiences to have a deeper engagement experience. As explained by the director of a university-based music organization, in searching for a proper connection to multilevel audiences, it is important to find a point of entry for each of these audiences—something that will resonate with people, and something that will bring them back:

> So now we have kind of built into those programs what I think is probably one of the best phrases I've come across to define it: "points of entry." It's like a vertical approach to education or a vertical approach to connection. At its very lowest level, you have somebody liking something on Facebook, or liking a picture, like a two-second or three-second brief, emotion-involved, meaningful interaction—it is a very brief one that can be shared by anyone—to something that is an in-depth, scholarly, professional interaction, like a 17-day residence, a master class on a PhD level. Those are the two extremes, and there are several points in between, depending on the level of sophistication, comfort, cost. All those points are just the way the festival has been structured. (Personal Communication, 2012)

Some organizations have also been experimenting with unconventional programming and various innovative approaches to public outreach. For example, the Opera Theater of Saint Louis designed a new program called "Opera Tasting," which combines listening to fragments from various operas with tasting food and drink samples (Dobrzynski, 2018). However, rather than bringing first-time operagoers to the theater, this program organized the tasting events in a variety of local places, including a historic district and a working-class neighborhood in St. Louis, as well as suburban locations and a college town further away from the city center. While evidence suggests that these programs tend to attract new audiences, they also tend to be labor intensive and may become financially unsustainable.

The focus on outdoor spaces as performance venues had also become a new trend for many music and performing arts organizations nationwide, even before the COVID-19 pandemic, as it helps connect with audiences in different ways and prioritizes open spaces as venues for community engagement. For example, civic leaders and the philanthropic community in Detroit have initiated the creation of a cultural district in midtown by creating a unified space for cultural institutions, local businesses, and architecturally significant historical buildings. Many cultural institutions located in this area have moved forward with plans to activate their outdoor spaces in the cultural district.

Another important recent development is the increasing emphasis on early outreach programs, which have grown in importance as many organizations recognize the need to engage with future generations of both patrons and musicians. The Opera Theater of Saint Louis, for example, has focused several of its outreach efforts on the new generations of patrons—Generation X and Millennials (Dobrzynski, 2018). They have created a Young Friends program for people under 45 that allows discounted tickets and special events access; they also started a tradition of performances in English and preperformance picnic events in outdoor spaces that also help them reach out to more diverse audiences. Other organizations have institutionalized their young musician recruitment programs by creating youth ensembles. For example, the Detroit Symphony Orchestra's Civic Youth Ensemble, initially created in 1970, today consists of two full orchestras, four string orchestras, three wind ensembles, three jazz ensembles, and one choir (in partnership with the Detroit Children's Choir), as well as several chamber ensembles and jazz combos.

These new public outreach initiatives, however, are good only if they are able to ensure access to the community at large, including traditionally underserved populations. Audience diversification, therefore, has become an increasingly urgent task for music and performing arts organizations. It represents egalitarian ethical principles and the idea that modern-day institutions have an ethical obligation to become more equitable, thus representing an important investment in future generations and upholding principles of intergenerational social equity (Frederickson, 2010). Both governmental and philanthropic support are important for enabling these forms of organizational socially responsible behavior.

**Utilizing technology and social media.** Increasing reliance on technology and social media has become another common adaptive strategy for many arts and humanities, reflecting the changing role of technology in people's lives as well as the changing nature of artistic consumption. Additionally, technological challenge is one of the common "future" challenges recognized by cultural managers (Appendix A). Furthermore, with the surge of the global COVID-19 pandemic, technology utilization has become even more urgent, in many cases defining both immediate organizational survival and long-term organizational sustainability. Some organizations, however, were unprepared for the pandemic turn of events, both technologically and mentally. Classical music and performing arts organizations, in particular, had relied on live performances as their mainstream mode of production, which distinguished them from museums and literary organizations. That mode, however, quickly became unsustainable during the pandemic.

Historically, the relationship of music and performing arts organizations with technology can be characterized as a duality. For the past 50 years or so, many organizations have viewed technology as a way of enhancing artistic experience, pushing them to invest in better light and sound equipment. However, some organizations, especially those with the classic repertoire, had reservations about technological solutions and viewed them as the antithesis of high-quality live performances: in other words, something that would damage the unique connection formed between performers and the audiences during a live performance. Another important rationale that hindered the use of live broadcasting and other forms of digital performance were the earned-revenue concerns. If concerts and performance were broadcast on radio or TV with free access to all, many were concerned about losing ticket sales revenues. Therefore, a certain path dependency has developed in the field, where technology was seen as a technical and supplemental tool rather than something that delivers actual music and performing arts experience to the audiences.

This was not, however, a universal logic, and some organizations, such as, for example, the Detroit Symphony Orchestra, have begun relying on technology to broadcast open performances as a way of enhancing public access to music and ensuring wider promotion for the organization itself. Leaders of this organization, which some refer to it as "the most accessible orchestra in the world," did not see online and media broadcasting as the antithesis of live performances; rather, they envisioned them as complementary modes of artistic delivery that meet the changing needs of their younger audiences. As expressed by a manager of this organization, live and virtual stages represent different types of experiences and complement each other:

> If we think that being together is the only way to experience an orchestra or anything else, that's probably naïve, and, with that in mind, we're seeing the day when people's home or community-entertainment systems are unbelievably sophisticated. And that's why our webcasts are so important. Having

said that, it depends on what you think our product is. If one thinks our product is music, then it works really well. You can listen to it anywhere. If one thinks our product is the shared coming-together to experience something that matters together, the community you know, the great human condition of coming together, then it's a different question. That's why I think it's going to be both. I think the institutions like orchestras that just say, "You come see us; we'll hit the rules, and we'll have all these rules, you know—no photo, no drink, no video, no social media." That's silly. That's not 21st-century. I can go see the most popular pop act at the largest stadium in town and take a million pictures and post them all over the world instantly. And I can't come to an orchestra concert and take pictures and post them celebrating where I am. (Personal Communication, 2015)

These reflections represent proactive adaptive thinking, and they also reflect a certain marketing logic, where classic performing arts organizations are seen as rule bound and too traditional, as compared to commercial types of entertainment institutions that allow their visitors to use personal technology and actually capitalize on it as free promotion. If visitors can take pictures and videos and post them on social media, they communicate and endorse these experiences within their friendship circle, which in turn serves as a form of direct and free advertisement for organizations.

Therefore, embracing social media and adopting technological solutions is increasingly seen as a "necessary evil" when it comes to adapting to audience preferences, but it is also a good way to expand outreach to both local and global communities. Some organizations, for example, have embraced the importance of digital technology as part of their global outreach strategies. For example, The Oregon Bach Festival, in addition to their traditional live performances and limited CD productions, started recording their music and distributing the recordings to a worldwide audience through an online platform. This strategy has increased their audiences globally and made them more accessible, as described by the organizational manager:

Specifically, with the recording, as that changed the industry, we moved from recording as a tactic of implementing that strategy to online. There is a digital Bach project that we are currently using, so, in a lot of ways, it takes the same place. It is a way to make our music, our scholarship, accessible to a wider range of people who might not be able to be here. It lets them be able to relive it during the course of the year, so now that is available online in a unique way rather than, say, like CDs. The strategy is kind of the same; it is involving people in as many typical ways and exposing people to music and scholarship, but the tactic is switching from a hard disk to online material. (Personal Communication, 2012)

When the COVID-19 pandemic unfolded in 2020, technological solutions and remote activities were no longer a choice but rather a mandate for music and performing arts organizations that wanted to stay alive. It was a do-or-die type of situation, and many organizations, by going virtual, adapted not only their performing styles but also their managerial approaches—for example, by running virtual fundraising campaigns. In their quest for sustainability, organizations had to adapt, and some did so quite successfully, including by adopting unconventional technology-based approaches to programming. One example is Barcelona's Liceu Opera House. This neoclassical venue, and one of Europe's largest opera houses, reopened its doors after three months of pandemic-related quarantine to hold a concert for nearly 2,300 house plants (Castilleja, 2020). The performance was broadcast online and caused quite a furor. Its intent was to highlight the absurdity of the human condition under the circumstances as well as the inherent connection between humans and nature. As the theater's producer, Eugenio Ampudio, described it, "Nature advanced to occupy the spaces we snatched from it. Can we extend our empathy? Let's begin with art and music, in a great theatre, by inviting nature in" (Castilleja, 2020).

Many other organizations were also able to keep their musicians and performers at home under quarantine while performing together via online technologies, while others increased live broadcasting of the previously recorded or new remotely produced performances. For example, the Detroit Symphony Orchestra and the Michigan Opera Theater launched virtual performances and video streaming accessible to their subscribers and members of the public at large. Michigan Opera Theater has also launched the "Learn at Home" virtual educational program, which connects the arts with at-home learners and features educational videos and classes for dancers of all ages. These adaptations involved reconsidering organizational structural and cultural norms, forcing cultural managers to rethink and reinvent both, which required a high degree of sustainable thinking and keeping future generations in mind, while figuring out how organizations can survive and sustain while staying true to their core missions. The COVID-19 pandemic has also underscored a fine line and the importance of a balance between resilience strategies needed for organizational survival and the distinctiveness of a particular art form or a particular organization. Moreover, if cultural managers have learned anything from this pandemic, it would be to expect the unexpected and be ready to handle it in the future.

### Institutional Distinctiveness Narrative: Capitalizing on Uniqueness

In our conversation about the changing role of music and performing arts in society, the CEO of a Detroit-based youth theater described music and performing arts as a unique kind of experience with a unique value and the ability to reveal to individuals their true-life purpose that goes beyond their day-to-day existence. In his view, among other arts and humanities, music and performing arts offer a distinct kind spiritual experience, which has, in some ways, been replacing the role that traditional institutions, such as churches, played in the past:

> Without art, there is no reason to be here because, if you have nothing besides "Wake up; do this; do that; do the same thing tomorrow," where does the meaning come in? This is something we can't live without. Especially now, because, two generations ago, there were some other things; it was normal for everybody to go to church, synagogue, temple, it was a part of life that goes beyond basic needs. Technically, you can live without it, but, from the very beginning, people lived with it. Something which was always present in old times—the religion. It's impossible that any village or nation would not have religion. In our time, it is art—it's not replacing religion, but, in terms of connection and understanding of the world, it's building a construct. (Personal Communication, 2016)

In a similar reflection by the CEO of a university-affiliated performing arts center, music and performing arts institutions are capable of filling the void for communal life experiences that humanity is going to increasingly feel as we continue moving toward a more digital and physically detached world; hence, music and performing arts experiences are likely to become even more precious and valued due to their distinct nature:

> There are all kinds of questions like that: "What has the electronic age done to us?" and "We are performing live; where is the value in that?" And I think that communicating and being involved with physical touch with people through the arts, as opposed to electronically, will always be there. And, in some ways, those experiences—as we get more decentralized, more electronic, more detached—those opportunities to come together will become more precious . . . Will we ever lose it? No, there will always be artists in our community; there will always be a community; there will always be people wanting to express and wanting to experience that. I don't think we should prescribe how it would look in the distant future, but we should understand that it is really the basis; it is just a very basic core of how we are as human beings. (Personal Communication, 2012)

This type of uniqueness that stems from the distinctiveness of the aesthetic experience itself supports the elements of the institutional distinctiveness narrative that, alongside the institutional resilience narrative, frames intergenerational sustainability of the music and performing arts sector. At an organizational level, specific strategies associated with the institutional distinctiveness narrative include staying true to the core mission; occupying a unique institutional niche; promoting and cultivating socially important values; shifting toward a semi-instrumental role; and capitalizing on the unique nature of art-based learning (Table 4.2).

**Staying true to the core mission.** The institutional distinctiveness narrative implies staying true to the core mission by establishing the value of an art form and a particular organization for a society without treating it as a commodity or as a mere source of economic capital. Among the elements of institutional distinctiveness, staying true to the mission is what allows managers to make pragmatic strategic decisions that move their organizations forward while making sure not to compromise the very identity of their organizations. Organizational missions, however, are not

Table 4.2. Evolving Missions, Managerial Roles, and Values Promoted to Current and Future Generations: Performing Arts

| Evolving missions | Forming symbiotic relationships with the community |
|---|---|
| | Embracing the value of social equity |
| | Focusing on audience:<br>　Access<br>　Diversity<br>　Inclusiveness<br>　Being up-to-date (reference to our time) |
| Evolving managerial roles | Manager as connector: building relationships with local communities |
| | Management as facilitation of arts-inspired communication, conversation, debate |
| | Management as adaptation |
| Values promoted to current and future generations | Performing arts as community-oriented institutions |
| | Sense of community and social bonding |
| | Shared experience and unique connection between artists and audience |
| | Educational value: music and performing arts as commitment to excellence |
| | Inspirational value (emotional appeal) |

set in stone; they have been evolving over time to reflect the changing nature of society and human condition (Table 4.2).

Missions of music and performing arts organizations have been increasingly reflecting contemporary reality and emphasizing being up to date. Being up to date is in natural alignment with the music and performing arts, as they are, to a lesser extent, historic experiences as compared to the visual or literary arts. Although a particular composition or play is created at a certain point in time and its contents reflect a particular period, it is enacted by contemporary artists who bring it to life in the present. One example of how this mission emphasis manifests itself in practice is when organizations adapt their repertoire or change the rules of what their audiences are allowed to do during a live performance (e.g., posting pictures on social media, recording fragments of a performance, etc.). Another example is the increasing adoption of digital technology for both artistic production and broadcasting.

Another prominent theme in music and performing arts missions' evolution is greater focus on audiences, as opposed to primarily focusing on the art and aesthetics. Mission emphasis on audiences could be explained by several factors, the most important of which is that sustainability of both live and recorded performing arts organizations greatly depends on mass audiences. Greater focus on audiences comprises many things: from reflecting aesthetic preferences of the audiences when choosing the repertoire to targeting underserved groups of population. For theaters, orchestras, and other music and performing arts organizations, including diverse groups of the population in their audience is a legacy of the historical past. Before commercial and nonprofit arts organizations split the territory in the early 20th century, performing arts organizations had a mixed repertoire, which reflected the tastes of both elite and ordinary audiences (McCarthy, 2001). In this sense, modern performing arts organizations are going back in history by more actively and consciously integrating the values of social equity, diversity, access, and inclusiveness into their missions. In practical terms, pursuing these values means having more accessible facilities, being more mobile and dynamic, being willing to reach audiences outside of the performing halls, and many other things.

Philosophically, focusing on diverse audiences implies embracing social equity as a guiding principle in both programming and management as well as pursuing such values as diversity, inclusion, and accessibility. Due to a strong connection between music and performing arts organizations and their communities, social equity has become a crucial element of the long-term sustainability of the sector. For instance, Ramnarine (2013) observes that classic orchestras are consistently working toward facilitating greater social equity by shifting the paradigm from serving the highly educated class to creating diverse opportunities, providing access, and fostering communities at large. By doing so, performing arts institutions can play an important normative function of promoting the value of social equity within their communities today and thus affect future generations and promote positive societal transformations going forward.

Music and performing arts organizations implement many deliberate strategies aimed at making their institutions more welcoming, including providing ticket discounts, arranging transportation to the performing arts venues, and organizing performances outside of the concert halls. Making performing arts more accessible also means finding languages to speak with people of various generations and socioeconomic groups. This could mean speaking the same language in a literal sense by providing programming in a language most spoken in the community although it might not be the original language of the work itself. One example of this is opera companies presenting classical Italian and other foreign-language performances in English, thus bringing down access barriers. Speaking the same language as the audience in a more figurative sense means finding the right balance of genres, forms, and repertoires in order to keep people interested.

Additionally, classic live music and performing arts are striving to become more inclusive by overcoming various access barriers associated with the perception of classical music, opera, dance, and theater as elite arts. Research shows that major barriers of access to the classic arts are not economic but rather psychological, and they often result from the lack of exposure to these art forms, particularly when there are no art classes in schools. As described by a composer who is also a cultural-management consultant, people from underserved populations often feel intimidated by the performing arts buildings, especially if they have never entered them before:

> The problem is that you have people who have never been in a concert hall; they are afraid to cross the door, to enter. They also never go to special restaurants, even if they might not be very expensive, but they are afraid to cross the border line between different parts of society. Cultural organizations can connect the different elements of society in a very easy way. The art, food and drink, and sport—this is one of the elements you can easily communicate among different cultures and parts of society . . . And my interest is that arts and culture will have an increasing importance in the future, and, besides super-star high-level performances and exhibitions, we need the system to involve people in different ways, come closer to the people, bring art to the people, and try to include them, try to make them partner, try to avoid any borderline between the performance hall and people who are afraid to move inside. This will be a very important step to bringing peace to society by introducing the beauty of art. (Personal Communication, 2012)

While mission emphasis on diversity, inclusion, and access is important for the long-term sustainability of the sector itself, it also represents a form of socially responsible behavior that facilitates more equitable and sustainable communities. Working with nontraditional and underrepresented audiences is another good example of such an ethic. By reaching out to the various publics, organizations include people who would not have otherwise obtained these opportunities, thus facilitating an overall sense of social justice. This is particularly important when programs target young generations, as such programs serve as a responsible long-term investment into a more just future, as expressed by the CEO of an opera company:

> When I came here, I thought it was very important for us to have extremely active education programs, to be in schools, to be working with young people . . . We established an education department, which is now extremely active. It is one of the most respected education programs in the United States. We commissioned children's operas; we had a summer opera camp bringing young people down to our theater. We go to prisons. We go to women's shelters with opera programs. We have an apprentice program for young singers at the university level. We sell discounted tickets to students. About 20 percent of our audience is 20 years old or younger, and we are very proud of that. (Personal Communication, 2012)

Music and performing arts organizations have also started exploring unusual genres, with the goal of targeting nontraditional audiences. One such example is the "Video Games Live" show performed by the Oregon Symphony for the first time in 2007 (Stabler, 2009). The show matches live symphonic music with big-screen projections of video games, and it is clearly aimed at the next generation of listeners. This project brought to the symphony a mixed audience of various ages, and about half of the audience was between the ages of 20 and 30, which is outside of the traditional age range for symphony music. One can argue that such a performance is also outside of the Oregon Symphony's mission; however, when diversity of audience is part of the organizational mission, then such an experiment is another way to fulfill that mission.

**Occupying a unique institutional niche.** When it comes to music and performing arts organizations, occupying a unique institutional niche implies two things: first, that it distinguishes them from more popular forms of entertainment existing within both arts and nonarts industries and, second, that it distinguishes them from other classical arts and humanities. Among other cultural industries, music and performing arts organizations most closely resemble the entertainment industry in terms of both the type of "product" that they deliver and their organizational modus operandi. First, in most cases, individuals' access to music and performing arts is based on the financial transaction of purchasing a ticket. While libraries are free, and many museums offer free admissions to certain groups, "free" concerts or performances have to be sponsored by someone, as they involve high production costs. Likewise, when it comes to organizational operations, with the increased adoption of corporate business practices, the distinction between how nonprofit music and performing arts organizations and their corporate counterparts are managed has become blurrier.

When it comes to differences from the other arts and humanities, the major one is the focus of music and performing arts on communal experiences. These experiences are frequently tied to a particular moment in time and require instant presence and engagement by both performers and audiences, which is quite different from a typical museum or literature experience. This type of aesthetics identifies a unique niche that music and performing arts occupy and allows them to draw in their own audiences, as expressed by the CEO of a music organization: "One-time concert experience is different than like a six-month-long exhibit, where you have a focused time, where you can bring people together, and give them something to talk about or share. It just makes it more special that way" (Personal Communication, 2021).

Furthermore, the relationship between theaters, operas, concert halls, festivals, and their audiences has been evolving; the audience is no longer viewed as a passive spectator but as an integral part of performance, reflecting the shift from a top-down performer—client orientation to a more collaborative co-production orientation. These modern-day transformations are rooted in the change in the performance aesthetics that happened in 1960s, when the theater was no longer considered a mere representation of a fictive world created for an audience to observe and interpret (Fischer-Lichte, 2008). The theater action was now supposed to happen between actors and spectators; it was supposed to produce and convey meaning rather than merely reproduce the text (Davies, 2011). Scholars of the modern performing arts aesthetics further argue that a performance should be considered both an art event and a work of art in its own right (Davies, 2011; Fischer-Lichte, 2008).

As a result of these transformations, live performances have gradually become more process oriented and more focused on interactions between actors and audiences, opening room for understanding the performing arts through the prism of wider social, cultural, and political processes (Fischer-Lichte, 2008). Erika Fischer-Lichte, for example, argues that, since the 1990s, the boundaries between theatrical and nontheatrical performances (festivals, amateur theater, street performance, political campaigns, fundraising events, and other types of community organizing) are merging. She calls this process "aestheticization and theatricalization of all types of performances" (Fischer-Lichte, 2008, p. 196). Her thesis essentially implies that performance aesthetics becomes an integral part of community life.

Moreover, there is an increasing recognition of a more networked nature of the music and performing arts production process. For example, Godlovitch defines a musical performance as "complex networks of relations linking together musicians, musical activities, works, listeners, and performance communities" (Godlovitch, 1998, p. 1). In this context, performers, listeners, and performance communities all become parts of the music and performing arts network, thus forming a community-level ecosystem that includes both arts and nonarts actors. All these evolutionary trends reflect the unique institutional niche that music and performing arts organizations occupy and that contributes to the sector's distinctiveness.

**Promoting and cultivating socially important values.** Over the course of their history, music and performing arts organizations, regardless of their institutional structure, have all shifted to some extent toward a more community-oriented model and positioned themselves as important civic institutions that are aware of and capable of responding to the issues and agendas that concern their local and global communities. An important way through which organizations support societal agendas is by cultivating and promoting socially important values (Table 4.2).

There are examples of organizations that have gone so far as to adopt a social mission and internalize local issues that their communities deal with as part of their core organizational goals. One such example is the Matrix Theatre—a Detroit-based youth theater whose mission is to build community, improve lives, and foster social justice by teaching, creating, and sharing theater as an instrument of social transformation. To that end, Matrix Theatre aspires to "create outstanding, affordable, and inclusive professional and educational theatre that addresses issues of community concern" (MatrixTheatre.com). Subsequently, many Matrix Theatre productions are focused on issues such as quality of environment, access to clean water, and matters of social justice.

More conventional performing arts organizations do not necessarily pursue community agendas as part of their core missions; however, they promote important values via their performances and community-based programming. By widening their audiences, initiating more extensive public outreach programs, and partnering with other organizations (such as public schools and social and human service organizations), music and performing arts organizations promote a sense of community and social bonding. The role of music and performing arts in forming a shared sense of community is part of their historical legacy, when performances of mixed repertoires were produced for mixed audiences, and people of various walks of life were gathered in the same spaces (Bayer, 2011). Hence, in a way, the increasing emphasis on promoting a sense of community and social bonding reflects earlier developments that persist today in more deliberate and systematic ways.

Modern-day music and performing arts organizations can be powerful actors in activating overall civic life in their local communities, as stronger engagement with the arts results in higher levels of social capital, and stronger, more attractive, and vibrant communities overall. Therefore, directly engaging one's community and fostering a sense of social bonding becomes an integral part of organizational goals, further supporting the symbiosis between organizations and communities, as expressed by the CEOs of a performing arts center and a dance organization:

> People who engage in the arts also tend to engage in more social capital, and we like that . . . So we are not just doing something aesthetic. We really want to have people engaged in the community; we love the fact that we could be some type of leverage, a motivator that encourages people to participate in the community, participate in the arts, and participate in the [organization], that it is all synthesized together. We just really love being in that role. (Personal Communication, 2012)

> The arts generally and this company specifically have a very important role in the advancement of a community and making this place an interesting and consistently new place to be . . . I think the arts really define cities as communities, where people are communities . . . (Personal Communication, 2012)

Aside from performing these important civic functions, live music and performing arts organizations offer powerful experiences that evoke inspiration and strong emotional appeal. Such a distinct impact of the performing arts is based on their aesthetics—in particular, the unique ability of the live performing arts to evoke strong emotions. These emotions are enhanced due to the effect of the interaction between performers and their audiences, and they facilitate a personal connection to the arts. Such strong emotional appeal is also likely to have a lasting psychological impact, and it tends to be more immediate and more intense by virtue of engaging multiple senses at once. (While looking at a thought-provoking painting and reading a critical novel may influence a particular museum visitor or a book reader, attending a music or a performing arts event is more likely to affect many people at once.) As explained by the CEOs of a music organization and university-based theater, these qualities of live performances are not easily substitutable by other kinds of experience:

> Well, we believe that great music is something that has almost a spiritual component that touches people; it refreshes them, and it enriches the quality of their life. And this is borne out by the reactions that are replayed to us by our audience . . . We work hard to deliver what we promised to people, so that they walk away feeling enriched personally by hearing some of the greatest works of art that man has ever created. (Personal Communication, 2012)

> The biggest thing for me is the value of live performance; that there is something that happens when the performer and the audience are in the same room and in the same physical space. It cannot be replicated by what Bill Gates or Steve Jobs will create; they will never be able to replicate that experience. We try to inculcate a sense of how exciting that can be . . . As a classical theater, we consider our work language-based, so [we foster] an appreciation for the power of language and that words have power that cannot be reduced to 140 characters, an appreciation for a more expansive view of how language works in communication than what it gets reduced to on Twitter. (Personal Communication, 2011)

Aside from an emotional appeal, engagement with music and performing arts can have educational value by modeling a long-term commitment to excellence. To be a successful performer—whether a musician or a dancer—one needs to invest a lot of time, energy, and persistence in, and personal dedication to, this occupation. One must practice with determination on a regular (and even everyday) basis. This type of commitment to excellence has value outside of the domain of the arts and humanities, and it carries certain standards and moral lessons with it. For example, when young people look at performing artists as role models, they may pick up their dedication and work habits and adopt them in their own approach to pursuing life goals. The CEO of a ballet company reflects on these community-level effects in the following way:

> Well, first of all, the arts generically are about the pursuit of perfection through the commitment to excellence, the pursuit of perfection through excellence. And I think that's a benefit to any community to have organizations—whether they are businesses, whether they are nonprofit, whether they are individuals, whether they are arts organizations—who are residents in the community, and who value excellence above all else. At the [organization] we have first of all a category of dancers who have committed their lives to the pursuit of perfection through the attainment of excellence. (Personal Communication, 2012)

The commitment to excellence is a crucial part of any area of the performing arts, since the acquisition of high-level artistic skills requires not only talent but also everyday hard work, discipline and persistence, creativity, and the ability to overcome challenges. Being a painter or a writer requires persistence as well; however, no other kind of art requires as much regular training as music and performing arts do. The commitment to excellence, as a virtue and a moral attitude, has broader implications for sustainability, since truly sustainable practices—whether in the arts or other social domains—also require commitment, dedication, and persistence.

These values that music and performing arts promote in their communities enhance the prospects of forming lasting connections between organizations, performers, patrons, and the community at large, which is beneficial for both organizations and their communities. Some organizations, for example, specifically recruit talented people with certain psychological attributes, as those would make for the best performers and musicians. There is also a realization that many of those artists will reside in their local communities, modeling these types of attitudes and traits from the stage to life. Managers of a dance organization explain how they target young people who have the right attitudes, personality traits, and leadership qualities, with the understanding that they will likely make a lasting impact on their community:

> I work with high-school kids. Inner-city high-school kids are a smaller program because it's more intense. And I will work with one or two high schools with their staff and identify prob-ably 12 to 15—maybe as many as 20—upper-level upper-grade students in what I call Project X: Project Exposure to the Arts. And what I'm looking for are high achievers because I'm seeing those are good candidates for future leaders in our community. Most likely they are going to stay in our community. And I want them to know about the arts. I want them to know this is something that they can do and participate in before, you know, it is too late for them to start on a professional dance track. (Personal Communication, 2012)

> Very few of our students will become professional ballet dancers because it is a highly demanding art form, and only one percent of any community becomes a serious professional classical-ballet dancer. But, in the process of committing themselves to the aspect of training, . . . they are beginning to understand commitment, they are beginning to understand creativity, they are beginning to understand teamwork, they are beginning to understand discipline, they are beginning to understand the importance of being on time. These are things that any employer would want very much to have within their organization, so we are basically in the work of building good citizens. (Personal Communication, 2012)

These individual-level values are foundational to the intergenerational sustainability of music and performing arts organizations because people are likely to practice these values and attitudes acquired through the artistic experience in their lives and transmit them to future generations. Such values and moral attitudes ensure a bonding connection between an individual and the arts, which creates lasting relationships.

**Shifting toward the semi-instrumental role.** The transformation of a classic music and performing arts organization into a community-oriented institution is related to another important element of the institutional distinctiveness narrative—shifting toward the semi-instrumental role. Such a shift is a form of mission broadening where arts and humanities organizations aim to engage with a variety of societal discourses in which art can be used as a powerful force for facilitating, inspiring, and moving societal agendas forward (Moldavanova, 2013, 2014). The engagement of music and performing arts organizations in the semi-instrumental role is important for local sustainable development, and it also contributes to the sustainability of the organizations themselves, as it capitalizes on the uniqueness of the sector and justifies its importance for society.

There are many examples illustrating music and performing arts' involvement in various societal agendas, public policies, and long-term community development initiatives (Causey, 2006; Higgins, 2012; McCarthy et al., 2001; Ramnarine, 2013). Music, for example, has been recognized as a universal language of cross-cultural communication that is capable of bringing down cultural barriers and stimulating intercultural learning and exchange (Higgins, 2012). When the issue of poverty became part of the global political agenda in the 1990s, music was used as a vital element in campaigns against poverty, organized by civic alliances between trade unions, nongovernmental organizations, and youth movements (Higgins, 2012; Ramnarine, 2011). Likewise, since the mid-1990s, music and performing arts organizations joined the environmental discourse, and there are numerous examples of using music and other performing arts to foster so-called ecological thinking (Ramnarine, 2013).

Contemporary music and performing arts organizations have also been actively engaged in social justice discourses. For example, following a series of national protests in the United States against police brutality and injustice after the arrest and killing of George Floyd, a 46-year-old Black man, in Minneapolis, Minnesota, in spring 2020 many arts organizations published statements condemning such violence, and some also created powerful artwork to raise social awareness of these issues. By engaging in these activities, arts organizations showed that they are active contributors to the social justice discourse.

An increasing number of music and performing arts organizations are also using the transformative power of music and performing arts to influence people's behavior and transform their lives. These types of programs often focus on marginalized and disadvantaged populations who may fall through the cracks of mainstream public policy initiatives, and thus they represent an important form of advocacy by arts organizations on behalf of such groups. One example of such a program is a theater-education partnership between the youth theater in suburban Detroit: All the World's A Stage and Macomb County Juvenile Justice Center. The program was designed for 14- to 17-year-olds who have been placed in the county detention program designed to provide a short-term, highly secure, and structured setting for youth who have come into contact with the court and require temporary removal from the community. The specific goal of the theater-based intervention was to influence attitudes and behaviors. While the program was initially met with skepticism, in the end, many of its participants experienced transformational thinking, as described by the representative of the theater:

> I said, "Today I'm going to introduce you to theater," and I'm getting guys like this: "Yeah, I ain't doing that crap"—and they weren't saying *crap*; they just, you know . . . So, we did theater; I introduced them to theater games. When we got done, I said to them, "How'd you guys like it?" And they said, "Eh, it was all right," which means "We loved it." They just weren't going to give you that satisfaction. I said, "Okay, now I have a question for you. We played four theater games; you guys cheated at every game we played. I'd say, 'These are the rules.' You all tried to figure out a way to circumvent the rules. So, answer me this. Why do people cheat?" Now it's not about theater. Now it's about life choices. Why do people cheat when nothing is on the line? "I could see, if I said the winner of each game gets $500—and, to be honest with you, if I was playing, I'd think of cheating too. So, don't think you think of cheating 'cause you are criminals. We all think of cheating. What separates us is we say, 'No, it's not the right thing to do,' but we all have that same basic thought because we're human. It's what we do with the thought. So why do you cheat?" One kid says, "Because we're scam artists." I said, "Okay, thank you for being honest." (Personal Communication, 2015)

As this example shows, bringing in an artistic experience, as opposed to engaging in traditional classroom instruction, stimulates critical thinking and makes participants more open to alternative behaviors. Another example of a program developed specifically for a marginalized population is the Detroit Public Theatre's signature community program "Shakespeare in Prison" (Dickson, 2020). The program seeks to empower incarcerated and formerly incarcerated people and helps them reconnect with their community by reflecting on their past, present, and future, while improving confidence, self-esteem, and other important attributes needed for recovery and subsequent social integration. The program's outcomes thus far have shown that its participants experience empowerment and transformational change that prevents recidivism and facilitates their positive community impact upon returning from prison.

The semi-instrumental role is often pursued in the broader context of public outreach, and it often involves partnering with other actors outside of the arts and humanities domain. One such example is the project that the Colorado Shakespeare Festival runs in collaboration with the Center for the Study and Prevention of Violence at Colorado University and the Boulder public school system. This project aims at the eradication of violence in public schools. In this project, after the performance of *Twelfth Night* at a public school, students participate in classroom workshops that focus on bullying. Through the exploration of the character Malvolio in the story, the festival actors encourage students to develop and enact alternatives to bullying. This program aspires to achieve important societal outcomes by impacting young generations and shaping their behavior via literature and performing arts. The program also represents an investment in more sustainable communities that is likely to benefit cultural organizations themselves.

All these examples demonstrate that music and performing arts organizations can be powerful agents for social change and supporters of positive individual and social transformations. They shape societal values and contribute to communities in many ways that exceed economic or artistic benefits, strengthening their communities from within while investing in the sustainability capital of their own organizations.

**Uniqueness of arts-based education.** Public education is important for all arts organizations, and, while museums and literature organizations rely on public education as a way to communicate with the public and as a pro-active audience-development tool, the educational function for music and performing arts organizations is part of both the art production process (recruiting new dancers, actors, musicians) and the art delivery process (communicating art to the public and developing art audiences). While visual artworks and books can be read in perpetuity, music and performing arts productions are experiences of the present, and organizations producing them need to work constantly on cultivating both their productive force and the audience. Therefore, as compared to the other arts and humanities, music and performing arts organizations have the longest and the strongest tradition of formalized public education, and their public education function tends to gain greater institutional support and be more developed and comprehensive than that of the other organizational types.

Music and performing arts organizations spend a great deal of time and effort developing large-scale outreach programs for the various segments of the population, but especially for young people. Additionally, there is a good number of related organizations in the private sector that provide independent arts education to youth as an after-school activity, and some of these organizations are run by musicians and performers themselves. Those organizations (e.g., dance studios, community youth theaters, chorales, music instrument schools, etc.) are also more numerous than writing, book, and poetry clubs or painting studios. They form a wholesome ecosystem in local communities that "feeds" into classical music and performing arts education.

Capitalizing on the strengths of their educational function, music and performing arts organizations implement a wide range of innovative outreach programs. One such example is the utilization of the idea of physical knowledge, or physical sensation, by engaging in an arts activity alongside performers or by having contact with an instrument. An example of this type of engagement would be the so-called Instrument Petting Zoos, which have become popular across the nation and are organized inside music halls and at special events, such as First Friday of the Month art walks, and in less common places, such as weekend farmers' markets. The idea is that musicians allow the lay public—both young people and adults who have no prior experience of playing an instrument—to touch an instrument and try making a sound. Public response to such initiatives has been fascinating: people overcome their fears and play an instrument for the first time in their lives, which shapes their perception of a performance by making it more personal and thus increasing the prospects of their engagement. The education director of a university-affiliated performing arts center describes the value of such experiences by making a sports analogy:

A lot of people looked at sports . . . almost everybody has some sport that they kind of like, or they might watch, or they might want to play or participate in . . . And, actually, some people realized that, when you participate in sports, you're building a physical knowledge as well a mental and emotional knowledge . . . So, when I'm watching football and the receiver goes out for the pass and makes a really great catch, you physically know what that feels like, right? And it just adds another element to that, and you want to experience that again because you experienced it when you were younger or whatever. If you've never held a violin in your hands, you don't know—you might like the music, but it still doesn't resonate the same way as if you have held the violin in your hand and played it, and felt that vibration in your body. The experience is a little bit deeper. It's more personal, and it resonates with you on a lot of different levels. It's not just hearing, there's an actual physical connection to the work. If you've experienced it, there is a deeper connection to what's happening on the stage. (Personal Communication, 2012)

These community-engaged activities are based on the uniqueness of the arts-based educational experience as compared to traditional classroom instruction. As noted above, arts-based experiences are capable of shaping individual attitudes and societal values, but they also have value in and of themselves. By virtue of engaging multiple senses and brain centers, arts-based education activates overall creativity, facilitates critical thinking, and allows us to see daily life in different ways. As reflected upon by the composer and art management consultant, art allows seeing life as it is, stripped of the daily distractions that obscure its essence:

I have a strong belief that these high superstar performances will exist always because people have the desire to be impressed by superstars, but, on the other hand, there is a different desire for people to be more active, more involved. Because of our electronic-media life, we have a feeling that we are able to know everything in the world, but, in fact, we are not well-informed. It is kind of information trash what we have, it is like a super trash, and it does not mean that we are informed.

It means really nothing if there is no analysis, if you do not have background information. So, there is a growing desire in people to create something that is unique, and which cannot be replaced easily. And to listen to the original . . . if you play it on stage—you cannot manipulate it; this is reality. And this is an interesting situation today that the reality on stage becomes more real than the reality of our daily life. We don't know what is being told us, because everything could be manipulated in media . . . The reality of our daily life gets more fragile; at the same time, the reality on [stage] gets more real because people see that it is not only the decoration of daily life. (Personal Communication, 2012)

Engagement with the arts offers nonartists an opportunity to reflect on the nature of the human condition. In this sense, a performance—whether it is a musical concert, a theater play, or a ballet—carries intrinsic value, and organizations that produce and promote this kind of value are likely to build lasting relationships with their audiences and sustain their organizations in the long run. A powerful way to communicate such value is to capitalize on the distinctiveness of arts-based education by reaching out to and cultivating the interest of younger generations, which further strengthens intergenerational sustainability of the sector and its organizations.

## Balancing the Resilience and Distinctiveness Narratives for the Long-Term Sustainability of the Music and Performing Arts: Evolving Managerial Roles

While both the institutional resilience and the institutional distinctiveness narratives carry their own independent value, it is the appropriate balancing between them that produces a sustainable organization. The act of balancing itself implies the presence of both structural and cultural organizational factors, but it typically occurs through the day-to-day engagement of the arts and culture managers in a special kind of logic—sustainable thinking and sustainable acting—which ensures that organizations thrive through hard times by translating challenges into opportunities while also steward-ing institutional missions and community values. Sustainable thinking is a future-oriented logic grounded in professional judgment and managerial intuition, and it capitalizes on the ever-evolving roles of organizational managers in the sector (Table 4.2).

Managers of music and performing arts organizations are responsible for an array of functions, ranging from their involvement in developing the repertoire and recruiting professional artists to fundraising and managing finances, maintaining productive relationships with the boards, promoting their organizations, coordinating public outreach and education, and dealing with day-to-day organizational routines (Stein & Bathurst, 2008). Music and performing arts managers wear multiple hats, and, while their official job descriptions have remained fairly stable, the vision of their broader role in supporting long-term sustainability of their organizations has been evolving to reflect an increasing need for institutional adaptation and greater engagement of organizations in community affairs. Specific managerial roles reflecting such evolution include manager as connector who deepens relationships with local communities; manager as facilitator of arts-inspired communication, conversation, and debate; and management as adaptation, which involves willingness to take risks, constantly learn, and adapt.

The first role, manager as connector, implies that managers of music and performing arts organizations envision themselves as connectors between their institution and other elements of their social, economic, and cultural ecosystem. Building relationships with their communities becomes one of the major priorities for managers of sustainable music and performing arts organizations, and this role tops the significance of stewardship, which is important in the museum and literature fields. The manager-as-connector role involves building relationships with four major groups of stakeholders: donors, partners, audiences, and the community at large (including future generations). This role, however, can also apply to internal organizational operations, where managers are seen as leaders who build relationships with their subordinates and colleagues, create shared understanding, and guide organizations toward a common goal.

The symbiotic connectedness between music and performing arts organizations and their communities is the main reason why emphasis on relationship building is such a vital managerial role. Those managers who are unable to establish productive relationships between their institution and the community at large may put their organizations on an unsustainable path by creating a sense of isolation and failing to achieve social and community relevance. As expressed by the CEOs of music and dance organizations, the ability of managers to develop relationships with communities has even more important bearing on organizational sustainability than standard managerial duties:

> In terms of sustainability, the success of any performing arts organization is contingent upon building relationships with audience, with donors, and with the larger community . . . You cannot teach good judgment; you can teach techniques; as I look at people in the field, you got a lot of very smart people, very sincere, who are struggling because their communities are not behind what they are doing. I think it is imperative—no matter how well trained someone is, how many degrees you have been through in arts administration—if your community does not fully support you, it will be nearly impossible to succeed. So, I would encourage whoever goes in[to] this business to first step back and make sure that the goals of the organization are as aligned as they can possibly be with the desires and objectives of the community in which they reside. (Personal Communication, 2012)

> Managers now have a much larger role in the community, and, when managers and artistic directors are partners, both have an obligation to the community; we have to be part of the political construct; we have to be part of the social fabric; we have to be part of the artistic fabric; we have to engage audiences; we have to engage in schools. There is a whole panorama of obligations and responsibilities that you have to be investing in. You can't just sit at the desk and try to raise money or try and manage the organization—you have got to be a face of the company, have got to be out there in the community. I don't think that has always been the case, I think sometimes the managers were considered back-room people who just dealt with numbers. (Personal Communication, 2012)

Stronger relationships with local communities allow organizations to serve audiences that are "greater in every sense: greater in enthusiasm, greater in size, greater in diversity, greater in socio-economic level" (Personal Communication, 2012) and that keep organizations "very relevant to this community" by making a particular community "distinctive and recognizable in other communities as well" (Personal Communication, 2012). Being able to achieve these goals means looking at management not "as a commerce transaction but as a relationship transaction" (Personal Communication, 2012). It means knowing one's community—its needs—and matching this knowledge with organizational goals. The CEOs of a university performing arts center and a nonprofit music organization describe this role and its unique importance for their sector in the following ways:

> I see art as a relationship; if I am the creator of the work, then what I am trying to create, communicate, say, is the story or the theme that is personal. That changes from production to production, but, as artists, we choose our productions and our topics based on what appeals to us inside . . . I personally see myself as a connector—you know, I mean, connecting what? Connecting person to person, connecting person to art, and connecting artist to artist. I try to be a translator and a little bit of a cheerleader and certainly a supporter. (Personal Communication, 2012)

> Every community is different, and we have had orchestras going out of business that otherwise should have been supported, and this includes Syracuse and New Mexico Symphony and Florida Philharmonic, and the Honolulu Symphony. Some have been resurrected in some fashion—hard to say whether they will continue . . . Aligning the objectives of the institution and the objectives of the community, and finding ways to create connections is essential . . . finding different ways in which to make themselves indispensable in their community, they need to come up with the role that makes it such that the community cannot imagine going on without an orchestra, and that requires the alignment of the goals of the orchestra with the larger goals of the community. (Personal Communication, 2012)

To be sure, finding proper alignment between organizational and community goals is not the sole responsibility of organizational CEOs; board members are also critically important in fostering community connectedness. For music and performing arts organizations that are sustained via audiences and artists, building relationships with communities is a necessary element of their sustainable management model. Such strong emphasis on relationships in the world of music and performing arts, particularly live arts, results not only from the fact that such organizations work with a mass audience but also because the majority of them are nonprofit corporations, which in and of itself brings their missions closer to the community (Frumkin, 2009).

The next important managerial function is management as facilitation, which is about the ability to use art as a way to stimulate communication, conversation, and debate. This managerial role is the reflection of the semi-instrumental role that arts organizations increasingly play and their ability to contribute to societal discourses outside of the domain of the arts and humanities. The purpose of management as facilitation, however, is not to simply transmit and replicate ideas; it is rather to stimulate conversation and debate about art, society, and the relationships between them. Such conversation, while spiked by artistic experiences, can lead to a broader discussion of human nature and the world, and it is important for the managers of music and performing arts organizations to be able to serve as catalysts of such a discussion. Managerial ability to tell a story and communicate through the arts is of critical importance for organizational sustainability, as reflected by the manager of a university-based music organization and a composer and cultural management consultant:

> [It's about] the story-telling, the brand and story that you have, and what is the richness and the humanity of what you do that you can talk about to connect people. Who are the people involved? What is unique about it? What is the history of the people on stage? What are the personal values of the conductors and musicians? What are the human things that the person can relate to? (Personal Communication, 2012)

> Well, managers have to communicate the subject, so people get interested in this. They have a message to tell, and they must be able to attract the people to listen to this message. It is getting more and more important not only to have very professional performances at a high artistic level, but also to communicate with people, transfer messages to people, to deliver this information to many people in different ways. (Personal Communication, 2012)

The third important managerial role, which is shared with the other arts and humanities, is management as adaptation. Management as adaptation is the key role in enacting the institutional resilience narrative, as it reflects an adaptive kind of thinking. While management as adaptation is important for both university-affiliated and freestanding organizations, institutional structure tends to mediate managerial choices for particular adaptive strategies. Being sensitive to such structural factors is, therefore, very important to managers. At an individual level, management as adaptation includes such elements as flexibility, willingness to take risks, and ability to constantly learn. It allows managers to transform the challenges and instabilities of their external environments into opportunities for organizational growth and development. The CEOs of a university-affiliated performing arts organization and a nonprofit music organization reflect how risk tolerance and adaptive qualities have become more important today than ever:

> The biggest thing about being a manager, going forward, that is different than before is being comfortable with being flexible. If you look at generations before, it's like . . . these are big scary things . . . Our creative campus grant, when we did that project, we heard so many of our colleagues saying they had to do so many—342 experiences before they had the successful one. Failure is more a part of life than winning. But you only remember the wins, so you have to never lose sight that the win is there, and you are always moving forward. You are learning something every time. It gets you a little closer every time, and so we talk a lot in our field now about risk management and assessing your comfort level with risk. I think risk management, and flexibility, and adaptability are essential . . . It is scary to risk, but you know that's life. (Personal Communication, 2012)

> Trying to do new and interesting opera but being sensitive to your audience. It is all of those things and it is constantly balancing everything and always being very open to changes and opportunities. The world of opera does change, and you have to be flexible to change with it. (Personal Communication, 2012)

The art of adaptation, however, does not always mean committing oneself to new modus operandi; it rather implies responding to the growing needs of society and more diverse audiences while also staying true to the mission. The key to a successful adaptation, therefore, is to keep a balance between organizational core missions and their strategic responses to the popular demand for artistic experimentation and innovation. In this regard, a manager who is acting sustainably is engaging in the balancing act aimed at reconciling these possible tensions.

## Concluding Thoughts

Long-term sustainability of music and performing arts organizations lies in their ability to establish a sense of connectedness and symbiotic relationships with their multiple publics—philanthropists and other donors; actors, musicians, dancers, and other performers; audiences; partner organizations—but, above all, with their local communities. Contemporary music and performing arts organizations are connected with their communities in a multiplicity of ways, including by their engagement in partnerships with other community organizations, their participation in socially important projects, and their important intrinsic and instrumental contributions to their communities. The larger the web of organizational relationships is, the better overall organizational social connectedness is, and the better the chances are that each element of the web is restorable, renewable, or substitutable. When some funding sources are in decline, organizations can resort to alternatives; when the audience shrinks, they are finding new and innovative ways to develop it; when there is an important societal matter on the horizon, they can work in partnership with other community actors to tackle it. Sustainable music and performing arts organizations, therefore, constantly work to build and sustain the web of their relationships.

Historically, the institution of private patronage was critical to the establishment of the professional music and performing arts sector in the United States, and it has been important for sustaining it throughout hard times. Furthermore, the introduction of the nonprofit business model in the 20th century had increased the number and variety of music and performing arts organizations and offered multiple tools to their managers for seeking greater financial sustainability. Moreover, partially because of the nonprofit model and partially as a matter of deliberate organizational strategies, modern-day music and performing arts organizations found themselves embedded in a web of social connections within their local communities. The very nature of the music and performing arts aesthetics has also been conducive to opening the doors to mass audiences and welcoming people from various walks of life. As a result of the sectoral distinctiveness, many music and performing arts organizations became accessible to wider audiences earlier than museums, which first existed as private collections, or literature that was accessible only to those who knew how to read.

Contemporary music and performing arts organizations no longer limit their missions to offering high-quality arts experiences; rather, they increasingly emphasize their civic roles and perform important normative functions in their communities by cultivating and implementing the ethic of sustainability through their organizational practices. Many also engage in socially responsible behavior and commit themselves to advancing the values of social equity, access, diversity, and inclusion. This brings music and performing arts institutions back to their core purpose and ensures that they serve the public interest in ways that remain distinct from the corporate business world.

After the separation between commercial and nonprofit institutional forms, music and performing arts organizations shifted from the mixed repertoire, with highbrow art being presented by nonprofits while more popular forms of entertainment were offered by commercial organizations. However, over time, as part of their institutional adaptation, both types of organizations started experimenting with mixed-art forms, and, regardless of their legal status, have directed substantial efforts to public outreach and audience development. The history of the sector in and of itself, therefore, serves as an example of institutional adaptation toward greater sustainability. The choice of adaptive strategies, however, is mediated by institutional structure. For example, university-based organizations take advantage of the extra-institutional protection provided by universities, as well as the web of internal connections, innovative ideas, and multiple opportunities available to collaborate with different university departments. On the other hand, nonprofit organizations enjoy greater flexibility and managerial autonomy; they can take advantage of a greater funding diversity, and usually have stronger connections with their communities.

At the end of the day, sustainable organizations result from balancing core institutional missions with the wide array of resilience-seeking strategies. Managers of music and performing arts organizations play a key role in the balancing process. Of particular importance is their ability to make sense of the intra- and extra-institutional environments and make decisions in the best interests of organizations and their communities, including both current and future publics. Prominent managerial roles associated with long-term sustainability include management as connection, which focuses on building symbiotic relationships with the community; management as facilitation of arts-inspired communication, conversation, and debate; and management as adaptation, which is associated with adopting a managerial style that is based on flexibility, adaptability, and risk taking. Managers of music and performing arts organizations are also accustomed to think about future generations as part of their decision-making. The moral obligation to future generations is embedded in their institutionalized and well-developed public outreach function, as well as through the recognition of the lasting intrinsic impacts of arts-based education on diverse audiences and communities.

Chapter 5

# Sustainable Thinking

## Lessons from the Arts and Humanities

This book makes the case for the importance of culture and cultural institutions as the fourth pillar of sustainable development, which complements the already well-established recognition of the environmental, economic, and sociopolitical pillars of sustainability (Adams, 2006; Dale, 2001; Edwards & Onyx, 2007; Fiorino, 2010; Nurse, 2006; Wang, Hawkins, Lebredo, & Berman, 2012; Stazyk, Moldavanova, & Frederickson, 2016). The book specifically elevates the importance of organizational thinking about sustainability by arguing that organizations are an important albeit often overlooked level of sustainability. Yet sustainability as an institutional logic unfolds in organizations, and it is enacted by managers who make decisions and engage in sustainable thinking on a daily basis, leading them to reconcile current organizational realities and the need to adapt to those realities with considerations of the interests and needs of future generations.

To this end, the book unpacks the idea of sustainability in a systematic way as an internal organizational logic pursued by a variety of organizational types (university-affiliated and freestanding) and in a variety of cultural subfields—museums, literature, and music and performing arts—thus arguing that principles and practices of internally sustainable management resonate with organizational external outcomes and enable cultural organizations to foster sustainability in their communities. Although the words "stability" and "maintenance" are not antithetical to sustainability, this book shows that organizational sustainability is more about active adaptation and change than it is about remaining in the same place for generations. Organizational and managerial discourses analyzed here, as well and numerous examples of organizational programs and practices aimed at sustainability, ultimately show that sustainable organizations are capable of achieving balance.

Arts and culture organizations engage in all sorts of balancing acts, such as balancing the artistic and the management sides of an organization, balancing internal capacity-building efforts with external outreach, balancing considerations of efficiency and effectiveness with equity, balancing decisions aimed at survival with long-term organizational sustainability considerations, and more. There are also field-specific balancing considerations that emerged for the various arts and humanities examined in this book. For example, sustainable museums strive to balance the value of their buildings and collections with the importance of reaching the public outside of these buildings. Music and performing arts organizations strive to balance the value of live performances with the use of online broadcasting technology to enable wider access. Literature organizations strive to balance their increasingly global reach with timeless relevance and deeper connectedness with local communities.

The most important balancing is, however, between the two narratives of intergenerational sustainability—institutional resilience and institutional distinctiveness. Specific organizational strategies aligned with both narratives strengthen institutional capital for sustainability, which is a critical resource organizations can lean on in the long term; however, there is often tension among those strategies. This book unpacks how the tension is mitigated and balance is achieved, as well as what role particular institutional structures, evolving missions, and managerial functions play in supporting intergenerational sustainability. It concludes that sustainable organizational management has both structural and cultural aspects, and such management often requires appropriate modification to both of these organizational layers affecting organizational daily functioning and relationships with the external environment.

These types of modifications can be challenging, especially when it comes to deeply ingrained organizational cultural assumptions. Yet, change is often inevitable, and the only choice that organizations may have is to embrace and accept change or else become irrelevant. In the arts and humanities field, adaptive organizational changes often result in hybrids that combine elements of diverse structural solutions with diverse cultural assumptions. These types of adaptations also often involve borrowing strategies from other social sectors and adopting ideas grounded in diverse artistic forms, thus creating a more interdisciplinary and synergistic organizational set-up going forward. This logic applies to all organizational types (university-affiliated and freestanding) and cultural subfields (museums, literature, and music and performing arts) examined in this book.

The key to long-term organizational sustainability is the ability of managers to act sustainably by making wise, incremental decisions on a day-to-day basis, which is referred to here as sustainable thinking. This special kind of managerial rationality enables this balancing act and allows for reconciliation of tensions between the two sustainability narratives: institutional resilience and institutional distinctiveness. It implies that truly long-term sustainability, one that secures the rights of future generations, requires sustainable stewardship today. Sustainable thinking is exercised by organizations with various institutional structures; therefore, it is not a particular arrangement that matters the most; rather, what matters is how any arrangement could be leveraged to enhance sustainability.

This chapter provides the summary of, and a broader reflection upon, these insights and key lessons learned about organizational sustainability. It highlights the ecosystem view of sustainability that embraces the inherent interconnectedness between cultural organizations and their communities and discusses the commonalities and variations in sustainability strategies developed by the three types of arts and humanities institutions covered in this book. Another goal of this summative chapter is to provide an opportunity to reflect upon the idea of sustainable thinking and its meaning and value for organizations aspiring to be sustainable now and for generations to come. The chapter develops the idea of sustainable thinking and explains how it differs from a more conventional strategic management, by integrating ethical assumptions aligned with intergenerational sustainability into the management process. The chapter underscores the book's broader relevance and its contributions to developing the theory and ethic of intergenerational organizational sustainability.

## Stress is Bad for Organizations, but Good for Innovation and Sustainability

The first important, albeit somewhat surprising, lesson about organizational sustainability is the role that external stress plays in supporting sustainable organizational management. As this book shows, stress is not an antithesis to organizational sustainability; rather, it can serve as a driver for innovation that activates organizational defense mechanisms, much like immunization enhances the ability of human bodies to productively fight infections. External stress, likewise, activates both institutional resilience and institutional distinctiveness narratives by prompting organizational managers to engage in various strategies that elevate organizational adaptive potential and reshape its core assumptions, especially about the broader community and social relevance.

Environmental stress, therefore, plays a similar role in the ecology of the arts that it plays in natural systems that also seek to renew and rebuild under the influence of environmental fluctuations and shifts. Moreover, stress affects organizations of all ages, sizes, and types, and no organization is fully immune to its effects. Consistently with the assumptions of organizational ecology perspective (Carroll, 1984; Hannan, & Freeman, 1989), generalist types of organizations, such as multipurpose arts and major cultural nonprofits, tend to have greater flexibility in the face of external shocks. At the same time, many niche-like organizations are also capable of coping with stress by capitalizing on their distinctiveness or, as in the case of some university-affiliated organizations, by leaning back on their "parent" institutions. While too much stress can be detrimental to the arts and humanities organizations if they are unprepared or unwilling to adapt, a certain degree of stress is highly beneficial for preventing organizations from stagnation, and it helps them to learn and develop.

In the aftermath of the Great Recession, Detroit's cultural organizations, for example, faced a number of externally induced pressures: financial problems associated with the declining public and private support; audience-related pressures such as changing demand; access and accessibility issues; audience aging; capacity-building and infrastructure-maintenance pressures; and higher levels of competition for both funding and audiences with other actors. Many of the immediate pressures—including financial, audience-related, capacity-building, and competition pressures, coupled with the changing socioeconomic environment of local communities—were also among the longer-term challenges. In response to these shocks, many organizations fell back on the traditional management strategies for cutting costs: temporarily closing the organization or suspending core programs, cutting staff positions and reducing hours, cutting programs to offset revenue shortfalls, as well as implementing administrative downsizing and contracting out. These were the kinds of cost-saving strategies aimed at economizing the use of organizational resources, and they are an example of short-term strategizing.

Looking into the future, however, three sets of adaptive responses to stress have emerged as those through which managers sought to achieve longer-term sustainability: (1) business-like practices, such as greater emphasis on marketing and advertisement, revenue diversification, and capacity building; (2) engagement in innovation, which include such common forms of innovation as technological, communication, and programming; and (3) connectedness-type strategies, which include increasing reliance on partnerships and interorganizational networks. Unlike the short-term strategies that were primarily focused on economizing organizational resources, the medium- and longer-term strategies were more about expanding and enhancing overall organizational capital and creating a safety net for the generations to come.

Connectedness-type strategies, in particular, were seen as holding the greatest promise, as they were focused on enhancing organizational social capital, which can be transformed into various other forms of capital that an organization may lack. Such a strategy involves establishing connections with communities that had a low prior exposure to certain arts, as a way of recruiting new stakeholders and donors, addressing both financial and audience-related pressures, and building relationships with future generations of patrons. Pursuing connectedness-type strategies often required organizations to venture outside their regular performing and exhibiting spaces in order to establish physical presence in their communities. Strengthening public outreach programs and building public education departments' capacities was also seen as necessary for achieving greater social connectedness. Many organizations developed new partnerships within and outside of the cultural sector. Some of these partnerships could be described as strategic relationships, as they supplied organizations with access to critical resources and connections, helped to broaden their missions and audiences, and expanded their market niches. Overall, managers pursued one common goal via the connectedness strategies—to ensure that their organizations fully embedded themselves within their communities.

Engaging in adaptive learning and organizational change in response to environmental stress, however, is not a trivial task, and sometimes it takes a significant financial shock and a major recession to activate organizational adaptive potential. One such example of a major stressor is the COVID-19 pandemic that spread throughout the world in 2020. The lockdowns and quarantines affected multiple sectors of the economy—but arts and humanities organizations were affected by it more than many other social sectors were (AAM, 2022; IPA, 2020; Newhouse, 2020). The effects of the pandemic-induced disruptions were especially salient in those areas that typically rely on live interpersonal communications, such as, for example, music and performing arts organizations. Additionally, while some organizations benefited from the governmental relief funds, those funds were inaccessible to many in the publishing industry (IPA, 2020). Overall, few organizations were ready for this pandemic, but many managed to successfully adapt: for some, this pandemic—like any other stress—brought an opportunity to learn, innovate, and reconsider their conventional models.

Specific adaptive strategies in the face of the pandemic included incorporating online technologies, utilizing outdoor spaces, and shifting to a more community-based type of programming. These adaptations involved reconsidering organizational structural and cultural norms, forcing managers to rethink and reinvent both, which required a high degree of sustainable thinking and the need to keep future generations in mind while figuring out how organizations could survive and sustain. The COVID-19 pandemic has also underscored the importance of a balance between resilience-type strategies and the distinctiveness of a particular art form or a particular organization. Moreover, while some of the adaptive strategies broke existing conventions, in many cases, they were a matter of choosing between life and death, and organizations that pursued them benefitted both immediately and in the long term, making their programs more accessible, wider reaching, and more global.

If cultural managers have learned anything from the COVID-19 pandemic, it would be to expect the unexpected and be ready to handle it in the future. Thus, even drastic stressors can be beneficial for organizational sustainability and should, therefore, be embraced. Moreover, being attentive and cognizant of the broader societal shifts on a daily basis is critically important to a proactive type of adaptation that supports both immediate survival and long-term sustainability. This perpetual need to have a forward-looking adaptive mindset is critically important for the sustainability of arts and humanities organizations going forward.

## Organizational and Community Levels of Sustainability are Interlinked

Another important lesson that can be gleaned from this book is the ecosystem view of sustainability, where arts and humanities organizations are treated as integral parts of their communities. The ecosystem view recognizes the critically important roles that arts and humanities organizations play in their communities, including by advancing sustainable development through a variety of intrinsic and instrumental roles they engage with (Moldavanova, 2013, 2014; Moldavanova & Wright, 2020). Importantly, the ecosystem view of sustainability brings together two levels of sustainability: organizational and community.

First, arts and humanities organizations that are cognizant of their communities' needs and willing to broaden their missions beyond their intrinsic value are also the organizations that are more likely to survive in the long term. Sustainably managed cultural institutions are increasingly realizing that their main value is not about their great buildings and collections per se; rather, it is about what those tangible assets mean to their communities and how they may help to meet their communities' needs. Sustainable organizations embed community needs in their programs and activities, allowing them to build symbiotic relationships with their communities. Examples of specific symbiotic activities highlighted in this book range from such pragmatic strategies as engaging in various partnerships with other community actors to enabling broader access to the arts being a part of local economic development agendas, and contributing to social and environmental discourses. Organizations engaging in these types of actions act as cognizant and socially responsible actors willing to invest in their communities and advance the rights of both current and future generations.

Second, organizational sustainability depends on operational environment broadly defined. Arts and humanities organizations are interlinked with their external environments: there are areas where they tend to thrive and others where they do not. While local economic conditions create a baseline for the arts and humanities to flourish, environments in which arts and culture organizations tend to thrive are not always economically wealthy, but these are the environments where the arts are valued, and there is a sense of community ownership over cultural assets. The presence of cultural assets is even more vital in marginalized and low-income communities, as, often, even modestly funded local libraries, museums, and theaters are the only "safe havens" for many youths and adults in such communities. These communities are willing to exercise their sense of ownership and step in where an organization might be struggling and may need support, as they understand the value of their cultural assets and the importance of safeguarding those assets for future generations.

Therefore, to a certain extent, organizational sustainability is also a product of organizational environment, rather than the sole responsibility of its managers.

Recognizing these realities, sustainable arts and humanities organizations engage in a variety of strategies that enhance their social connectedness—a highly valuable form of organizational social capital that can be converted into a variety of other resources. To that end, managers of sustainable organizations alter their own management styles, to shift away from solely focusing on internal organizational operations towards focusing more on external relationships. They envision their institutions, as described by a museum director, as "a set of relationships, a constellation of people and ideas." (Personal Communication, 2013). As described by a manager of a community-based theater, organizational social connectedness that obtains from such an approach is key to long-term sustainability, "The long-term answer for [organization name], and for probably any community organization, is to become so deeply embedded in the culture that people can't conceive of their community without it." (Personal Communication, 2016). Moreover, aligning organizational and community values is seen as an important goal for managers who pursue this type of ecosystem approach, as described by the director of a university-affiliated museum: "We have gone from a kind of lone idea of leadership and management to understanding that we all are part of an ecology, and we are an ecology that is focused on values, beliefs, meaning, interpretation, social good, creating a better society—and that society then, now, has exploded. It's huge." (Personal Communication, 2012).

Sustainable organizations act as integral parts of their social ecology, and they rely on it to enhance mission fulfillment both now and in the longer term. For example, several Detroit-based organizations benefitted from being recognized as important actors in the local ecosystem. One example is the Detroit Institute of Arts; the DIA received $23 million in annual support for 10 years via the passage of the 2012 property-tax millage, which was approved by the majority of citizens in three counties in the Detroit metropolitan area. After the city of Detroit filed for bankruptcy, the DIA was also able to save its collections from creditors by capitalizing on its connections with foundations, private individuals, other cultural organizations, and citizen groups (Stryker, 2015). On the other hand, organizations that "fell out" of the ecosystem had near-death experiences. One example is the closure of the oldest continually operating public aquarium in the United States, the Belle Isle Aquarium. Originally established in 1904 in Detroit, the Aquarium closed its doors to the public in 2005, right before the onset of the financial recession (Boardman 2010). The Aquarium was reopened in 2012 by a dedicated group of volunteers, and today it is a much better-connected organization.

Overall, the ecosystem approach that bridges sustainability at organizational and community levels is supported via an overall sense of connectedness that exists within local communities, as well as between arts and humanities organizations and other community actors. It is about a healthy symbiosis between organizations and their communities as much as it is about the ability of organizations to adapt to the various environmental stressors that they face. The goal of these strategies is to embed cultural assets within broader social fabrics by instilling a sense of the cultural assets' importance for current generations, their children, and grandchildren.

## Sustainability Engages All Organizational Levels: Structure, Culture, Leadership

Another important lesson about organizational sustainability that can be gleaned from the examples in this book is that it affects all organizational facets, such as structure, culture, and leadership. Structure, in particular, is used by managers of sustainable organizations to effectively navigate external pressures and reinforce productive relationships with key stakeholders, and it can reinforce a particular adaptive path chosen by organizational managers. For example, the move toward greater institutionalization of the public outreach function observed across all the arts and humanities is an example of how structural solutions are sought to build up institutional capital for sustainability. Another example is the adoption of the various hybrid forms of structure, such as university affiliation combined with nonprofit status or nonprofit-like strategies adopted by university-affiliated organizations (e.g., the creation of a board of directors).

Structure, however, can also be a hindrance, for example, when comparing the strengths and weaknesses of university-affiliated and freestanding models of operation. Differently structured organizational types are not created equal: they operate differently, their relationships with communities are different, and they often see their future through different lenses. For example, university-affiliated institutions generally have less autonomy to develop their external connections, as they are dealing with multiple layers of the "parent" organization's bureaucracy and university's own policy priorities. Freestanding organizations, on the other hand, often do not have the baseline support that their university-affiliated counterparts often do, which is a disadvantage. Therefore, it is important to know about these structural factors and be able to navigate them. One way to do so would be to develop mitigating approaches and learn from the strategies that work well for organizations of different structural types. As an example, university-affiliated organizations may consider achieving a better balance between focusing on their internal stakeholder (the university itself) and investing in their external relations. Likewise, freestanding organizations should develop endowments and other forms of safety net, foreseeing future financial crises and recessions.

In addition to accounting for structure, managers should also be mindful of organizational cultural assumptions. Arguably, it is even more important to cultivate a culture of sustainability. As a reflection on the importance of cultural assumptions that support organizational sustainability, the director of a community-based theater makes an analogy with a church, where values, faith, and commitment of individual members, regardless of their financial abilities, is what carries an institution through time:

> A church has strengths that really allow it to exist. It has lots, and lots, and lots of interactions with people where people are giving regularly, giving a little bit of money, and it's very typical in this community, even where there is a great deal of poverty for people to go to the church and give money every week. It's built into the culture; it's built into the expectation of how one is supposed to function in a society . . . If we are able to build it into the very culture, then we will get there. (Personal Communication, 2016).

A culture of sustainability has two dimensions: an internal one that relates to how day-to-day decisions are being made without compromising organizational identity and its long-term prospects, and an external one that is about the degree to which organizations are willing to act and capable of acting as socially responsible institutions that care about both the short- and long-term impact that they make on sustainability in their communities (Table 5.1).

Table 5.1. Organizational Cultural Assumptions and Sustainability

| Internal Assumptions | Balancing operational decisions with organizational identify and intergenerational prospects | Examples:<br>• striving to be more up-to-date, being able to make a reference to our time and be relevant to current and future generations, while not deviating from the mission;<br>• adopting new digital technologies (e.g., digital collections, e-books, recording and broadcasting performances). |
|---|---|---|
| External Assumptions | Balancing operational decisions with care about organizational impact on sustainability in communities now and for the generations to come | Examples:<br>• embracing of the value of social equity and equal opportunity of access as a cornerstone of sustainable development, while being mindful of an organizational bottom line;<br>• achieving better cultural representation by diversifying organizational governance and staff. |

An example of the first type of cultural assumption that has been gaining prominence across the different arts and humanities is their focus on being more up-to-date, being able to make a reference to our time and be relevant to current and future generations. Many museums, literature, and music and performing arts organizations have realized that their short- and long-term survival depend upon their ability to find a common language with people from different generations. An example of the second type of assumption is the embracing of the value of social equity, defined as providing equal opportunity of access to the arts for various population groups and serves as a cornerstone of sustainable development. Many organizations in the arts and humanities field have embraced this value and adopted programmatic innovations aimed at reducing various access barriers for the populations whom they serve.

What this book discovers, however, is that the two levels of cultural assumption are related, and those organizations that commit themselves to improving broader viability and both short- and long-term sustainability of their local and global communities are also the organizations that are more likely to be managed sustainably internally. As part of their adaptation toward greater sustainability, arts and humanities organizations have taken on a course of transforming themselves into more socially responsible institutions that both build up their own institutional capital for sustainability and advance sustainability in their local and global communities. These changes foster organizations that are cognizant of their impact on future generations. This type of transformation in organizational cultural assumptions toward greater engagement of the arts and humanities in community sustainability has been growing in importance for all organizational types researched in this book.

## EVOLVING CULTURAL ASSUMPTIONS AND LEADERSHIP ROLES: INSIGHTS FROM THE DIFFERENT SUBFIELDS

When it comes to the differences among the cultural sub-fields, museums have been shifting their core institutional assumptions to accommodate a more egalitarian focus, and they have also been shifting from serving the humanities to a more interdisciplinary focus by plugging into various social discourses. Many classical museums are also dealing with the long history of elitism that still permeates their operations by diversifying their governing structures and staff. This helps to increase the representation of traditionally underrepresented cultures and points of view in their exhibitions and programs (Acevedo, & Madara, 2015; Olivares & Piatak, 2022; Sandell, & Nightingale, 2012). Museums are also increasingly positioning themselves as educational institutions, shifting away from the mere preservation of objects and moving toward the promotion of a connection between objects and social discourses that shape our current and future world. Museums have employed a number of structural solutions, such as audience-diversification initiatives and more extensive public outreach programs, further positioning themselves as catalysts for social change capable of spreading progressive ideas and sustainable logics. Establishing formal—public education departments and developing educational programs for all ages—but especially for young people, in particular—presents evidence of museums' commitment to future generations.

Music and performing arts organizations particularly stand out when it comes to the degree of embeddedness that they can establish within their communities. By providing high-quality performing arts experiences and expanding their public outreach programs, music and performing arts organizations promote a sense of community and social bonding. Furthermore, evolving institutional missions make it clear that the performing arts are attempting to form not just productive but symbiotic relationships with their communities, which translates into increased focus on audience development and on such values as access, diversity, and inclusion. The promotion of social equity has gained increasing prominence for the music and performing arts organizations as well, further capitalizing on the strengths of their public education function.

Likewise, literature organizations increasingly emphasize access and accessibility in their missions. Literature, as we know it today, is able to transcend the boundaries of time and space, and such inventions as the electronic format and the institution of literary translation make this property even more important. Furthermore, an increasing emphasis on the multiplicity of viewpoints and cultures, and the richness of human experiences, are all embedded in the evolving institutional missions of literature organizations. Literature has become a creative force for globalization and the engine for the transmission of cultural capital globally; it also serves as a language of communication between generations, transmitting human heritage from one generation to the next. The value impact of literature is embedded in its story-telling power. Through stories and narratives, literature organizations raise cultural awareness and foster creativity and openness to new ideas. Structurally, literature organizations are catching up with museums and music and performing arts organizations by establishing an institutionalized public education function that assures the integration of literature as an ongoing creative force in community development.

The third element that is as important as organizational structure and cultural assumptions is leadership. The ability of organizational managers to convey institutional missions to their stakeholders and the public at large, as well as connect organizational missions with the communities and their needs, defines whether organizations are going to succeed in their paths to sustainability or fail. To accommodate these various rationales, key roles of organizational managers have been evolving, and there are both differences and similarities in this regard among the arts and humanities. The traditional role of management as stewardship appears to be most prominent in museums and literature organizations. Museum managers increasingly view stewardship as the balance between preservation and sharing, with the greater emphasis placed on education and sharing with both local and global communities. Management as stewardship is the most prominent role for literature organizations as well; however, it is more prevalent in the world of print literature, where the book is viewed as a valuable art object. Stewardship is less prominent for electronic literature, where such themes as management as innovation and managing opportunities prevail. This is because, among all three subfields examined in this study, literature is the most dynamic industry, the one that relies most heavily on technological progress and market mechanisms. To ensure the long-term sustainability of their organizations, literature managers have to be innovative, adaptable, and able to take advantage of opportunities as they come along.

Managers of music and performing arts organizations, on the other hand, primarily view themselves as connectors to their communities, and management as building relationships with communities appears to be their most prominent managerial role. Among all organizational fields examined in this study, the sustainability of music and performing arts is most directly dependent upon the quality of their relationships with local communities. Performing art is a collective experience that relies on the symbiotic relationship between artists and audiences. Moreover, as generations pass, music and performing arts organizations are forced to constantly replace both their audiences and their productive force to a greater extent than other arts and humanities do. Furthermore, building relationships with the community is important for both chief executive officials and artistic directors.

Aside from the differences in the evolving managerial roles, there are also shared assumptions among the different arts and humanities. The most important shared assumption that supports organizational sustainability is the ability of managers to engage in sustainable thinking and sustainable action, as well as their deep commitment to future generations. This commitment serves as an underlying logic guiding both day-to-day and long-term decision-making in which managers engage in order to both carry their organizations through urgent storms and ensure continuous learning and adaptation going forward. Sustainable management is first and foremost ethical management that ensures that organizations will be socially responsible and internally cognizant, capable of considering their internal needs as well as external societal realities and the needs of the communities that they serve, and to include both current and future generations into these considerations.

## Organizational Sustainability Involves Various Tensions and Requires Balancing

When one thinks about the idea of sustainability, one often envisions harmony, stability, and durability. All these properties are not antithetical to the idea of organizational sustainability; however, the key idea that emerged in this book describes organizational sustainability as often a contradictory, rather than a harmonious, concept that requires various kinds of balancing. Some examples of balancing among the different aspects of organizational sustainability discussed in this book include balancing short- and long-term considerations, greater local relevance with more global outreach, quality of in-person experiences with greater accessibility that comes with online formats, emphasis on object preservation with knowledge sharing considerations, etc.

An example of a unique kind of balancing in the arts and humanities field are the tensions between the artistic and the management sides of an organization. These tensions stem from the fact that artistic directors tend to focus on artistic missions of their organizations and how to best deliver those missions; by contrast, managing directors or CEOs tend to focus on implementing strategies aimed at increasing organizational efficiency and competitive advantage as well as improving stakeholder relations. The tensions are exacerbated when organizations face increased levels of competition due to financial recessions and other exogenous factors. The CEO of an opera company reflects on these, often contradictory, dynamics in the following way:

> There are a number of things that are contradictory. I think, first of all, you need to be honest and true to the art form, and you want it to be as excellent and as good as possible. The challenge is to find a way to do that and still pay your bills. If you have year after year of deficits, if you are doing brilliant opera but you can't pay for it, eventually, you're not going to exist. So, you have to do really good opera, but do it in such a way that you can pay for it. I think there is a world of opera where we have to do certain basic repertoire, and it

is important to do opera that is less well known. There has to be a good balance . . . And you have to find the proper blend of these things. (Personal Communicaiton, 2012)

In a smaller organization, the same person often performs as both the artistic director and the managing director, which requires an internal balancing. In larger organizations, the balance between the management and artistic sides is ensured through the dual leadership structure, where the leadership is carried through the synchronized work of an executive director and an artistic director. In some ways, this is the resemblance of the city-government structure in U.S. cities, where elected and appointed officials are responsible for different sets of roles but with an overlap between political representation and effective administration. In this respect, some managers find the symbiosis between management and art to be a more sustainable approach, as reflected upon by the CEO of a nonprofit music organization:

There are some organizations where the artistic director simply says, "I am going to go forward with my vision, and it is simply everyone else's job to simply find the money, find the resources"—which is a very naïve and impractical approach to have, especially in this economy—and those companies tend to get into significant financial distress at some point because the money is being spent, and maybe it is being spent to further a high-quality previous product, maybe not. It doesn't always happen that way, but, if at some point resources are no longer available, the companies begin to have shortfalls in their annual budgets; the companies begin to accumulate deficit; the companies begin to have to cut back on expenses; and then all of a sudden, the organization itself becomes very quickly in distress. One of the things that has made this one a sustainable institution has been the ability of the executive leadership and artistic leadership to find common ground on how to ensure quality within the context of available resources. (Personal Communication, 2012)

Keeping the balance might not be an easy thing to do, especially when managers of the same institution come from different professional backgrounds. An artist who becomes an artistic director and a general manager who joins an organization have different styles, and finding common ground could be a serious challenge. Even at the discourse level, the language used by artists who are in management positions is very different from the language used by professionally trained managers. The first quotation describes how a person with an artistic background defines management, and the second quotation offers the definition from a professionally trained manager:

> The term "culture management" has two parts—one is culture, and one is management. How to attract sponsors and manage the structures are both important questions, but culture management means thinking very carefully what is your message, what is culture, what is the subject, which is different from selling chocolate or cars. This must be clear in your mind, so it is more philosophic . . . it is very hard to think how to warm the heart of the people. For instance, even finding a title for a cultural project is very important. And I would recommend to cultural managers, "Please do your work and study the economic part of management, but, then, please, take care and study very carefully what art means and what culture means . . . do it in a responsible way." (Personal Communication, 2012)

> Before I became the executive director, I was in a general manager position, and then in 2002 I became the executive director . . . The things that were most important to me were to instill the most sound business practices, to ensure that we had accurate data and record keeping, so we can properly measure what we were and were not accomplishing, to make changes in the staff that were necessary—to ensure that we had competent people to execute what we were trying to do, and then challenge the organization to perform at a higher level, and I am not talking only about on the administrative side, but to encourage the organization to raise its sights in terms of what we hope to accomplish, to make sure that we dealt with the known revenue and known expenses, and that we cannot depend on wishful thinking to make future plans. (Personal Communication, 2012)

The most critical type of balancing for long-term sustainability, however, is that between the two narratives of intergenerational sustainability—institutional resilience and institutional distinctiveness. Institutional resilience is a product of continuous organizational learning and adaptation, and it benefits from both organizational structural elements and cultural assumptions, as well as the ability of managers to navigate the strengths and weaknesses embedded in a particular structural arrangement. Within the institutional resilience narrative, there are specific strategies that over time translate into organizations' greater social and community relevance, such as the ability of organizations to utilize technology and social media, actively engage in public-private partnerships, implement sound audience development programs, and engage in interdisciplinary initiatives. Resilience narrative on its own, however, presents an incomplete view of how arts and humanities organizations achieve long-term sustainability. The second narrative of intergenerational sustainability is the institutional distinctiveness narrative, which applies to individual organizations as well as the sector as a whole. The distinctiveness narrative safeguards institutional missions and their unique positioning. We can think of it as "intrinsic significance" of the arts, with the caveat that arts and humanities exert not only implicit and indirect but also very explicit and direct influence on their communities. The distinctiveness narrative is fundamentally about values that arts and humanities institutions promote to both current and future generations, and connections that they make among generations by accumulating and transmitting cultural capital over time.

In a sustainable organization, the two narratives constitute a duality, both complementing and contradicting one another. For instance, distinctiveness allows an organization to occupy a unique institutional niche, which ensures both its survival in the process of natural selection and long-term sustainability; likewise, proactive strategic choices by institutional managers aimed at enhancing institutional resilience also result in more sustainable organizations. Although institutional resilience and institutional distinctiveness narratives are both necessary for institutional survival and sustainability, there is also a tension between them. A common tension between the two narratives arises when some organizations are strategically inclined to make their experiences more entertainment-like, as a way of appealing to a wider range of visitors and achieving greater resilience: but this may compromise institutional distinctiveness. For example, in response to declining budgets, some museums organize blockbuster-type exhibitions, with the hope that those exhibitions will spark popular demand, enhance their overall social relevance, and reach out to previously untapped audiences. However, such a strategy may conflict with the educational purpose of museums, as described by a manager:

There is a big trend in museums—all institutions, symphonies, not just museums, symphonies, zoos, you name it—to try to provide an entertaining experience while providing an educational experience, and so the two often clash. The curators and the educators want to keep things very academic. The marketers, visitor-service people, want people to have a good time. So, it's a battle kind of within the institution. Sometimes you might go too far in one direction or the other direction. Hopefully, it will work out. (Personal Communication, 2015)

Aside from their "side-effects" on organizational missions, these types of exhibitions may also be costly and may mean a higher admission price, thus raising accessibility concerns. As an example, during the Great Recession, in 2009, Michigan Science Center (then called the Detroit Science Center) was loaned a special exhibition of 36 mummies from the Museo de las Momias de Guanajuato in Guanajuato, Mexico (Walsh, 2009). One hope was that this unusual exhibition that celebrated the Day of the Dead in Mexico would draw attention from a Hispanic population in Detroit—the population that had not been among the core visitors and patrons of the center at the time. While the exhibition had some educational significance by educating visitors about "natural" mummification processes, it was mostly a blockbuster-type exhibition aimed at delivering sensational effects to the public. The deviation from the scientific mission was not the only problem; the exhibition also did not result in revenues expected from its sensational value, in part due to its high admission price. This positioning was not only shortsighted in terms of organizational strategy, but it was also unsustainable by perpetuating the social and economic inequalities within the community itself. Subsequently, it contributed to the demise of the center in 2011.

The institution was resurrected a year later under the new name: Michigan Science Center. Since then, it has been pursuing an educational mission that is consistent with its original intent. Sustainable thinking eventually led the board to a realization that, in some ways, the center had been offering its programming to traditional audiences of science enthusiasts while neglecting the broader audience and stakeholders. The center has eventually adopted a more diverse approach to programming and hired more diverse staff, while also expanding its public outreach programs. This new path has allowed the strengthening of the center's core educational mission, which is the cornerstone of its institutional distinctiveness. The center has also been able to establish broader social and community relevance and reach out to previously underserved audiences: thus appropriately reconciling the resilience and distinctiveness narratives.

Another example of a typical tension between the two narratives of sustainability is when a collaborative imperative that is embedded in the institutional resilience narrative may prompt some organizations, especially smaller ones, to consider partnering with larger organizations or even doing a merger, especially in times of stress. These types of partnerships, however, may compromise institutional identity, as missions of smaller institutions are likely to be subsumed by their larger and more powerful partners. Therefore, an imbalanced approach to such a positive strategy as partnering with others may also be detrimental to organizational sustainability.

These tensions affect different institutional types and can cause both freestanding nonprofits and university-affiliated organizations to experience mission drift issues. In the world of university-affiliated cultural organizations, mission drift is likely to manifest itself as the subordination of the organization's mission to the university's goals. The primary goal of a university is education; therefore, in many cases, university-affiliated arts organizations tend to justify their existence by adopting this goal as their own mission. While there is nothing wrong with an educational mission, in some cases, an artistic mission may suffer. For example, cultural organizations tend to integrate into university-wide projects and spend a great deal of effort competing for grants and serving as a source of additional revenues for university research, which can detract from their own core missions, thus serving as an example of tension between institutional resilience and institutional distinctiveness narratives.

For freestanding institutions, visitor dollars become an increasingly important source of operational revenues, and as a result, they are more inclined to treat the public as customers and attempt to reflect their customers' preferences. They are also increasingly reliant on the adoption of other business-like strategies, such as, for example, an increasing emphasis on marketing at the expense of the arts. However, excessive marketization is something that cultural organizations need to manage carefully if they hope to maintain their institutional distinctiveness. In the short run, customer-driven logics may attract bigger and more diverse audiences; in the long run, however, these strategies may put organizations in competition with the entertainment industry, a competition they are unlikely to win.

Since these types of tensions between resilience and distinctiveness narratives are not uncommon, what becomes critical is the ability of managers to reconcile these tensions by making balanced decisions that are ultimately more favorable to their institutions as well as the current and future publics that their institutions serve. The manager of a historical museum reflects on his daily thought process in attempts to build up sustainability capital for his institution while remaining loyal to its core mission now and for the generations to come:

> In terms of sustainability, there's a couple directions that we're looking at, and there's an infinite number of choices. One, is there an opportunity for public funding for this organization like [names of organizations] have? We're looking at that as an option. It's quite unlikely because of what's come before us, and [because of] the thought of asking taxpayers to increase their tax load for an organization that is perhaps not top of mind for many of them. It may be difficult, but nevertheless we're looking at that as both a short- and long-term strategy. We're also looking at whether it makes sense for our organization to merge, collaborate, or somehow become a part of another— [university name], . . . the State of Michigan, . . . [another cultural organization]. Another one is, do we shift what we do? Do we shift from an organization that is primarily supported by contributions to an earned-revenue model? Do we get in the business of selling Detroit posters and t-shirts? Selling a lot of them, which is really focusing on the earned revenue, renting this place for private functions every single night. We're doing some of that now. We have events here five days a week, but shifting to an earned-revenue model, which is really kind of a drift from your mission, is another thing that could be considered. (Personal Communication, 2015)

When it comes to balancing the various tensions embedded in the idea of organizational sustainability, such as those described above, it is important to think about sustainability as a process rather than a mere outcome. The process-oriented view of sustainability embraces the limitations of organizational structure as well as the instability and unpredictability of external environments. Economic recessions, public health crises, and a variety of internal organizational issues (that often unfold unexpectedly), all create a fluid environment in which arts and humanities function. Unlike, for example, human-service organizations that can often lean on public support at times of stress, arts and humanities organizations are frequently left to their own devices during crises. Their long-term sustainability greatly depends on the ability of their managers to reconcile the various tensions that they encounter, as well as the various immediate organizational survival logics, with more forward-looking organizational legacy imperatives.

## Organizational Sustainability Is an Ethical Concept Guided by Commitment to Future Generations

Why do organizations and their managers act in ways that support long-term organizational sustainability, ways that include making decisions that go beyond immediate efficiency and mere organizational survival? The answer to that question often lies within the domain of ethics rather than the domain of management, as seemingly "unprofitable" or "inefficient" decisions may be quite beneficial for organizational long-term sustainability. As many examples in this book show, these types of decisions can be both explicitly and implicitly motivated by managerial commitment to future generations.

The best example of an explicit commitment by cultural organizations to future generations is the expansion and development of the public education and outreach function. Arts organizations that have institutionalized, professionalized, and financially supported public education functions are more likely to be intergenerationally sustainable. Public education departments have been growing in importance for various organizations in the sector since the 1970s. The institutionalized approach to public outreach is becoming more common across all arts and humanities fields, including literature organizations, which traditionally targeted adult audiences and did not invest as much in the public education function as some other fields did. Aside from a greater degree of public outreach institutionalization, there is also an increasing emphasis on early outreach, in some cases to children as young as three years old (Genoways & Ireland, 2003; Hooper-Greenhill, 1999; Packer, 2006). As described by the director of a university-affiliated museum, institutionalized public outreach allows achieving "generational branding":

My sense of it is that the education classes especially, made the museum almost iconic for the regional community. There are generations of people from around the regional area—now third, fourth generations have taken summer classes, public education classes. And, for them, the museum is iconic. And it has achieved, I guess we can call it "generational branding"—one generation informing the next. . . . that is why there would be such an outcry if someone decided to shut it down, even though it is just a small part of other systems . . . I think the public education program really invested the museum into the consciousness of the public now and over generations. (Personal Communication, 2012)

Importantly, public education programs are becoming more equitable and inclusive, which also signifies a direct organizational commitment to future generations of both artists and patrons. On the one hand, more equitable outreach is supported by strategic pragmatic considerations, such as expanding the stakeholder base and addressing audience shortages and revenue shortfalls. On the other hand, it is also motivated by an ethical organizational commitment to a more just and inclusive future and a sense of greater social responsibility. Equity-based outreach initiatives are often enabled via partnerships with educational, human-service, and business organizations and local and state governments; they employ a shared responsibility model that engages appropriately with the wider societal fabric and ecosystem surrounding cultural organizations.

An implicit type of commitment by cultural managers to future generations is embedded in the discursive framing and decision-making logic that aims to think beyond short- and medium-term time horizons to incorporate care for future generations. As managers make specific operational and strategic decisions, the sense of importance that they give to building relationships and connecting with younger generations is illustrated by the following reflections expressed by the director of a university-affiliated museum and the CEO of a performing arts organization:

I want to know what art has to say to you about your life . . . So that is what happens to *your children* in a world where the ice sheets are melting . . . So when *your grandchildren* come to the [museum], they will say, "That's very interesting; in 2011 the ice sheets were still melting, and here's the sense of loss and longing that human beings felt about that," rather than saying, "Okay, that's the world of science, and here is the world of art" [emphasis added]. (Personal Communication, 2011)

We are counselors to *young* dancers because even our professional dancers are often 18 years old—they are still young, they are still kids, *they could be my granddaughters—so you have that obligation, you have an obligation to encourage and engage the rest of your staff to make sure that they continue to remember why we are all here.* Which is about the art form, and what is going on in the studio, and why we are raising money, so there is a whole palette of responsibilities that management now has in order to maintain a successful organization that remains at the tip of the spear in terms of its focus and importance in a community [emphasis added]. (Personal Communication, 2012)

What is fascinating about these quotes is the language that these managers use to describe their decision-making processes. Both managers describe the rationale for their decisions as a commitment, or an obligation, to their own children and grandchildren. Hence, they personalize organizational decisions as if they were deciding for their own descendants, which, according to the philosopher Derek Parfit, is the most appropriate way of interpreting and implementing the idea of intergenerational equity in practice (Parfit, 1984).

From a managerial standpoint, fulfilling an obligation to future generations might be a challenging task, especially at times of economic recession, when the arts and humanities are often the first ones to be cut from the list of budget priorities and when arts education tends to be the most vulnerable budget line. Hence, staying true to the obligation to future generations often involves good judgment and an ability to push things through in any situation. As one of the managers described it, when one of the programs for young people is under the threat of being cut, she personally steps in to defend the program:

I suppose *the biggest role I've played with that, with the adventures program, is I'm like a dog with a bone; I won't let it go.* Because, one, it's about the art in our schools; it is about the art; it is about children, and the exposure, and I've seen so many wonderful things happen over the years, and I've seen so many moments and . . . it is it right that we do it this way [emphasis added]. (Personal Communication, 2012)

The commitment to future generations may not be directly voiced in formal strategic plans that many arts and humanities organizations started adopting, especially in the past decade. Due to its practical nature, the strategic planning process typically focuses on short- or medium-term goals rather than on planning for the generations to come. Many managers are aware of this type of issue and also recognize their own cognitive limitations when it comes to their ability to be fully accurate in designing the strategic visions and plans for their organizations. As described by the managers of a university-affiliated museum and of a nonprofit arts center, being aware of these limitations, exercising critical thinking, and leaning on their commitment to future generations are important considerations for making sustainable decisions:

I would never want to say, "Here's my idea of a good society, and here's how we're getting there." . . . meanwhile, our environmental issues may shrink us to where we have a staff of three. . . . so, it's that frame of reference, of never seeing yourself as always having the right idea but trying to be self-skeptical, yet optimistic. It is really flipping that management from "I'm telling you where we're going, and you come along" to "I'm watching; I'm tinkering." It's constantly tinkering. (Personal Communicaiton, 2013)

I don't know what will happen in 30 years. I hope that . . . it is less expensive for families to be here, that we never have to say no to someone who would like their children to be in a class here because of money. I think, we can, perhaps, be in that situation because I know what we all believe at the arts center, [just as] as museum people do—that we sometimes feel that we are safeguarding something that is extremely important, and, at the end of the financial downturn, we want to still be here and still be standing, and to have provided the experiences and performance and visual arts that make us human. (Personal Communicaiton, 2011)

Commitment to future generations is, therefore, embedded in the various institutional logics and managerial decision-making, and it eventually results in accountability to future generations. Importantly, this type of thinking supports an organizational quest for long-term sustainability, as described by the manager of a community-based theater: "If we were to look at it in that real long-term macro perspective, our goal is to get to the point that we are completely embedded into the cultural life of the community. And, so, the people can't conceive of having their kids and grandkids not grow up participating in [organization name] in some part" (Personal Communication, 2016).

## Organizational Sustainability
## Is a Product of Sustainable Thinking

Contrary to a dictionary definition of this concept, organizational sustainability does not necessarily equal stability, maintenance, or absence of change. Many examples, quotes, and testimonies in this book illustrate that, while stability is an important organizational consideration, appreciating change and taking on a learning-and-resilience mindset is even more important, all while keeping an eye on the organizational core mission and its impact on both current and future generations. Furthermore, organizational sustainability is a concept replete with various tensions, and the key to an organization's ability to stand the test of time is the dynamic interplay of the institutional resilience and distinctiveness narratives achieved through day-to-day choices of organizational managers aimed at reconciling these various tensions. These types of managerial decisions over time translate into institutional capital for sustainability—an intangible, yet powerful, endowment that sustains arts and humanities organizations for generations to come. The question is this: How is the balance among the various, and often contradictory, aspects of organizational sustainability achieved?

The key to achieving that balance is the process-oriented view of organizational sustainability that embraces the idea of sustainability as a process rather than an outcome; this view capitalizes on both unconventional strategic management to achieve organizational competitive advantage and employs sustainable thinking focused on longer-term organizational legacy. Such a process-oriented view of organizational sustainability embraces the value of consistency and respects not only change but also tradition when it comes to sustainable management. Good management is not something that can be done on an ad-hoc basis—it requires practice and persistence.

The importance of both breaking with convention and being respectful of traditions is yet another paradox of organizational sustainability. In the context of arts and humanities organizations, this paradox stems from their purpose of serving as the accumulators and transmitters of collective cultural heritage from one generation to another, which is a part of tradition. Therefore, when it comes to managing sustainably in the context of such organizations, it becomes important to strike a balance between new and innovative ideas and respecting traditions. It also becomes important not to allow arts and humanities organizations to serve as mere economic engines or providers of entertainment in their communities. The remainder of this chapter unpacks the differences and the complementary nature of two institutional logics—strategic management and sustainable thinking—that both unfold in sustainably managed organizations.

Strategic planning, as "a disciplined effort to produce fundamental decisions and actions that shape and guide what an organization is, what it does, and why it does it" (Bryson, 2010; cited in Bryson, 2018, p. 24), helps organizations to develop a decision-making framework that allow managers to think, act, and manage strategically, thus enhancing the prospects for organizational survival. Likewise, the two narratives of intergenerational sustainability are not just abstract concepts but also have a concrete management aspect. A closer examination of the similarities with and differences between the two narratives and strategic-management literature, which addresses the problem of alignment and coherence among management practices (Brown, 2010; Koteen, 1997; Varbanova, 2013), is therefore necessary.

Between the two narratives of intergenerational sustainability, strategic management most directly resonates with the institutional resilience narrative, which seeks to improve the strategic positioning of a given organization through the building of partnerships, adoption of technology, and other means. However, strategic management takes into account data regarding the internal and external organizational environment, and often aims to produce measurable outcomes that increase an organization's competitive advantage (Brown, 2010). The sustainability paradigm, on the other hand, does not have a direct way of quantifying long-term inputs and outputs. Instead, the resilience narrative presupposes an increase in the sustainability capital of organizations via greater social and community relevance and structural adaptation. The idea of differentiation, which at first glance appears similar to the distinctiveness narrative, is also present in strategic-management literature, since it is important for organizations to distinguish themselves in order to gain a competitive advantage and secure stable funding (Brown, 2010). Arguably, however, the differentiation strategies described in strategic management literature are ultimately strategies for ensuring short- or medium-term institutional survival. This is different from the distinctiveness narrative, which seeks to maintain an institutional legacy across generations by promoting particular kinds of values in society more generally.

In conventional terms, then, the focus of strategic thinking is on achieving results. Strategic thinking asks, "What is my mission, and what are my goals? What steps do I need to take to accomplish these goals? How do I effectively use internal and external resources for maximizing outputs and outcomes?" The rationale below describing an adaptive strategic path taken by a music organization in the aftermath of the Great Recession illustrates the idea of strategic thinking:

> Other than our signature of innovation here through technology, I think everything else that we are doing is a return to a set of fundamentals that everyone will agree is required. We have a summary statement in our annual report that talks about that, the formula for our future sustainability: the presentation of more concerts in more places, serving our community, prioritizing the resources that we do have as an investment in people rather than other things, and not letting the growth of expenses outpace the growth of income, while at the same time we significantly recapitalize. Those are the four points of the summary of this whole plan. That's not our philosophy, but we do acknowledge that they all four have to work together. (Personal Communication, 2015).

Sustainable thinking, on the other hand, transcends this logic. Instead of seeking immediate results, sustainable thinking asks, "What is important for my organization, and what kind of legacy would it to leave for the future? What are its core values, and what would it take to preserve them?" In other words, strategic and sustainable thinking are different, albeit connected, ideas. Indeed, sustainability often builds on strategic thinking. The quotes below from university museum directors illustrate the connection between short- and long-term thinking, between being strategic about creating a value for the community and producing a powerful and long-lasting impact on multiple generations:

> I don't think we are here to add to their life economically; we are here to add to their sense of stewardship, sense of citizenship in a larger environment in which we are all part. And if can reach the public with a sense of responsibility . . . if they start appreciating that, then I think our chances are improved that they will be more responsible citizens . . . And if that's the case, it increases the chances of museums having a longer life. I am not being prescriptive here; for some people, it might be short-term; for some people, it might be long-term. We want to turn people on, whether it is to turn on a kid, or an adult, or a family. (Personal Communication, 2011)

> Our role is to try and inculcate the best minds. We are not going here to tell people what to do; we are not here to make policy, whether it is a personal policy or a government policy. We are here to provide the best information so that people can make their own decisions about the policies that they want to follow, the policies that are in their best interest short-term, or long-term for their kids. So, we can present exhibits and programs on how we use our collection and information to do predictive model, and that will leave them thinking . . . (Personal Communication, 2011)

Sustainable thinking, therefore, is about legacy and creating something that will last, not just something that will be immediately effective. It is an idea spanning multiple generations and paving the way for a more just future. The focus of sustainable thinking on organizational legacy also naturally brings ethics and value-driven considerations into the decision-making process, as it becomes important to consider how current decisions and strategies would affect future generations. Chief among these ethics is intergenerational social equity that is a proper balance of the rights and interests between current and future generations (Catron, 1996; Frederickson, 2010; Parfit, 1984). Sustainable managers keep the needs of future generations in mind when approaching specific decision situations and dilemmas. For them, doing the right thing is what is important, rather than what would set their organizations apart from others in the market, or what would give them a competitive advantage. Organizations that follow these types of considerations effectively enable a sense of intergenerational justice within their ecosystems.

Implementing intergenerational social equity in practice, however, necessarily involves recognizing and dealing with the various path dependencies and historical dynamics that still exist in the field today. This includes the history of elitism and the lack of institutional diversity when it comes to arts and culture supporters and donors (Ostrower, 2020), organizational boards, staff, and, subsequently, specific programming choices (Acevedo, & Madara, 2015; Olivares & Piatak, 2022; Sandell & Nightingale, 2012). These issues perpetuate social inequities and reduce cultural representation rather than improve intergenerational equity, and they need to be addressed in systematic ways so that cultural organizations can become equitable now and for the generations to come.

Furthermore, socially responsible thinking that takes place in sustainable organizations considers the ethics of current organizational actions, especially the proper balance between the various potentially competing organizational values, such as efficiency, effectiveness, responsiveness, and equity. Organizations achieving a proper balance among these values exert a positive impact on their communities by both remedying the consequences of previous injustices and imbalances and by advancing more sustainable communities going forward. For example, many arts and humanities organizations featured in this book care about social justice, environmental sustainability, and providing better access to the arts for underserved groups; they act in socially responsible ways that prioritize ethical considerations and social equity over bottom-line considerations or a narrow focus on the artistic aspect of their work. These are the organizations that embed themselves within their communities by taking more of a servant role and actively pursuing egalitarian ideals. Their managers embrace such values as equity, access, diversity, and inclusion and act not merely in reactive, adaptive ways but also proactively—to produce more just and sustainable communities.

When it comes to their perceptions, organizational managers do not necessarily have an explicit definition of a "sustainable organization," but they have an intuitive vision that guides their perceptions and decision-making. This intuition is informed by years and years of experience, professional education, networks, and all sorts of personal backgrounds. When they discuss their approaches to sustainability, they often use conventional language, but the conventional terms combine to result in a qualitatively new concept, and that concept reflects the broader themes about organizational sustainability discussed in this book. The director of a university-affiliated performing arts center defines a sustainable organization as a "healthy organization," which implies both professional management and establishing the value of their organization for society:

> I think a healthy organization—I mean, obviously, there are some key factors, like, you know, fiscal health and, you know, good management, business practices, accountability, and, particularly, when you are looking at the health of the organization, you know, heart health versus mind health—is where the ideas are coming from. And I believe it starts with a spark, and that's how I do work. I say, "I want to find a way to have dance to be stronger because it just feels right to me." Obviously, you need branding and identity, those good business marketing practices that are part of a healthy organization . . . but, when you hear people talk about how the project happened . . . it just warms my heart to hear people in the community say, "We need to do another jazz-train project; we need to do that again." Because they've taken ownership of it . . . That's like a healthy thing, that holistic approach . . . and just creating that environment to where it is part of your everyday life. (Personal Communication, 2012)

Importance in goal alignment between communities and organizations is, therefore, an element of sustainable thinking focused less on the immediate goals and more on legacy, community ownership, and shared leadership overall. Many managers realize that a sustainable organization comprises more than one person and more than one leader. Therefore, good managers should be inclusive and make sure that their organization keeps functioning effectively, even when they retire, as expressed by the CEO of a performing arts organization:

> Many people say, "Oh, now you are retiring, how is the company going to survive without you?" I'll say to them that the point to what I've been trying to do for all these years is I've been trying to institutionalize the way to do things. The company is not me. It is an institution, and, yes, I play an important role, but the company will continue to exist without me because

the company is so much more than me. And you try to sur-
round yourself with good people, to have a vision or sense of
what you want the company to be doing . . . That is how it
works. You set that tone, and then you have people moving
ahead . . . (Personal Communication, 2012)

In summary, strategic thinking improves the chances for organizational survival—a necessity for intergenerational sustainability—and it
often becomes a baseline for sustainable thinking. By contrast, sustainable
thinking allows for the reconciling of the various tensions and contradictions embedded in the idea of organizational sustainability, including
between the resilience and distinctiveness narratives. Sustainable decisions
over time translate into sustainability capital, which can be conceived of
as an unseen endowment that sustains organizations in the long term and
safeguards the needs of future generations.

While there are many examples of managers recognizing the role of
their organizations in serving both current and future generations, explicit
concerns about intergenerational sustainability are not necessarily voiced
directly in organizational strategic documents, such as mission statements
and strategic plans. Furthermore, cultural managers frequently acknowledge
the limitations of formal strategic plans as documents that are usually
designed for five to eight years in order to support near- and medium-term
strategizing. Instead, managers signal their long-term commitments on a
very pragmatic level and trust their intuitive judgments, as expressed by
the managers of a university-affiliated museum and a university-affiliated
performing arts center:

We usually have strategic plans for five years, but I believe in
strategic doing, not strategic planning. Strategic planning is
fine in an ideal world, but the world is not ideal. You end up
running a place by taking advantage of opportunities that were
never imagined in a university strategic plan, and having to
deal with crises that no strategic plan could foresee . . . when
I talk about strategic planning, I mean what do we need to do
in the next two or five years to continue being competitive;
what are the next big things out there; what niche should we
be occupying that no one else does? (Personal Communication,
2011)

Instead of always worrying that they have their belt and they have their suspenders, they have their rain, because you can't plan for everything. You can plan for a lot; you can absolutely think you have a plan for everything and that you'll have no worry when the thing you thought of occurs. You have to trust that you built a good enough toolbox that, somewhere in there, is that resource, or you've partnered with somebody with the resources and thought about something you haven't thought about, and you will be able to recognize that genius when it comes forward: "Oh, my god, yes! Thank you!" (Personal Communication, 2012)

The abovementioned quotes belong to the managers of different institutional types who describe the idea of sustainable thinking using different language. However, the overall message of both is essentially the same: sustainable management is more about guiding and shepherding organizations through difficult times and for the generations to come than it is about performing more traditional managerial functions (organization, planning, motivation, delegation). To that end, being flexible and responsive to the extra- and intra-institutional pressures appears more important than following a strategic plan. This observation is consistent with recent developments in strategic management literature, regarding the limitations of strategic planning, which is frequently used as a framework designed to fulfill donors' requirements rather than provide tangible benefits to organizations (Varbanova, 2013). In fact, strategic managers are often forced to go beyond formal plans by becoming entrepreneurs (Fitzgibbon, 2001; Phillips, 2011), capable of performing "economic as well as sociocultural activity, based on innovations, exploitation of opportunities, and risk-taking behavior" (Varbanova, 2013, p. 17). However, this kind of strategic thinking does not fully explain how organizations achieve intergenerational sustainability.

The ultimate evidence of sustainability in the arts and humanities world is found primarily in the realm of sustainable thinking and sustainable acting, rather than in simply declaring sustainability as a formal goal and including it in policy documents. Acting sustainably in the first place appears important for building institutional capital for sustainability, and both sustainable thinking and care for future generations are embedded in particular management choices and institutional actions aimed at achieving long-term outcomes. This does not mean that strategic plans are unimportant in the world of arts and humanities organizations; they function as a valuable framework that supports decision-making. However, sustainable thinking takes decision-making to a whole new level; it implies making the right choices now, including by elevating both organizational structure and culture to create socially responsible organizations that care about their own sustainability and that advance sustainability in their own communities as well. In the long run, sustainable thinking produces outcomes favorable to future generations.

The key to long-term sustainability is the ability of managers to act sustainably by making wise, incremental decisions on a day-to-day basis, similar to the incremental decision-making described by Charles E. Lindblom (Lindblom, 1959), rather than attempting to predict the future based on incomplete and often contradictory information. In line with classic studies in other policy contexts (Wildavsky et al., 1988), since it is impossible to make accurate predictions about the long-term future, the strategy of long-term planning (risk aversion) appears less important for arts managers than resilience (an immediate system response, risk taking). Because of our limited knowledge of the future, traditional decision theory exemplified in the rational choice paradigm, and that assumes individuals have valid and nearly complete information about the environment and are able to competently evaluate alternatives, expectations, and preferences, is ill-suited to understanding decision-making in the name of future generations.

Instead, the neo-institutional view is better suited to understanding managerial decision-making processes in pursuit of favorable long-term outcomes. In particular, March and Olsen's decision-making framework and the logic of appropriateness are fitting in this context, to explain how particular institutional norms and managerial routines result in more sustainable organizations (March, 1994; March & Olsen, 1989). The sense of appropriateness embedded in sustainable thinking allows organizational managers to reconcile the various tensions and contradictions embedded in organizational sustainability, including the tensions between the resilience and distinctiveness narratives. Consistently, say March and Olsen (1989), managers of sustainable arts and humanities organizations would not simply act as rational strategic planners in considering the longer-term sustainability; they would be trying to make sense of the existing environmental settings and institutional conditions, while making decisions with practical implications for future generations.

While doing so, managers navigate systems of organizational rules, formalized procedures, organizational forms, and conventions, as well as collective roles, informal beliefs, codes, and internal organizational cultures. Such institution-based behavior is grounded in institutional history and reflects subtle lessons of arts organizations' cumulative experience. While the logic of appropriateness is based on past institutional experiences and is backward looking (March, 1994; March & Olsen, 1989), it is perfectly applicable to guiding cultural managers' decisions in the name of future generations, exemplifying the idea of learning from the past about the future. Subsequently, following certain everyday routines by managers eventually results in organizational accountability to future generations.

Furthermore, when it comes to intergenerational sustainability, organizational managers devise strategies that vouchsafe the interests of future generations, but they sometimes do so unconsciously; it is instead a personal sense of what is right and what is ethical that guides their everyday work. They do so without even realizing the full potential of their current actions for future generations; it is rather their personal sense of what is right and what is ethical that guides their everyday work. Directors of a university-based art museum and of a freestanding art center explain their actions in the following way:

> It's that understanding that doing the best work you know how to do, [although] it's not always right, is all you can do. And if you do that, you sleep better. (Personal Communication, 2011)

> We are also extremely nimble; I mean, one of the reasons we're surviving financially right now is because our staff works so hard; they make fast decisions; they work smart; and they work constantly. And that's not a viable, possibly long-term strategy, but it's working for us right now. (Personal Communication, 2011)

In the long run, sustainable thinking produces outcomes favorable for future generations. In many respects, thinking in the long-term implies making the right choices right now and designing programs that connect organizations with the day-to-day life of their communities. According to a museum manager, any kind of intergenerational impact would have been impossible without the exploration of what is current and what concerns people today: "And the things that we make, the issues that we address, the things that we find important, shape the community in the future. So, [we manage] to find ways to connect that and bring different aspects of the community, or explore different issues that are of importance for us right now—maybe by making a historical comparison, but by making it about what it important in the community right now" (Personal Communication, 2012). The practical implication of the distinction between these two modes of thinking is that both strategic and sustainable thinking are important for organizational sustainability, and having a sound organizational strategy is very important for sustainable organizations. Several more distinctions between strategic and sustainable thinking are worth discussing here (Table 5.2).

First, both sustainable thinking and strategic thinking imply the presence of a certain mindset, and the ability of managers to think beyond short-term time horizons and adjust the course of actions initially defined in the strategic plan (Bryson, 2018). However, as compared to the paradigm of intergenerational sustainability, strategic management is much more concerned with near-term outcomes. The process of strategic management mainly focuses on the present, while considering the vision of a desired future; it typically involves planning only for several years ahead rather than thinking in terms of future generations (Varbanova, 2013).

Table 5.2. From Strategic Thinking to Sustainable Thinking

| Strategic thinking | Sustainable thinking |
|---|---|
| • Improving decision-making and strategic positioning<br>• Using internal and external data to achieve measurable outcomes<br>• Results oriented, practical<br>• Concerned with "here and now," more nearsighted (three- to five-year typical plans) | • Preserving and fostering long-term institutional legacy<br>• Outputs and outcomes are not always quantifiable<br>• Value-guided, intuitive<br>• Less concerned with growth and clients, more concerned with ethics and future |
| Questions to ask: What steps do I need to take to accomplish my mission/goals? How do we maximize outputs? | Questions to ask: What is important for the organization in the long run, and what kind of legacy should it leave? |

Second, the practice of strategic management requires developing a more or less exact assessment of organizational capacities, resources, and expected societal impacts (Bryson, 2018; Varbanova, 2013). At the same time, it is quite challenging to quantify the value of arts experiences and assess the precise impact that arts and humanities organizations have on society, particularly if one is speaking in the language of tangible outcomes. Even qualitative indicators of arts performance are problematic (Varbanova, 2013). Therefore, sustainable thinking is less about the performance indicators and more about the mission and organizational long-term legacy.

Third, as compared with sustainable thinking, strategic management is much more results oriented and practical. It focuses on the dynamic interaction of internal organizational capacities and external environments, and it seeks to take advantage of opportunities for advancement, growth, and development. Sustainability, on the other hand, is not about growth or maximizing returns; it is more about institutional purpose, values, and responsibility rather than performance per se. Additionally, an important element of strategic management is a strong client orientation (Koteen, 1997), where the needs of a client are often put above the consideration of an institution itself. However, such an orientation is problematic for cultural organizations that rely on distinctiveness for their sustainability. In fact, sustainable thinking, as a philosophy, is ultimately about the ability of institutions to pursue a broader public interest, as evidenced, for example, by organizational commitment to social equity.

Finally, in the face of future uncertainties, sustainability implies the presence of an ethical imperative—a concern for the rights and welfare of future generations—embedded in both organizational routines and managerial practices. Being intergenerationally sustainable means not only being effective but also being equitable toward future generations. The sustainability imperative is concerned with the legacy of public institutions and how modern-day policies and actions affect the ability of public institutions to carry out their purpose across generations. Therefore, we can think of sustainable thinking as a process that extends strategic management by bringing it to a new level.

## Concluding Thoughts

This book has sought to unpack the idea of sustainability as an organizational logic and routine, and to show that sustainable organizations are those capable of achieving their own immediate survival and longer-term sustainability while also advancing sustainable development in their communities. The book has established the importance of the organizational level of sustainability as a setting in which sustainable thinking, as a special kind of institutional rationality, develops and unfolds. Moreover, organizations are an important level of sustainability, and their various contributions to sustainable development should be viewed as central, rather than peripheral or merely complementary, to those provided by other actors.

The book's specific discoveries about sustainability as an organizational logic have been grounded in the experiences of a variety of U.S.-based arts and humanities organizations located in seven states and one metropolitan area (Detroit). While the book focuses on the classical forms of culture, questions of sustainability also affect new and emerging cultural industries, such as streaming companies and virtual arts, and the key lessons presented here are also relevant to them. Importantly, the theoretical framework presented in the book is grounded in both a zoom-out approach that sketches the differences and similarities among the arts and humanities subfields included in the study, and a zoom-in approach that places organizations within a particular local ecosystem (Metropolitan Detroit). This approach, as well as the diversity of the organizations themselves, has allowed telling a story about organizational perseverance and immediate adaptation in the face of significant external shocks, the chief of which was the Great Recession of 2007–2009.

This book has specifically proposed a theoretical framework that unpacks the idea of intergenerationally sustainable organization as one that combines internally sustainable management practices with socially responsible behavior aimed at advancing sustainable development in local and global communities. The value of this framework is the connection that it makes between the ideas of intergenerational equity and organizational sustainability, showing how sustainable management today leads to enhanced institutional capital for sustainability in the long run. Furthermore, the key idea that emerged as a central concept describing organizational sustainability is the idea of balance, which can be a balance between the two narratives (institutional resilience and institutional distinctiveness), between art and management, local and global, socially relevant and institutionally distinct, rational and intuitive, traditional and innovative, sophisticated and accessible, preservation and sharing. All these and many other, often contradictory, ideas are embedded in the concept of organizational sustainability, and it takes a certain kind of decision-making process—sustainable thinking and acting and, above all, commitment to future generations—to reconcile these types of contradictions. This final chapter has summarized the key lessons learned about organizational sustainability, further developing the idea of sustainable thinking and specific institutional logics that enable it and distinguishing sustainable thinking from mainstream strategic management.

The many examples derived from the institutional context of the arts and humanities organizations support the reframing of the idea of sustainability at the macro, or societal, level as a multi-color concept that incorporates diverse systems and entities, including institutions and organizations belonging to the cultural sector, as opposed to framing macro-level sustainability as a unicolor-green concept that focuses primarily on the environment. As the book illustrates, cultural institutions represent collective cultural heritage that has been preserved by many previous generations of humans for their posterity and that carries important intrinsic significance. Furthermore, arts and humanities institutions also play various instrumental roles in their communities by promoting economic development, cultivating important societal values and sustainable attitudes in a variety of domains from environment to social justice, and contributing to a community-level culture that fosters sustainability locally and globally. An appropriate recognition of the role of the arts and humanities in society and their inclusion in sustainable development agendas, therefore, promotes an ecosystem view of sustainability, where cultural organizations are always treated as integral parts of their local and global communities.

The normative implication of this view is that current generations ought to have a strong commitment to supporting and preserving organizations within the domain of the arts and humanities, whether this includes creating a strong system of incentives for individuals and philanthropic communities to invest in the arts or allocating public support to cultural institutions. This view also supports the inclusion of the arts and humanities in the public educational curricula, as an important condition for ensuring equitable and continuous access to this critical resource to the public at large. Using the example of Metropolitan Detroit as one of the geographies included in this book, urban areas in the U.S. still lack inclusive access to public arts. This issue is particularly problematic in terms of ensuring equitable intergenerational transfer and accumulation of cultural capital from one generation to the next.

While formal organizations functioning within the three subfields of the arts and humanities (museums, literary organizations, music and performing arts) have served as the focus of this book, highlighting both unique and universal messages and themes that describe intergenerationally sustainable organizations and their management, lessons about long-term sustainability discussed in this book carry significance beyond the arts and humanities institutions, and they are relevant for any organization committed to pursuing the ethic of sustainability. The broader implications of the findings are clear: long-term sustainability that secures the rights of future generations requires sustainable stewardship today. Sustainable thinking guided by ethics and organizational legacy considerations goes beyond the principles of strategic management, helping managers to make decisions that are good for the organizations and for the communities they serve. Sustainable organizations direct their efforts toward achieving equitable outcomes for both current and future generations.

# Appendix A

## Recession Induced Pressures and Common Organizational Responses

| Current Pressures | Future Pressures |
|---|---|
| • Financial pressures (endowment, operating revenue, losses/expenses)<br>• Audience-related (audience decline, aging; meeting the demand; underserved populations)<br>• Infrastructure (space, technology, building, and exhibition maintenance)<br>• Capacity building (human resources, skills, volunteers)<br>• Leadership succession ("founder syndrome")<br>• Public recognition and publicity<br>• Competition (for funding, among each other) | • Financial pressures (recessions, contributor base)<br>• Changing audience preferences (generational, entertainment versus art)<br>• Technology<br>• Capacity building (human resources, skills, volunteers)<br>• Professionalization (strategic plan, marketing, business approaches, etc.)<br>• Competition with the entertainment industry<br>• Identity (repertoire, how art is delivered, perceived)<br>• Changing environment (reemergence of the city)<br>• Sustainability challenge (thinking beyond short-term) |

# Appendix B

## Institutional Factors of Resilience

Freestanding Nonprofit Organizations

| Advantages | Limitations |
|---|---|
| • Greater managerial autonomy and flexibility<br>• Greater adaptability and response to change<br>• Proximity to the communities of service<br>• Greater accessibility<br>• More developed public outreach<br>• Access to broader funding opportunities<br>• Ability to build networks of clients and supporters | • Mission drift as a result of commercialization<br>• Shift toward entertainment (dependence on visitor/audience numbers)<br>• Reliance on individual and corporate sponsors (affects programmatic decisions)<br>• Higher participation fees (limit the audience)<br>• Preoccupation of managers with fundraising at the expense of a creative work<br>• Competition with the commercial sector |

University-Affiliated Organizations

| Advantages | Limitations |
|---|---|
| • Baseline support and institutional shield from environmental pressures<br>• Access to intellectual and human resources, new ideas and creativity<br>• Opportunities for interdisciplinary projects, long-lasting collaborations<br>• Access to a highly educated audience<br>• Positive impact on image and identity<br>• Less emphasis on commercial strategies | • The subordination of the mission to the goals of a larger institution<br>• Lack of institutional and managerial autonomy<br>• Bureaucratization<br>• Utilitarianism: using arts organizations for fundraising and public relations<br>• Funding and membership limitations<br>• Distance from the larger public (elitist perceptions)<br>• Vulnerability of the public education function |

# Appendix C

## List of Organizations: Data Collection I & II

Data Collection I

| | Name | Genre | Type | Year created | Location | Interviewees | Interview Yr |
|---|---|---|---|---|---|---|---|
| 1 | Kansas City Ballet | Performing arts | Freestanding | 1957 | Kansas City, MO | 2 | 2012 |
| 2 | Kansas City Symphony | Performing arts | Freestanding | 1982 | Kansas City, MO | 1 | 2012 |
| 3 | The Lied Center of Kansas, University of Kansas | Performing arts | University-affiliated | 1993 | Lawrence, KS | 2 | 2012 |
| 4 | The Kauffman Center for the Performing Arts | Performing arts | Freestanding | 2011 | Kansas City, MO | 1 | 2012 |
| 5 | Oregon Bach Festival, University of Oregon | Performing arts | University-affiliated | 1970 | Eugene, OR | 1 | 2012 |
| 6 | The Lyric Opera of Kansas City | Performing arts | Freestanding | 1958 | Kansas City, MO | 1 | 2012 |
| 7 | Colorado Shakespeare Festival, University of Colorado | Performing arts | University-affiliated | 1944 | Boulder, CO | 2 | 2011 |
| 8 | Kenneth Spencer Research Library at the University of Kansas | Literature | University-affiliated | 1953 | Lawrence, KS | 1 | 2012 |

Data Collection I (Continued)

| | Name | Genre | Type | Year created | Location | Interviewees | Interview Yr |
|---|---|---|---|---|---|---|---|
| 9 | Words Without Borders | Literature | Freestanding | 2003 | Brooklyn, NY | 1 | 2012 |
| 10 | The Iowa Review | Literature | University-affiliated | 1970 | Iowa City, IA | 1 | 2012 |
| 11 | National Endowment for the Arts, Literature Program | Literature | Govern-mental organ-ization | 1965 | Washington, DC | 1 | 2012 |
| 12 | Allen Press Inc. | Literature | Freestanding | 1935 | Lawrence, KS | 1 | 2012 |
| 13 | Center for Digital Scholarship at the University of Kansas | Literature | University-affiliated | 2010 | Lawrence, KS | 1 | 2012 |
| 14 | Open Letter Books | Literature | Nonprofit, University-based | 2012 | Rochester, NY | 1 | 2012 |
| 15 | Creative Writing Program at the Douglas County Prison | Literature | University-affiliated | 2001 | Lawrence, KS | 1 | 2012 |

Data Collection I (Contiuned)

| | Name | Genre | Type | Year created | Location | Interviewees | Interview Yr |
|---|---|---|---|---|---|---|---|
| 16 | Spencer Museum of Art at the University of Kansas | Museums | University-affiliated | 1928 | Lawrence, KS | 4 | 2011 |
| 17 | The University of Kansas Natural History Museum | Museums | University-affiliated | 1864 | Lawrence, KS | 2 | 2011 |
| 18 | Lawrence Arts Center | Museums | Freestanding | 1975 | Lawrence, KS | 1 | 2011 |
| 19 | Boulder Museum of Contemporary Art | Museums | Freestanding | 1972 | Boulder, CO | 1 | 2011 |
| 20 | Colorado University Art Museum | Museums | University-affiliated | 1939 | Boulder, CO | 1 | 2011 |
| 21 | Watkins Museum of History | Museums | Freestanding | 1975 | Lawrence, KS | 1 | |

Data Collection II

| | Name | Genre | Type | Year created | Location | Interviewees | Interview Yr |
|---|---|---|---|---|---|---|---|
| 1 | Detroit Symphony Orchestra | Performing Arts | Freestanding | 1887 | Detroit, MI | 1 | 2014 |
| 2 | Belle Isle Aquarium | Museum | Freestanding | 1904 (closed 2005, re-opened 2012) | Detroit, MI | 4 | 2015 |
| 3 | Museum of Contemporary Art Detroit | Museum | Freestanding | 2006 | Detroit, MI | 2 | 2016 |
| 4 | Grosse Pointe Theatre | Performing Arts | Freestanding | 1948 | Grosse Pointe, MI | 1 | 2016 |
| 5 | Wild Swan Theater | Performing Arts | Freestanding | 1980 | Ann Arbor, MI | 1 | 2016 |
| 6 | Detroit Repertory Theater | Performing Arts | Freestanding | 1957 | Highland Park, MI | 3 | 2016 |
| 7 | Chamber Music Society of Detroit | Performing Arts | Freestanding | 1944 | Farmington Hills, MI | 1 | 2015 |
| 8 | All the World's a Stage Theater | Performing Arts | Freestanding | 1986 | Clinton Township, MI | 1 | 2015 |

Data Collection II (Contiuned)

| | Name | Genre | Type | Year created | Location | Interviewees | Interview Yr |
|---|---|---|---|---|---|---|---|
| 9 | Mosaic Theatre Detroit | Performing Arts | Freestanding | 1992 | Detroit, MI | 1 | 2015 |
| 10 | Matrix Youth Theater | Performing Arts | Freestanding | 1991 | Detroit, MI | 1 | 2015 |
| 11 | Charles H. Wright Museum of African American History | Museum | Freestanding | 1965 | Detroit, MI | 1 | 2016 |
| 12 | Grosse Pointe Historical Society | Museum | Freestanding | 1980 | Grosse Pointe Farms, MI | 2 | 2016 |
| 13 | Ann Arbor Hands-On Museum | Museum | Freestanding | 1978 | Ann Arbor, MI | 1 | 2016 |
| 14 | Detroit Institute of Arts | Museum | Freestanding | 1885 | Detroit, MI | 1 | 2015 |
| 15 | Ann Arbor Symphony | Performing Arts | Freestanding | 1982 | Ann Arbor, MI | 1 | 2016 |
| 16 | Hilberry Theater at Wayne State University | Performing Arts | University-affiliated | 1956 | Detroit, MI | 2 | 2016 |
| 17 | Michigan Science Center (Detroit Science Center until 2012) | Museum | Freestanding | 1970 (closed 2011, re-opened 2012) | Detroit, MI | 2 | 2016 |

Data Collection II (Continued)

| | Name | Genre | Type | Year created | Location | Interviewees | Interview Yr |
|---|---|---|---|---|---|---|---|
| 18 | Detroit Historical Society and Museum | Museum | Freestanding | 1914 | Detroit, MI | 1 | 2015 |
| 19 | Music Hall Center for the Performing Arts | Performing Arts | Freestanding | 1878 | Detroit, MI | 2 | 2015 |
| 20 | Detroit Puppet Theatre | Performing Arts | Freestanding | 1990 | Detroit, MI | 1 | 2016 |
| 21 | Henry Ford Museum of American Innovation | Museum | Freestanding | 1929 | Dearborn, MI | 1 | 2015 |
| 22 | Pewabic Pottery | Museum | Freestanding | 1903 | Detroit, MI | 1 | 2016 |
| 23 | Edsel and Eleanor Ford House and Fair Lane, Home of Clara and Henry Ford | Museum | Freestanding | 1927 and 1909 | Grosse Pointe Shores, MI and Dearborn, MI | 1 | 2016 |
| 24 | Berkeley Historical Museum | Museum | Municipal | 1993 | Berkley, MI | 2 | 2016 |
| 25 | Meadow Brook Theatre at Oakland University | Museum | University-affiliated | 1966 | Rochester, MI | 1 | 2016 |
| 26 | Arab American National Museum | Museum | Freestanding | 2005 | Dearborn, MI | 1 | 2015 |
| 27 | Grosse Pointe War Memorial | Museum | Freestanding | 1949 | Grosse Pointe Farms, MI | 1 | 2016 |

# References

AAM. (2022). *American Alliance of Museums.* National snapshot of COVID-19 Impact on United States museums. https://www.aam-us.org/wp-content/uploads/2022/02/COVID-19-Snapshot-of-the-Museum-Field-Dec-Jan.pdf

Alivizatou, M. (2016). *Intangible heritage and the museum: New perspectives on cultural preservation.* Routledge.

Abbey-Lambertz, K. (2011, December 21). Detroit libraries closing: 4 branches will shutter due to budget cuts. *Huffpost.* https://www.huffpost.com/entry/detroit-libraries-closing-4-branches_n_1162872

Acevedo, S., & Madara, M. (2015). The Latino experience in museums: An exploratory audience research study. Retrieved from: https://blog.americansforthearts.org/sites/default/files/Latino-Experience-in-Museums-Report-Contemporanea.pdf

Adams, W. M. (2006). *The future of sustainability: Re-thinking environment and development in the twenty-first century.* Paper presented at the Report of the IUCN Renowned Thinkers Meeting, 29–31 January 2006, IUCN.

Alexander, E. P. (1983). *Museum masters: Their museums and their influence.* American Association for State and Local History Book Series.

Alexander, E. P., & Alexander, M. (2008). *Museums in motion: An introduction to the history and functions of museums.* AltaMira Press.

Amburgey, T. L., & Rao, H. (1996). Organizational ecology: Past, present, and future directions. *Academy of Management Journal, 39*(5), 1265–1286.

Anderson, G. (2004). *Reinventing the museum: Historical and contemporary perspectives on the paradigm shift.* AltaMira Press.

Anonymous. (1993). Betrayal of trust. *The Burlington Magazine, 135*(1078), 3.

Antelman, K. (2004). Do open-access articles have a greater research impact? *College & Research Libraries, 65*(5), 372–382.

Astley, W. G., & Van de Ven, A. H. (1983). Central perspectives and debates in organization theory. *Administrative Science Quarterly, 28*(2), 245–273.

Bansal, P., & DesJardine, M. R. (2014). Business sustainability: It is about time. *Strategic organization, 12*(1), 70–78.

Barry, B. (1997). Sustainability and intergenerational justice. *Theoria, 44*(89), 43–64.

Barton, D., & Hamilton, M. (1998). *Local literacies: reading and writing in one community.* Psychology Press.

Battles, M. (2003). *Library: An unquiet history.* W. W. Norton.

Beamer, G. (2002). Elite interviews and state politics research. *State Politics & Policy Quarterly, 2*(1), 86.

Belfiore, E. (2002). Art as a means of alleviating social exclusion: does it really work? A critique of instrumental cultural policies and social impact studies in the UK. *International Journal of Cultural Policy, 8*(1), 91–106.

Belfiore, E., & Bennett, O. (2008). *The social impact of the arts.* Palgrave Macmillan.

Berry, D. M., & Fagerjord, A. (2017). *Digital humanities: Knowledge and critique in a digital age.* Polity.

Binelli, M. (2013). *Detroit city is the place to be: The afterlife of an American metropolis.* Picador.

BIODOME: An experiment in diversity. (2011). Boulder Museum of Contemporary Art.

Blair, W. (2005). *The history of world literature.* Kessinger.

Bloom, H. (1994). *The western canon.* Harcourt Brace.

Bobinski, G. S. (1969). *Carnegie libraries: Their history and impact on Amerian public library development.* American Library Association.

Bowman, W. (2011). Financial capacity and sustainability of ordinary nonprofits. *Nonprofit Management and Leadership, 22*(1), 37–51.

Brooks, V. W. (2012). *On literature today.* Literary Licensing, LLC.

Brown, W. A. (2010). Strategic management. In D. O. Renz & R. D. Herman (Eds.), *The Jossey-Bass Handbook of Nonprofit Leadership and Management* (pp. 206–228). Wiley.

Bryson, J. M. (2018). *Strategic planning for public and nonprofit organizations: A guide to strengthening and sustaining organizational achievement.* John Wiley & Sons.

Carroll, G. R. (1984). Organizational ecology. *Annual Review of Sociology, 10*(1), 71–93.

Catron, B. L. (1996). Sustainability and intergenerational equity: An expanded stewardship role for public administration. *Administrative Theory & Praxis, 18*(1), 2–12.

Center for the Art of Translation, The (2012). *About us.* Retrieved from http://www.catranslation.org/

Cerisola, S. (2019). A new perspective on the cultural heritage–development nexus: The role of creativity. *Journal of Cultural Economics, 43*(1), 21–56.

Clarke, A. E., Friese, A., & Washburn, R. S. (2018). *Situational analysis: Grounded theory after the interpretive turn.* 2nd ed. SAGE.

Community Foundation for Southeast Michigan (2019, August 7). *Wash and learn program brings the library to Detroit laundromats.* Retrieved from https://cfsem.org/story/wash-and-learn/

Community of Literary Magazines and Presses. (2012). *About.* Retrieved from http://clmp.org/about/

Conn, S. (1998). *Museums and American intellectual life, 1876–1925.* University of Chicago Press.

Conn, S. (2010). *Do museums still need objects?* University of Pennsylvania Press.

Corbin, J. M., & Strauss, A. L. (1990). Grounded theory research: Procedures, canons, and evaluative criteria. *Qualitative Sociology, 13*(1), 3–21.

Corbin, J. M., & Strauss, A. L. (2008). *Basics of qualitative research: Techniques and procedures for developing grounded theory.* SAGE.

Dale, A. (2001). *At the edge: Sustainable development in the 21st century* (Vol. 6). University of British Columbia Press.

Davis, J. H., Schoorman, F. D., & Donaldson, L. (1997). Toward a stewardship theory of management. *Academy of Management Review, 22*(1), 20–47.

Dewey, J. (1934). *Art as experience.* Minton, Balch & Company.

Dexter, L. A. (2006). *Elite and specialized interviewing.* European Consortium for Political Research.

DiMaggio, P. (Ed.). (1986). *Nonprofit enterprise in the arts: Studies in mission and constraint* (Vol. 3). Oxford University Press.

Domask, J. J. (2007). Achieving goals in higher education: An experiential approach to sustainability studies. *International Journal of Sustainability in Higher Education. 8*(1), 53–68.

Dunlap, L. W. (1972). *Readings in library history.* R. R. Bowker.

Dunne, C. (2011). The place of the literature review in grounded theory research. *International Journal of Social Research Methodology, 14*(2), 111–124.

Duxbury, N., Cullen, C., & Pascual, J. (2012). Cities, culture and sustainable development. In H. Anheier, Y. R. Isar, *Cultural policy and governance in a new metropolitan age* (pp. 73–86). SAGE.

Edwards, M., & Onyx, J. (2007). Social capital and sustainability in a community under threat. *Local Environment: The International Journal of Justice and Sustainability, 12*(1), 17–30.

Elkington, J. (1994). Towards the sustainable corporation: Win-win-win business strategies for sustainable development. *California Management Review, 36*(2), 90–100.

Emmison, M. (2003). Social class and cultural mobility. *Journal of Sociology, 39*(3), 211–230.

Epstein, J. (2002). *Book business: Publishing past, present, and future.* W. W. Norton.

Falk, J. H., & Dierking, L. D. (2000). *Learning from museums: Visitor experiences and the making of meaning.* Altamira Press.

Farley, R., Danziger, S., & Holzer, H. J. (2000). *Detroit divided.* Russell Sage Foundation.

FastCompany (2019, September 25). *Hundreds of thousands of people read novels on Instagram. They may be the future.* Retrieved from https://www.fastcompany.com/90392917/the-next-big-reading-platform-may-be-instagram.

Feld, A., O'Hare, M., & Schuster, J. (1983). *Patrons despite themselves: Taxpayers and arts policy.* New York University Press.

Feldstein, M. S. (1991). *The economics of art museums.* University of Chicago Press.

Ferris, W. P. (2011). Sustainability, leadership, ethics and aesthetics usher in the spring for OMJ. *Organization Management Journal, 8*(1), 1–2.

Fiorino, D. J. (2010). Sustainability as a conceptual focus for public administration. *Public Administration Review, 70,* s78-s88.

Fitzgibbon, M. (2001). *Managing innovation in the arts: Making art work.* Greenwood Press.

Foster, K. J. (2010). Thriving in an uncertain world: Arts presenting change and the new realities. Retrieved from https://www.researchgate.net/publication/281557619_Thriving_in_an_Uncertain_World_Arts_Presenting_Change_and_the_New_realities

Frederickson, H. G. (2010). *Social equity and public administration: Origins, developments, and applications.* ME Sharpe. Inc.

Fuller, D., & Sedo, D. R. (2013). *Reading beyond the book: The social practices of contemporary literary culture.* Routledge.

Garibay, C. (2009). Latinos, leisure values, and decisions: Implications for informal science learning and engagement. *The Informal Learning Review, 94,* 10–13.

Garvare, R., & Johansson, P. (2010). Management for sustainability—a stakeholder theory. *Total Quality Management, 21*(7), 737–744.

Geiser, E. A., Dolin, A., & Topkis, G. S. (1985). *The business of book publishing: Papers by practitioners.* Westview Press.

Genoways, H. H. (2006). *Museum philosophy for the twenty-first century.* Altamira Press.

Genoways, H. H., & Andrei, M. A. (2008). *Museum origins: Readings in early museum history and philosophy.* Left Coast Press.

Genoways, H. H., & Ireland, L. M. (2003). *Museum administration: An introduction.* AltaMira Press.

Gifford, S. (2007). National Endowment for the Arts announces new reading study. *National Endowment for the Arts.* Retrieved from http://www.nea.gov/news/news07/trnr.html

Glaser, B. G. (1978). *Theoretical sensitivity: Advances in the methodology of grounded theory.* Sociology Press.

Goddard, S. (2010). *Trees and other ramifications: Branches in nature and culture.* Spencer Museum of Art, Lawrence, KS.

Greenberg, M. L. (2015, March 7). Keeping the wheels turning or why students need foreign languages more than ever. Retrieved from http://slavist-semistrunnik.blogspot.com/2015/03/keeping-wheels-turning-or-why-students.html

Greenblatt, S. (2011). *The swerve: How the world became modern.* W. W. Norton.

Greenblatt, S., Županov, I., Meyer-Kalkus, R., Paul, H., Nyíri, P., & Pannewick, F. (2009). *Cultural mobility: A manifesto.* Cambridge University Press.

Grigar, D., & O'Sullivan, J. (2021). *Electronic literature as digital humanities: Contexts, forms, and practices.* Retrieved from: https://library.oapen.org/handle/20.500.12657/58859

Griswold, W., McDonnell, T., & Wright, N. (2005). Reading and the reading class in the twenty-first century. *Annual Review of Sociology*, 127–141.

Gunderson, L. H., & Pritchard, L. (2002). *Resilience and the behavior of large-scale systems* (Vol. 60). Island Press.

Guthrie, J., Ball, A., & Farneti, F. (2010). Advancing sustainable management of public and not-for-profit organizations. *Public Management Review, 12*(4), 449–459.

Hadley, S. (2021). *Audience development and cultural policy.* Palgrave Macmillan.

Hannan, M. T., & Freeman, J. (1989). *Organizational ecology.* Harvard University Press.

Hansberry, J. (2000). Denver's scientific and cultural facilities district: A case study in regionalism. *Government Finance Review, 16*(6), 13–16.

Hansmann, H. (1981). Nonprofit enterprise in the performing arts. *The Bell Journal of Economics*, 341–361.

Harris, M. (1999). *History of libraries of the western world.* Scarecrow Press.

Hassan, R. (2011). *The age of distraction: Reading, writing, and politics in a high-speed networked economy.* Transaction Publishers.

Hayles, N. K. (2008). *Electronic literature: New horizons for the literary.* University of Notre Dame Press.

Hooper, R. P. (2019, June 20). Cranbrook's sprawling, ambitious "Landlord Colors" exhibit connects Detroit to the world. *Detroit Free Press.* Retrieved from https://www.freep.com/story/entertainment/arts/2019/06/20/cranbrook-landlord-colors-exhibit-detroit-material/1490300001/

InsideOut (2019). About us. Retrieved from https://insideoutdetroit.org/our-story/

Iowa Review Enhanced Access Project, The. (2011). Retrived from https://iowareview.org/

IPA (2020) International Publishers Association. *From response to recovery: The impact of COVID-19 on the global publishing industry.* Retrieved from https://www.internationalpublishers.org/images/aa-content/news/news-2020/ipa-post-covid-action-plan-report.pdf

Jameson, F., & Miyoshi, M. (1998). *The cultures of globalization.* Duke University Press.

Jung, Y., & Love, A. R. (Eds.). (2017). *Systems thinking in museums: Theory and practice.* Rowman & Littlefield.

Katz, W. A. (1995). *Dahl's history of the book.* Scarecrow Press.

Kangas, A., Duxbury, N., & De Beukelaer, C. (2017). Introduction: Cultural policies for sustainable development. *International Journal of Cultural Policy*, *23*(2), 129–132.

Khair, T., & Doubinsky, S. (2011). *Reading literature today: Two complementary essays and a conversation*. SAGE.

Kim, M. (2016). Characteristics of civically engaged nonprofit arts organizations: The results of a national survey. *Nonprofit and Voluntary Sector Quarterly*, 0899764016646473.

King, N. (2004). Using interviews in Qualitative research. In C. Cassell & G. Symon (Eds.), *Essential guide to qualitative methods in organizational research* (pp. 11–22). London: SAGE.

Koteen, J. (1997). *Strategic management in public and nonprofit organizations: Managing public concerns in an era of limits*. Praeger.

Kotler, N. G., Kotler, P., & Kotler, W. I. (2008). *Museum marketing and strategy: Designing missions, building audiences, generating revenue and resources*. John Wiley & Sons.

Krasny, M. E., Lundholm, C., & Plummer, R. (2011). *Resilience in social-ecological systems: The role of learning and education*. Routledge.

Lansisalmi, H., Peiro, J.-M., & Kivimaki, M. (2004). Grounded theory in organizational research. In C. Cassell & G. Symon (Eds.), *Essential guide to qualitative methods in organizational research* (pp. 242–255). SAGE.

LeDuff, C. (2014). *Detroit: An American autopsy*. The Penguin Press.

Leuenberger, D. Z., & Bartle, J. R. (2009). *Sustainable development for public administration*. M. E. Sharpe.

Lindblom, C. E. (1959). The science of "muddling through." *Public Administration Review, 19*(2), 79–88.

Lindenberger, H. (1990). *The history in literature: on value, genre, institutions*. Columbia University Press.

Lowry, M. (1978). *The performing arts and American society*. Prentice Hall.

MacDonald, C. (2019, December 5) Effort to stave off Detroit foreclosures leaves many deeper in debt. *Detroit News*. Retrieved from https://www.detroitnews.com/story/news/local/detroit-housing-crisis/2019/12/05/detroit-foreclosures-effort-wayne-county-treasurer-puts-many-residents-into-deeper-debt/1770381001/

MacDonald, T., & Bean, A. (2011). Adventures in the subatomic universe: An exploratory study of a scientist-museum physics education project. *Public Understanding of Science, 20*(6), 846–862.

March, J. G. (1994). *A primer on decision making: How decisions happen*. The Free Press.

March, J. G., & Olsen, J. P. (1989). *Rediscovering institutions: The organizational basis of politics*. Free Press.

Markusen, A. (2014). Creative cities: A 10-year research agenda. *Journal of Urban Affairs, 36*(2), 567–589.

Matarasso, F. (2001). *Recognising culture: A series of briefing papers on culture and development*. Department of Canadian Heritage: UNESCO.

McConnaughey, J. (2019, June 4). Touchable art: More museums making art accessible to the blind via technology. *Associated Press*. Retrieved from https://www.detroitnews.com/story/life/2019/06/04/art-blind/39545029/

McGhee, G., Marland, G. R., & Atkinson, J. (2007). Grounded theory research: Literature reviewing and reflexivity. *Journal of Advanced Nursing, 60*(3), 334–342.

Merritt, E. (2006). Root of all evil? The ethics of doing business with for-profit entities. Retrieved from American Alliance of Museums https://www.aam-us.org/.

Miragaia, D., Brito, M., & Ferreira, J. (2016). The role of stakeholders in the efficiency of nonprofit sports clubs. *Nonprofit Management and Leadership.* doi:10.1002/nml.21210

Moldavanova, A. (2013). Sustainability, ethics, and aesthetics. *The International Journal of Sustainability Policy and Practice, 8*(1), 109–120.

Moldavanova, A. (2014). Sustainability, aesthetics, and future generations: Towards a dimensional model of the arts' impact on sustainability. In D. Humphreys & S. S. Stober (Eds.), *Transitions to sustainability: Theoretical debates for a changing planet* (pp. 172–193). Common Ground Publishing.

Moldavanova, A. (2016). Two narratives of intergenerational sustainability: A framework for sustainable thinking. *The American Review of Public Administration, 46*(5), 526–545.

Moldavanova, A., & Goerdel, H. T. (2018). Understanding the puzzle of organizational sustainability: Toward a conceptual framework of organizational social connectedness and sustainability. *Public Management Review, 20*(1), 55–81.

Moldavanova, A. V., & Wright, N. S. (2020). How nonprofit arts organizations sustain communities: Examining the relationship between organizational strategy and engagement in community sustainability. *The American Review of Public Administration, 50*(3), 244–259.

Moldavanova, A. V., & Akbulut-Gok, I. (2022). Inter-organizational networking and the Great Recession: Lessons from Detroit arts and culture organizations. *International Journal of Public Administration, 45*(3), 213–227.

Moldavanova, A. V., Meloche, L., & Thompson, T. L. (2022). Understanding the geography of access to cultural amenities: The case of Metropolitan Detroit. *Journal of Urban Affairs, 44*(4–5), 614–639.

Nazarov, A. R. (2011). Death with dignity. Retrieved from American Alliance of Museums https://www.aam-us.org/

NEA. (2004). Reading at risk: A survey of literary reading in America. *National Endowment for the Arts*. Retrieved from http://www.nea.gov/news/news04/readingatrisk.html

NEA. (2006). The arts and civic engagement. *National Endowment for the Arts*. Retrieved from http://www.nea.gov/pub/civicengagement.pdf

NEA. (2007). To read or not to read: A question of national consequence. *National Endowment for the Arts*. Retrieved from https://www.arts.gov/publications/read-or-not-read-question-national-consequence-0

NEA. (2018). U.S. trends in arts attendance and literary reading: 2002–2017. *National Endowment for the Arts*. Retrieved from https://www.arts.gov/publications/us-trends-arts-attendance-and-literary-reading-2002-2017

Newhouse, C. (2020). The 2020 nonprofit employment report: The 3rd largest employer faces the COVID-19 crisis. *John Hopkins Center for Civil Society Studies*. Retrieved from http://ccss.jhuedu/2020-nonprofit-employment-report/

Nurse, K. (2006). Culture as the fourth pillar of sustainable development. *Small states: Economic review and basic statistics, 11*(1), 28–40.

Odendahl, T., & Shaw, A. M. (2002). Interviewing elites. In J. F. Gubrium & J. A. Holstein (Eds.) *Handbook of Interview Research: Context & Method* (pp. 299–316). SAGE.

Olave, M. A. T. (2020). Book love. A cultural sociological interpretation of the attachment to books. *Poetics, 81*.

Olivares, A., & Piatak, J. (2022). Exhibiting inclusion: An examination of race, ethnicity, and museum participation. *VOLUNTAS: International Journal of Voluntary and Nonprofit Organizations, 33*(1), 121–133.

Osborne, S. P., Radnor, Z., Vidal, I., & Kinder, T. (2014). A sustainable business model for public service organizations? *Public Management Review, 16*(2), 165–172.

Ostrower, F. (2020). *Trustees of culture: Power, wealth, and status on elite arts boards*. University of Chicago Press.

Packer, J. (2006). Learning for fun: The unique contribution of educational leisure experiences. *Curator: The Museum Journal, 49*(3), 329–344.

Packer, J., & Ballantyne, R. (2002). Motivational factors and the visitor experience: A comparison of three sites. *Curator: The Museum Journal, 45*(3), 183–198.

Parfit, D. (1984). *Reasons and persons*. Oxford University Press.

Paulraj, A. (2011). Understanding the relationships between internal resources and capabilities, sustainable supply management and organizational sustainability. *Journal of Supply Chain Management, 47*(1), 19–37.

Peterson, R. (1986). From Impresario to Arts Administrator: Formal Accountability in Nonprofit Cultural Organizations. Chapter 7 in DiMaggio, P. (Ed.). *Nonprofit enterprise in the arts: Studies in mission and constraint*. (Vol. 3) (pp. 161–184). Oxford University Press.

Phillips, R. J. (2011). *Arts entrepreneurship and economic development: Can every city be "ostentatious"?* Now Publishers Inc.

Pierson, P. (2000). Increasing returns, path dependence, and the study of politics. *American Political Science Review, 94*(2), 251–267.

Poetry Out Loud. (2012). *Competition*. Retrived from http://www.poetryoutloud. org/

Poets & Writers, Inc. (2012). *Mission*. Retrieved from http://www.pw.org/

Portney, K. E., & Berry, J. M. (2016). The impact of local environmental advocacy groups on city sustainability policies and programs. *Policy Studies Journal, 44*(2), 196–214.

Portney, K. E., & Cuttler, Z. (2010). The local nonprofit sector and the pursuit of sustainability in American cities: A preliminary exploration. *Local Environment, 15*(4), 323–339.

Pollock, L. (2009). Public art for private gain? *The Art Newspaper*. Retrieved from http://indianartviews.blogspot.com/2009/01/public-art-for-private-gain.html

Ramnarine, T. K. (2013). The orchestration of civil society: Community and conscience in symphony orchestras. In *The Ethnomusicology of Western Art Music* (pp. 42–66). Routledge.

Romzek, B. S., LeRoux, K., & Blackmar, J. M. (2012). A preliminary theory of informal accountability among network organizational actors. *Public Administration Review, 72*(3), 442–453.

Rubio, D. F. (2014). Preserving the unpreservable: Docile and unruly objects at MoMA. *Theory and Society, 43*(6), 617–645.

Rushton, M. (2005). Support for earmarked public spending on culture: Evidence from a referendum in Metropolitan Detroit. *Public Budgeting & Finance, 25*(4), 72–85.

Rushton, M., & Landesman, R. (2013). *Creative communities: Art works in economic development*. Brookings Institution Press.

Russell, J. S. (2014). On elite campuses, an arts race. *The New York Times*. Retrieved from https://www.nytimes.com/2014/11/16/arts/design/on-elite-campuses-an-arts-race.html

Sandell, R., & Nightingale, E. (2012). *Museums, equality and social justice* (p. 344). Routledge.

Sapp, G. (2002). *A brief history of the future of libraries: An annotated bibliography*. Scarecrow Press.

Schaltegger, S., Burritt, R., Beske, P., & Seuring, S. (2014). Putting sustainability into supply chain management. *Supply Chain Management: An International Journal, 19*(3), 322–331.

Schober, R. (2023). *Spider web, labyrinth, tightrope walk: Networks in US American literature and culture*. Walter de Gruyter GmbH & Co KG.

Skocpol, T., & Fiorina, M. P. (1999). *Civic engagement in American democracy*. Brookings Institution Press.

Smith, A., Voß, J. P., & Grin, J. (2010). Innovation studies and sustainability transitions: The allure of the multi-level perspective and its challenges. *Research Policy, 39*(4), 435–448.

Smith, P. A. (2012). The importance of organizational learning for organizational sustainability. *The Learning Organization, 19*(1), 4–10.

Snow, D. A., Morrill, C., & Anderson, L. (2003). Elaborating analytic ethnography linking fieldwork and theory. *Ethnography, 4*(2), 181–200.

Spaeth, E. (1960). *American art museums and galleries: An introduction to looking.* Harper.

Stazyk, E. C., Moldavanova, A., & Frederickson, H. G. (2016). Sustainability, intergenerational social equity, and the socially responsible organization. *Administration & Society, 48*(6), 655–682.

Stead, J. G., & Stead, W. E. (2013). *Sustainable strategic management.* ME Sharpe.

Stone, J. (2017). *Detroit 1967: Origins, impacts, legacies.* Wayne State University Press.

Strategic Plan 2010. (2010). *Colorado University Art Museum, University of Colorado at Boulder.* Retrieved from https://www.colorado.edu/cuartmuseum/

Strauss, A. L. (1987). *Qualitative analysis for social scientists.* SAGE.

Taylor, S. S. (2011). What poetry brings to business. *Organization Management Journal, 8*(1), 64–66.

Temple, E. (2019, December 12). The 10 best literary film adaptations of the decade. *LitHub.* Retrieved from https://lithub.com/the-10-best-literary-film-adaptations-of-the-decade/

Thistlethwaite, J., & Paterson, M. (2016). Private governance and accounting for sustainability networks. *Environment and Planning C: Government and Policy, 34*(7), 1197–1221.

Thomas, T. E., & Lamm, E. (2012). Legitimacy and organizational sustainability. *Journal of Business Ethics, 110*(2), 191–203.

Thompson, J. B. (2012). *Merchants of culture: Th publishing business in the twenty-first century.* Penguin.

Throsby, C. D. (2005). *On the sustainability of cultural capital.* Sydney: Macquarie University, Department of Economics. Retrieved from https://www.researchgate.net/profile/David_Throsby/publication/5165805_On_the_Sustainability_of_Cultural_Capital/links/00b4953b362c8cb840000000.pdf

Throsby, D. (1995). Culture, economics and sustainability. *Journal of Cultural Economics, 19*(3), 199–206.

Tremmel, J. C. (2009). *A theory of intergenerational justice.* Edward Elgar Publishing Limited.

Tubadji, A. (2010). See the forest, not only the trees: Culture-based development (CBD). Conceptualising culture for sustainable development purposes. In F. Le Duc (Ed.), *Culture as a tool for development. Challenges for analysis and action.* (pp. 183–200). ARCADE.

Tubadji, A., Osoba, B. J., & Nijkamp, P. (2015). Culture-based development in the USA: Culture as a factor for economic welfare and social well-being at a county level. *Journal of Cultural Economics, 39*(3), 277–303.

Van der Heijden, K. (2004). Can internally generated futures accelerate organizational learning? *Futures, 36*(2), 145–159.

Varbanova, L. (2013). *Strategic management in the arts.* Routledge.

von Schlegel, F., & Frost, J. (1878). *Lectures on the history of literature, ancient and modern: From the German of Frederick Schlegel.* Moss & Co.

Walsh, D. (2009, October 8). Detroit Science Center's Eekstein Workshop creates exhibit of "accidental" mummies from Mexico. *Crain's Detroit Business.* Retrieved from https://www.crainsdetroit.com/article/20091008/FREE/910089977/detroit-science-centers-eekstein-workshop-creates-exhibit-of

Wang, X., Hawkins, C. V., Lebredo, N., & Berman, E. M. (2012). Capacity to sustain sustainability: A study of US cities. *Public Administration Review, 72*(6), 841–853.

WCED. (1987). Our common future. *World Commission on Environment and Development.* Retrieved from https://sustainabledevelopment.un.org/milestones/wced

Week, The (2011, May 6). Detroit's "shocking" 47 percent illiteracy rate. *The Week.* Retrieved from https://theweek.com/articles/484910/detroits-shocking-47-percent-illiteracy-rate

Wildavsky, A. B. (1988). *Searching for safety.* University of California Press.

Williams, R. (1983). *Culture and society, 1780–1950.* Columbia University Press.

Woods, A. (2017, December 6). Write A House is giving writers free homes in Detroit. *HuffPost.* Retrieved from https://www.huffpost.com/entry/write-a-house-detroit_n_4474976?guccounter=1&guce_referrer=aHR0cHM6Ly93d3cuZ29vZ2xlLmNvbS8&guce_referrer_sig=AQAAACN8zn9d2cSjILtu22XunP4u7Cw2RPaBuhWjvLES7sk84hdW4fdxEtZ7Ic4KtJPL__l6a6ad8LZAK20mGfHXUB1YfiTuVXXAmarg_GaGyQWdgo9ZqtaXEE3wwiqWcdHE3kptYnsohsmy5eQc0Mrp6WalG9xD6E6qKHcEsy1wI4iv

Yang, K., & Bergrud, E. (2008). *Civic engagement in a network society.* Information Age Publishing.

Young. E. (2018, September 4). What was lost in Brazil's devastating museum fire. *The Atlantic.* Retrived from https://www.theatlantic.com/science/archive/2018/09/brazil-rio-de-janeiro-museum-fire/569299.

Zaniewski (2017, August 19). Reading Works aims to boost adult literacy. *Detroit Free Press.* Retrieved from https://www.freep.com/story/news/education/2017/08/19/reading-works-metro-detroit/569495001/

# Index

*Page numbers followed by the letter t refer to tables.*

investment and, 19; argument, 8–10, 32; balancing nature of, 20–21, 140, 145, 147, 162, 214, 227, 232, 233, 238, 239, 244, 250; as both internal and external construct, 11, 28–29, 42; change as its "second" nature, 42, 213; clear institutional identity and, 21; cultural assumptions and, 222, 226; Detroit (city) and, 29; Detroit (metropolitan area) and, 31; as ethical concept, 234; intergenerational equity and, 250; intergenerational sustainability and, 10; institutional continuity and, 36; institutional distinctiveness and, 128, 244, 250–251; institutional resilience and, 42, 110, 128, 244, 250–251; museums and, 17, 41, 42, 77; operational environment and, 219, 220; organizational capacity and, 15; as a process, 33; process-oriented view of, 238–239; relationships with communities and, 55, 205; semi-instrumental role, 84, 110; social connectedness and, 14; strategic planning and, 15, 88; strategic thinking and, 240; stress and, 17, 21, 27, 75, 215–216, 218; sustainable thinking and, 215, 238, 244, 248, 250–251; technology utilization and, 183; theoretical framework for, 8, 28; as a two-level concept, 7; what it is, 15, 16; what it is not, 12–13, 15, 16. *See also* organizational capital, organizational social capital

Parfit, Derek, 236
Poetry Out Loud, 124
Poets & Writers, 125
*Public Space, A*, 135

PuppetArt Theater. *See* Detroit Puppet Theatre

Ramnarine, T[ina] K., 189
"Reading & Rhythm on the Riverfront" program. *See* Detroit Riverfront Conservancy
Reading Works (adult literacy program), 139–140
Rose Art Museum (Brandeis University), 37, 50

San Antonio Symphony (California): ceased to exist, 12, 159; and the Great Recession, 12
San Jose Repertory Theatre: ceased to exist, 12
San Jose Symphony (California): ceased to exist, 12, 159; and the Great Recession, 12
semi-instrumental role: arts and humanities and, 5, 6, 140; cultural organizations and, 11; institutional distinctiveness and, 128, 137, 187, 198; instrumental role and, 11, 81–82, 140; intrinsic role and, 11, 81–82, 140; literature organizations and, 137–138, 140; managers and, 207; museums and, 81–84; music and performing arts and, 198; public outreach and, 200; social responsibility and, 138. *See also* intrinsic role, instrumental role
science centers, 18, 36, 38, 54, 85
Scientific and Cultural Facilities District (CO), 55
"Shakespeare in Prison" program. *See* Detroit Public Theater
Smithsonian American Art Museum, 69
Smithsonian Institution (Washington, D.C.), 39, 49. *See also* Smithsonian American Art Museum

www.ingramcontent.com/pod-product-compliance
Lightning Source LLC
Chambersburg PA
CBHW020505270326
41926CB00008B/741